ENDSLEIGH
THE MEMOIRS OF A RIVERKEEPER

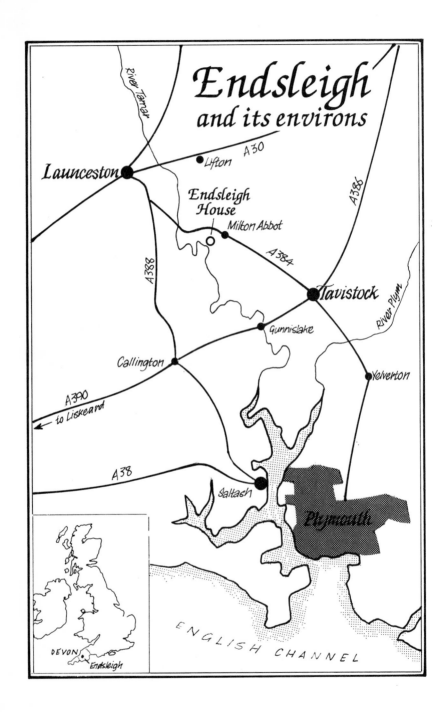

ENDSLEIGH
THE MEMOIRS OF A RIVERKEEPER

Horace Adams

Edited by
Clive Murphy

MERLIN BOOKS LTD.
Braunton Devon

British Library Cataloguing in Publication Data

Adams, Horace
Edited by Clive Murphy
Endsleigh
Memoirs of a River Keeper
I. Title

Cover design, artwork: Edward Taylor

ISBN 0–86303–685–6
Printed in England by
Antony Rowe Ltd., Chippenham, Wilts.

For Jill

My thanks are owed to:

Mr Allan Reid for suggesting the collaboration; Mr Peter Medd and his fellow directors for enabling it; Mr and Mrs Derek Bradbury and staff for hospitality; Miss Jean Vigars for motoring me to cigarettes; Captain and Mrs David Bailey and Mrs Jennifer High for camaraderie; Rear-Admiral P. R. Marrack for piscatorial promptings; Mrs Virginia Bunyan for providing an epigraph; Mrs Fay Cattini for expert typing; Mrs Horace Adams, Mr and Mrs Rodney Hill and Lady Pamela Peppiatt for calming influence; and, above all, to Horace for being Horace — Malvolio and Feste rolled into one.

Clive Murphy

Photographs between pages 56 and 57, 168 and 169.
Map of Endsleigh pages 112-113.

Of all the charms of Endsleigh, there's one of them unique:
Whenever Endsleigh comes to mind, it's of Horace first we speak!

Virginia Bunyan

One

The old brain's been stuck back there in the corner. How can I *begin* to recreate in words the beauty and excitement of Endsleigh?! The house itself, or 'cottage' as it was called first, was built on the River Tamar in 1810 as a hunting lodge for the 6th Duke of Bedford but, during my lifetime, it's been used mostly for fishing. The Tamar is the best salmon river in the West Country, the most civilized part of Great Britain, and one way and another the fourteen mile of water from Greystone Bridge to Gunnislake, the cream, have been my master and my friend since 1933 — under the 11th Duke who died in 1940; under the 12th Duke, *my* Duke, who died in 1953; and under the 13th Duke and the Bedford Trustees till 1962. In 1962, the Endsleigh Fishing Club, a syndicate, became my bosses, though they've always said I boss them. Last year [1983], the Marquess of Tavistock, who caught his first salmon with me as a boy, became a member. I'm awfully pleased because, as one of the offsprings of the Bedfords, he *is* Endsleigh and, to finish my days off, I'm becoming a little bit more ducal again.

Today [Monday, July 23] is a good time to start talking: the fishing's completely out — the water's coloured and it's only half an inch on the gauge-board. 'Glorious Devon. Five rainy days out of seven,' they used to say. Well, so far, we've only had one day's real rain since before Easter: this have been the hottest summer since '76. April was so warm there were young ladies on the river bank in their bikinis. In May the river gradually dropped down to seven inches. Then, on the 23rd, it rose to one foot eleven and everybody was jumping for joy. But the water didn't hold. The next day it was down to eleven inches and the next day it was back to seven again, though Mr Peter Medd, our Chairman, he and his wife got two salmon each out of Bush Pool. When he come here first Mr Medd was very raw but I'd now put him in the top ten. Of course, he's got a sixteen foot carbon fibre rod and it's the rod that does the fishing.

1

I wonder how he'd have got on with the split cane and Greenheart rods of days gone by.

'Change-over' isn't till Thursday but, because of the conditions, some of this week's fishers have left already. Brigadier and Mrs Oldrey, not members of the Syndicate, they're leaving today — instead of fishing they was concentrating more on butterflies, that sort of thing. Mr Holland, not a member either, he's one of the eight or nine that's staying on (the house can take about thirty). He's just been up to the Rising Sun on the Taw at Umberleigh, and he was the only person in the hotel for four days! *He* could write a damn good book. After the Second World War until four years ago he farmed fourteen thousand acres in the Argentine and he knows everybody that's worth knowing everywhere. The trouble is he might mention names and he'd be had for scandal. The Harris twins, Mr Mick and Mr George, and their twin wives, Joan and Audrey, they're staying on too. Mr Mick was born half an hour before Mr George. When they joined the Syndicate in '68 they were really identical but I twigged the ladies from the word go. You'm a bit observant when you've been on the river so long, as you'm always looking for clues for poachers and watching things very mistrustful, and I spotted Mr Mick's wife, Joan, wore little ear studs. I call the Harris twins 'the Oxfam boys' because they're tiny little men and they buy their clothes cheap at Oxfam shops where their wives work voluntary. They all live in the same house in Romsey with a mongrel terrier.

A lot, like the Harrises, bring their dogs to Endsleigh, but you're the first person that have brought a cat. A lady this year brought a parrot. She took it down on to the river bank, chained by its leg to a perch on a little stand. I said, 'Madam, if you leave that on the river bank the buzzard mightn't have it but the sparrowhawk or the kestrel will. They'll dive down and grab it by the head and probably kill it.' Whether you like a person or whether you don't like the person you don't want to see anything happen to the animal. We've a member called Mrs Floyd. In '78 I was proceeding up river and, to my astonishment, I say her playing a cow. The cow was galloping across a field followed by Mrs Floyd. I approached her and I said, 'What's wrong?!' She said, 'In my back cast I hooked this cow!' I said, 'Well, keep your rod up or otherwise the cast'll break!' Any rate, sure enough, it *did* break. Then we were a little perturbed because it was a fair-sized fly, a 2/0, and it was stuck in this

2

cow's neck. I had to go and tell the farmer. He had a pair of pliers and he broke the barb of the hook and it slid out easily so all was well. Fancy a woman coming here to catch a salmon and she caught a damn great cow! We couldn't have got it in the boot of the car for her!

So, you see, I've met all sorts here, not just the aristocracy, especially since the days of the 12th Duke — and even *he* allowed non-family to visit and, eventually, paying guests. There's now a real cross-section including doctors, scientists, lawyers, and big business people, and there are far more women and children than before. We even get babies in arms. Pregnant wives are on the river bank and then the babies are born and you, the riverkeeper, is asked to rock the baby while mother's fishing! It's got to that!! Some people you just don't know why they come at all. I had a lady here once. If you told her where to go to fish, she was liable to go back in the *wood* and fish. She didn't know if it was Christmas or Easter: probably she'd had an illness. I caught a twelve pound fish for her and I wanted her to play it, but she couldn't.

During the early days of the Syndicate, a gentleman arrived here in an old coupé with the canvas hood covered in bird droppings. Dear old Lady Hayter-Hames, she said to me, 'Whoever do that car belong to?!' I said, 'I'll look him up presently,' and he turned out to be just a day rod from Cornwall, invited here by a member. I ran up against him at Gravel Pool and we had a yarn. I left him fishing and, when I came back later in the day, I said, 'Have you had any fish?' 'Yes,' he said. 'Three.' I said, 'Where are they?' He said, 'In the car.' So I had a look in the car and there was no fish there. I met up with Sir Kenneth Peppiatt later on and he said, 'That gentleman's got five fish.' I said, 'Well, he told me he'd had three and,' I said, 'I can't even find the three.' Any rate, the day came to an end and the gentleman booked six salmon in the Register. I rung up a water bailiff who lived in his area and he informed me this was a good-living man, yet I'll swear to God Almighty he never caught one fish. Nobody *else* caught a fish that day on the whole river nor even *seen* a fish, and one of the fish he entered was as heavy as seventeen pound.

There's quite a good fisherman, a different kind of eccentric, who comes to Endsleigh. He's called Victor Canning. Like you, he smokes tremendous. I think it's undermining him because he's always coughing and spluttering, and he's shaky though I wouldn't have said he was all that old. [He died, aged 74, in February, 1986.] He's easy to get on with,

3

you'd like him — or maybe you wouldn't because he writes and you write. If I left you here and now and went straight to Tavistock Market, there'd be a stall with second-hand paperbacks by Victor Canning — adventure things, a bit of gun stuff, a lot of what I call fantasy. He makes these yarns up and he sells them. I've never read one. I can't pick up a book and read it very well; I fall asleep. Instead, I like to pick up the paper and read the scandal: 'While Clive Murphy was staying at Endsleigh his wife ran off with another man because, she says, he's always interviewing people. She's got bored and she's bolted…': that sort of thing. But this Victor Canning, he writes fiction. I said to him, 'How do you get it?' He said, 'Listening to you for a start!'

It's true: I *do* keep rabbiting on. I believe in it. If people get fed up with you, they'll walk away without their say. They were probably going to tell you off and they've forgotten how. A Mrs Simmons, who painted my portrait in '79, at the invitation of Lady Caffyn, one of our directors, she *asked* me to keep talking. I was stood wearing a jacket with my elbow on a bookcase in the Quiet Room and she said, 'I want you to be natural. Tell me all about your family and I'll tell you all about mine. I want you to keep talking all the time you're with me.' Later she went down the river and took a sketch of Black Rock and painted it in behind me. The portrait's been hung about in different places. It's hung now in the Small Sitting-Room where the bar is. The only trouble is that it's got this damn great table-lamp in front of it and it'll get dirty. The last Saturday of the season, the Syndicate hold a party, a big dinner, after the General Meeting. *I* don't go to the dinner itself, but I come in to the table for the speeches when everybody's half cut and I always make the winding-up speech and tell them what have been happening on the river. In '79 I said, 'This year has been a great year for me because I've had the honour not of just having my portrait painted but also to be hung in the house.' I said, 'Some people say it's not a bit like me but', I said, 'the artist put on canvas what she saw, and no one else was present at the time.' I said, 'My mother always taught me two things as a kid: "Do your best and, if you've failed, all right, you've tried," and "Charity begins at home. Put your own house in order first. It's no use for people to start criticizing when they can't do it better theirselves." ' I said, 'The main critic has been a person who has never held a paintbrush in their hand, and', I said, 'one lady went so far as to say she loved the frame. But *I* congratulate the artist. She had a bad subject and she made a good job of it. My wife, among others, says she doesn't think the mouth is right but, after all, how could the mouth be right when it was always on the move?' So everybody then stood up and toasted Mrs Simmons, which was nice. People still say the portrait's not me. They say things like it don't glorify me enough and that I'm looking sour and worried, but I *am* always worried. And they still say that the mouth is wrong and I still have to explain that Mrs Simmons painted it as though it's moving. But one woman who came here had been to Italy and had learned everything in the art world, and she wanted to know who did this and how long I sat and whatnot, and she said, 'Well, it's a wonderful painting, Adams, and you should be very, very proud of it.' And I am.

Yes, I'm a *bit* deaf, but I can hear *you* all right — you're quite plain for Irish. My sister-in-law on the telephone, she goes burorarorarorar. She's Northern Irish and she's *terrible*, I can't understand a word her says. You don't *sound* Irish. I'm relieved at that. Before I met you I said to the wife, 'A bloody Irishman!' — you know how people talk. No disgrading to an Irish person because there's good English, good Irish, good Germans, good everything. It's just the *few*. Most of the Irish are well respected in the West of England, though they used to be looked down on because they liked a drop of the hard stuff and they'd get fightable. When the dual carriageway bypassed Launceston, it was all Irish labourers, what they used to call 'navvies'. Same with the telephones and gas down through from Tavistock to Liskeard. It's sad one's got to be falling out with one another but, if we gave up Northern Ireland and there wasn't some real agreement, the Russians would come in and it would be a hell of a sight worse. That big roadworks linking the Tamar Bridge with the Marsh Mills roundabout, there's Irish working there now. Some people say they'll probably blow up the new Theatre Royal in Plymouth. But it's not *they* boys that's going to blow the theatre up. When Irishmen kill our soldiers and do this and that, then *all* the Irish gets a bad name.

The Irish work hard, and frankly, a lot of the West Country boys are lazy buggers. There are too many of these idlers around now, expecting all for nothing. Except a person is ill, no one should have a wage unless they work. 'Unemployment' crops up every day of the week. But there's a lot that's unemployable! I've had four or five youngsters to help me here, and they just didn't *want* a job! About two year ago I had a lad and he was damn good in a sense — a good-looking boy and well turned out, not slobby, and he was interested in fishing and he was interested in carrying a gun. But they're *all* interested in fishing and they're *all* interested in carrying a gun, full stop — they don't want the slasher or the digger or the shovel. The fishing was slack, there wasn't much water, so I decided to clean up a little pool called Beech Tree which was getting a bit overgrown, and I cut down eight biggish sticks, about ten inches in circumference, with a chain-saw. After cutting these down, I decided to cut them in lengths. I said, 'Now, come on! You throw them up the bank!' and he stood there watching me. I said, 'Now come on! Throw the sticks up the bank!' He said, 'Well, *you've* cut them down!' I think that was bloody cheek! He was stood with his hands in his hipsters and they were stuck there: instead of sniffing glue, he'd got glue in his pockets. Poor old Adams, the old boy, had to throw the sticks up the bank. Unemployable. Had to be phased out. A waste of time.

But now, since the 1st of July, I've a young man of about thirty to help me called Wesley Lee who's all there and half way back. He knows quite a bit about farming and he's a good mechanic. In other words, he's a real old country jan. There's promise there if he's treated properly. [During '85 Mr Lee departed, and, at the end of the season, a Mr Bob Wellard became Horace's successor. Horace now assists individual fishermen on a voluntary basis.] He's already very popular with the main people, and I shall willingly show him all the tricks of the trade and try to pass my knowledge on to him. He's never fished in his life so I've been looking after the guests and he's been trimming the banks, repairing gateposts. Being a riverkeeper is not just catching fish: there's a tremendous lot of jobs to do. With poachers to watch out for, so much to tidy and repair, and so many people to attend to, you haven't got a minute that you can call your own, you've got to be dedicated. The trouble is people want the weekly agricultural wage which is round the £80 mark. This day and age everybody wants more, more, more; it's all money, money, money. How the hell are you going to conquer unemployment when it's the wage combustion that have partly caused it?!

Which brings me on to the unions. You come down here of a morning and you're all starry-eyed or you're yawning and a guest may say, 'Did you have a rough night, Adams? Didn't you sleep well?' I say, 'I've never had a *chance* to sleep because I've been out all night looking for the poachers! It's all very fine. When you're tucked up in bed snoring away and probably dreaming about tomorrow's fish, *we*'re still out on the river protecting them! We waterkeepers, we've got no hours at all. Our hours is to perform our duty whether it takes five hours, twelve hours or twenty-four hours in a day, and sometimes it takes thirty-six hours! It's as simple as that.' Then they ask, 'What does your union say?' and I say, 'We riverkeepers haven't *got* a union! *We* can't strike. We're not like the miners or the shop assistants or what have you who just because they don't like a person drop tools and walk out!'

In fact, I don't *want* a union. I don't personally believe in strikes. Why should one section of the community hold the rest of the community at stake? We'll talk about the present miners' strike. There's old-age pensioners not sure if they're going to get their next hundred-weight of coal. *They* can't strike! They're being held at ransom. And it's not the fault of the miner himself. It boils down to one individual, the *leader* of the miners, who happens to be Arthur Scargill. After the war there was so much written about Hitler and how it could never happen in England. Well it's already happened in England: in 1984 it's really happened. There's a little Hitler — Scargill. There's no mistake about it. The union says he's fighting for the worker. How's he fighting for the worker?! He's keeping the worker on strike without much pay, and starving their children; he's just having a fight with Margaret Thatcher. It's like these striking schoolteachers. They say they've got the pupil at heart. Well, *have* they got the pupil at heart?! *I've* got the fisherman at heart because that's my job and therefore I'm down here trying to protect the river and showing him what fly to use for his enjoyment to make his holiday a real holiday. If I'm 'out', it's out so others can 'strike' fish.

Some miners are fighting the police, calling them bastards. Well the police aren't bastards, the police are the friends of the people, they're trying to protect the miner who is *willing* to work! The miner, poor devil, he's attached to a union, he's got to do what he's told and, if he doesn't, he's on the wrong horse. One always ridicules the police, but the police have got the hardest job to do. They talk about them being overpaid. I would say, 'Double the police pay!' They've got to be tough, and yet on the other hand they're so gentle, they're so kind. Four year ago, me and

7

the wife was involved in an accident near Devonport. I stopped at a belisha crossing for a young lady, and a car came down behind me, bang, right into the boot. The police at the station brought us cups of tea and put some flowers we had into water. People have no reason to run down the police. If you break the law, the police is there to amend, and that's your funeral. I blame ourselves for the state of things. We haven't been strong enough with our children. Our parents were strict with us, and we've been too simple. You don't need to have wars to ruin a country: you can ruin it from within. I back the police all the way.

Even aside from catching the poacher, a riverkeeper's a bit of a policeman. Take for instance one Sunday about five year ago. I was down river at a stretch called Beera and I met two young ladies and a young gent and a couple of kids. I said, 'Excuse me, but you're not allowed up here.' They said, 'We're going picnicking on the river.' I said, 'Well, it's not allowed.' So one of the ladies was a little sarcastic devil, she said, 'Who's going to stop us?' I said, 'I shall have to.' She said, 'How are *you* going to stop us?!' I said, 'I shall make myself a bloody nuisance, because I shall just hang on with you. I'm not going to allow you to pass this Land Rover.' I've had a Suzuki for three year come November, though I can't understand the Syndicate having a foreign car here *and* a red one — it's like a mail van up and down the river. Any rate, I said to this lady, 'I've got all afternoon and all evening. I'm not bothered. I've got nothing else to do but to stay here with you. It's as simple as that.' I said, 'Where do you live?' She said, 'Stoke Climsland.' I said, 'I suppose you've got a nice cottage?' She said, 'Oh, we've got a beautiful house and a beautiful lawn!' — you know, very biggety. So I said, 'All right then, madam,' I said, 'what happens if I bring my wife and daughter and we come over and have a picnic on your lawn?' 'Oh,' she said, 'you couldn't do that!' I said, 'Exactly!' I said, 'This field may be much bigger than your lawn, but you're still not allowed here. If there's a bull come down and cross the field and toss you in the air, your husband or your boyfriend or whoever it might be with you is going to sue the farmer.' Then she got a bit hot under the collar so the man said, 'He's right. We shouldn't be here. We'll turn tail and we'll go and we'll sit in the old disused quarry down the road and have tea.' Probably if the lady'd been nice I'd have said, 'Well, go on. You can sit down here and have your picnic, but I don't want you wandering around. And don't get leaving any litter because this is very expensive fishing. And let's be fair about it, we don't want the children in swimming.' Swimming's not allowed on my stretch, only on the tidal water between Blanchdown and Gunnislake Bridge. The Dukes gave permission there because it didn't interfere so much with the fishing, and it's been handed down like that ever since.

Going back further to eleven, twelve year ago. I'd come in at Greystone Bridge, the top end late one afternoon and, when I got to Lord and Lady Trenchard who was fishing Hardstone, he said, 'Have you seen what I've seen?!' I said, 'No. What's that?' He said, 'There's two canoes, two boats and a raft gone down with five or six people. It's like two families.' I said, 'Well, why didn't you stop them?! You're one of the directors!' He was Chairman later, before Mr Peter Medd. He said, 'I thought you might be downstream and I'd leave it to you.' I said, 'How long ago did they go down?' He said, 'Only about five minutes.' Well, they'd reached Cartha-martha Pool where Giles, a grandson of Sir Kenneth and Lady Peppiatt, was fishing. I asked Giles to stop fishing and I challenged them. There was two men, two women and four youngsters with this flotilla of sailing craft. I said, 'Excuse me,' I said. 'Have you had permission to come down through here?' They said, 'No, but we've got every right down here so much as you have!' I said, 'Well that's where you're wrong! This is private fishing, I'm in charge, and I want you to come in on to the shingle!'

So they were sensible enough to pull in, one behind the other, and I talked to the two men. One of them looked pretty tough like if he wanted a rough house he could be better than you. But it turned out that the other, a decent-looking bloke, was the one that was argumentable. He said, 'What damage are we doing?!' I said, 'Well, probably you're not doing any damage at all, but that doesn't signify that you're *allowed* here!. Canoes come down occasionally, but only if they've got permission. If there's anybody come down without permission we stop them, which we've got every right to do because this is very expensive fishing.' I said, 'Now, look,' I said, 'let's face it, you know you're in the wrong. I've just come in from Greystone Bridge. There's a big van up there with racks on. Does that belong to you?' He said, 'Yes. And we've another at Horsebridge where we're going to get out and load up.' So I said, 'Where do you come from?' He said, 'St Austell.' 'All right now,' I said, 'I want to know how you got in here.' He said, 'At Greystone Bridge. We've got the map here. We've been canoeing and boating all over the West Country during the holiday period with the kids, and you're the first person ever to stop us!' I wouldn't know if I *was* the first person — this is what he was telling me. I said 'Look, you've got to see *my* point of view. I'm just employed, I'm only a working fellow. Probably you're working people. But you're in the wrong so I'm asking you to come out. Otherwise I'll have to go and get the Water Authority bailiffs or, if necessary, the police, and I don't want to do that.' So one of the ladies said to him, 'We're in the wrong, darling. It's better for us to come out,' and I ran the two men back to Greystone to get their van to go to Horsebridge, which is seven mile around, and, meanwhile, the ladies was very chatty and very nice and asked could they see Giles fishing so Giles put on a demonstration. Later, I had to hang around out of sight until seven o'clock to watch them pick up their craft and see they didn't do any damage such as pull stakes up or cut the rope of one of *our* boats.

I've an awesome job in a way. There was a local celebrity with plenty of money and his own private stretch of water above us. He wanted to join the Syndicate, and he used to come and fish here quite regular — you know, take a day rod if there was one going vacant. I'd treated him as a gentleman and I still do now. Well, I happened to come in to the top part of the river with my friend Bert Moore — a general handyman who retired about eight year ago — to clear a big branch from across a path. I said, 'My God! There's somebody poaching there on the Cornwall bank!' Bert said, 'You always see people bloody poaching! That's all you'm looking for!' I said, 'I'll drive straight on as though we haven't spotted him,' and this gentleman was stood beside a tree and, as soon as I seen his dog, I knew who he was instantly. So we moved down river with the Land Rover and got out of sight, and Bert started sawing with the chain-saw and the sound is coming up the valley. I thought, 'I'll creep up under cover of the bushes between me and the gent.' I crept up, and he must have spotted me because all of a sudden he reeled in and he kept looking back on his shoulder as he moved away. Then, when Bert stopped sawing, he put his best boots on because he probably thought Bert had spotted him as well and we were going to apprehend him. Of course, I should have crossed Greystone Bridge and went up to him and said, 'Look here, sir! This is a bit bad!' but I was so embarrassed to think it was a man like him that was so respected I done nothing about it, I just let it go to see what happened, and I kept watch pretty closely, early mornings, evenings, so much as I could to catch him out red-handed and pounce.

About a fortnight later, a friend of his came to Endsleigh and we got talking and I said, 'I saw Mr So and So on the Cornwall side. I'm bound to report this to the Chairman.' 'Well,' he said, 'he told me all about this and he *thought* you spotted him and he says he regrets it now. He's had a lot of worries and he wandered down without thinking.' But this is what everybody says, and I put the Chairman in the picture and there was a letter sent telling him that this time the matter would be over-looked seeing as I didn't challenge him.

No, I've never been *asked* to retire, but last year on the report of the Annual General Meeting it said, 'Adams have now reached the age of seventy and he must have help of some kind. It's up to Adams to find someone that can replace him in due course.' So this is how Wesley Lee came on to it, and I've promised that, if I've got my health and strength, I'll do everything for the benefit of the Syndicate and the benefit of the river till the end of 1985, and then us got to be getting to think again. In '78 when I was coming up to sixty-five I said, 'It's about time somebody else was brought in. I think I'll retire,' and I can remember Lord Trenchard saying, 'Whatever for?! You've got the best job you can have. You've got free transport; you've got free fishing, free drinks, free lunches — everything free. You'm having a whale of a time.' He said, 'You'll carry on until you drop dead. Probably you'll have a stroke and roll straight in the river!' — they've said that *many* a time, a lot of people. But, now, I was slowing up, and I had at the back of my mind that, though I'm always saying there's so much unemployment and people don't want to work, I *might* be keeping someone out of a job. So, in '78, I went into *semi*-retirement, and I seem to be doing more now than when I was in full employment. I'm not here quite so much in the winter, but I put in enough hours in the summer to last for two or three winters if you went by union hours.

That year, a girl up the terrace where I live in Milton Abbot thought I was going to retire completely because I got a garden seat. I'd been out in the boat fishing with Mr Medd below Woodtown Croy after a big flood. 'Oh, look!' he said. 'There's a seat up there! A garden seat!' And this flam new seat had washed down and caught in the bushes, and it was made with this here Burma teak that's not supposed to rot. So his son climbed the bushes and relieved it and we lifted it down, and Mr Medd said, 'You'd better put that in the back of your Land Rover.' So I put it in the back of the Land Rover and took it home and put it out on our lawn. That same evening I was reading the local rag, the *Tavistock Gazette*, in bed, and on the back page was a little portion: 'Vandals destroy new Coronation seat ... Smashed to smithereens and thrown in River Lyd' — the Lyd's a big stream but they call it a river, and this is where our salmon goes up to spawn at Lifton. I thought to myself, 'My God! That's that seat!' The next morning, seven o'clock, I picked the phone up and I dialled the Chairman of the Council of Lifton and told him how I'd found this Burma seat in the bushes on the River Tamar down at Endsleigh, and I read him out the portion in the *Tavistock Gazette*. He said, 'I'll intercede about that and ring you back.' So he rung me back later in the day — this was a Friday — and he said, 'You're right,' he said. 'That's the seat.' I said, 'Well, it's in good nick.' He said, 'You hang on to it and we'll make arrangements to collect it. Thank you very much.'

The following Thursday I walked in the door — I'd got half a day and I wanted to get into Tavistock that afternoon to get my hair cut — and the telephone was ringing so I rushed to it, and someone said, 'Oh, this is the *Tavistock Gazette*. Apparently you found a Burma teak seat which had been washed down from Coronation Park. We thought vandals had destroyed it. Can you give a description?' So I gave a description and I said, 'What I can't understand is it had to come past four or five croys [jetties built out from the river bank to create salmon lies and to fish from] and all down through the rapids, and it was washed right up on top of the bank yet it had only got one little mark on it, no scratches, no digs, no nothing.' He said, 'Well, it was very good of you to report the matter.' So that was that. I got my lunch — the wife was out — and went to Tavistock. The paper comes out just after lunch, and there on the front page was 'Endsleigh water bailiff finds Coronation Park seat in the bushes six to eight mile down river...' They'd got a whole column and they'd enlarged on every word I said. I met an old farmer and he said, 'You've made history today! Your bloody name's the leading thing!' Really he thought it was a load of bullshit, and it was. The police rang me up that evening, and I left it by the side of the wall outside our back door for them to collect.

So I lost my retirement seat though I wasn't going to retire yet anyway and I'm glad I didn't because it's a wonderful life being a riverkeeper. If only youngsters would look at it that way and didn't want to be listening to the transistor instead of working hard with a capital aitch. I mean, for instance, they can become a blacksmith and, of course, they may like the idea in *theory* — there's a lot of things in *theory*. But, when it comes to the practical point, they don't want to get their hands or their slacks or their overalls dirty. And, when the horse kicks out and knocks them for a six, they don't want too much of that, either. Like the younger boys coming into fishing this day and age, they don't want to be called a bloody fool when they'm doing their best for a person. They'm just as liable to turn around and say, 'Hey, wait a minute! Who the hell are *you* talking to?!'

I've been called a hell of a lot of names in my day on the river, but nobody can offend me, I don't go home and lose no sleep. You're accused of knocking the fish off the fly with the net — 'You bloody fool, Adams! I could have got that fish!' It's sad really that a lot of the young people can't take it because, if they want to survive, they'll have to. Mr Mick Harris, for instance, he's very fiery. If you miss tailing or netting a fish, my God he goes on. But it's only that split second. He'll bang you down quick and then he'll turn around and say, 'What do you want? A drop of cider or a drop of Scotch or a sherry?' — although the Harris twins don't drink much theirselves, they really look after you on the river to warm you up or cool you down.

I remember Sir Thomas Russell fishing off a croy in the 12th Duke's days and, while he was playing a fish, his chauffeur shouted, 'Well done, sir! Well done!' and Sir Thomas shouted, 'Keep your bloody mouth shut!' You see?! Just like that! Well, I said to the chauffeur, I said, 'Don't take any notice of him because', I said, 'you're talking to one of the nicest gentlemen that you could talk to, but', I said, 'he's excited. He doesn't realize what he's said to you.' And, right on the same, the fish got off. *Now* Sir Thomas wasn't angry, he didn't throw his rod down on to the croy and go to bash it, but he took his hat off to the fish because it got away. And then, when he come up on the bank, the first thing he did, he went to this young chauffeur and said, 'I'm sorry, no offence but when someone shouts to me and takes off the concentration, I just say, "Keep your bloody mouth shut!"' Young people have got to be prepared to take this sort of thing. You've got to take a lot of knocks in life. It's all excitement at that moment, and words is said without any meaning.

About five year ago, there were two gents — I'll call them Mr Jack Frost and Mr Willie Robins — fishing Beat 4 which is from Leigh Wood Gate to Horsebridge and, if I was to tell this story to other people in front of 'Mr Robins', he'd be delighted: he'd say, 'You're ridiculing me!' and I'd say, 'The truth always stands. What about it?' and he'd say, 'You bugger!' and he wouldn't half tell them something about *me*! ... Any rate, during the morning, Mr Frost had said, 'There's no need for you to come down to look after Willie and myself. We'll be all right. You look after the people that don't know their way round.' So I said, 'All right, but probably I'll come down about half past five to see you.' He said, 'That's to please yourself. I'll take Willie out in the boat by Leigh Wood Waterfall.'

So I arrived at six o'clock in the Land Rover. I parked and came up to this Mr Robins sat in his Jag. He looked at me pretty solemn and he said, 'You told Jack Frost you were going to be down here at half past three.' I said, 'I didn't tell Mr Frost that. I told Mr Frost that, if I came down here, it'd be around five-thirty and it's now six o'clock. And', I said, 'Mr Frost said to me there was no need for me to come down because *he* could look after you if you wanted to go out in the boat.' Mr Frost was fishing, standing in the river just below us, and he said, 'You'd betterway keep your mouth shut, you know, Willie, because otherwise Adams will go home.' So I said to Mr Robins, I said, 'You fish a lot in Scotland, and I've always been given to understand that the ghillies there leave work at five to five-thirty. It's now six o'clock and I'm here offering you my services and you'm angry with me.' I said, 'It doesn't make sense. If you don't want to go out in the boat, I can just say good-evening and go home because I've got plenty of work to do in the garden. It's up to you.' So Mr Frost said, 'Go on, Willie! You've been put in your place. If you want to bloody fish, get in the boat!'

Mr Robins got out of the car, didn't speak, got in the boat, and I took him down the stream — Leigh Wood is quite a long pool. And he'd been fishing for a little while and he was into a fish! I just stayed there, rowing the boat, and he said to me, he said, 'Where should we land the fish?' He'd come to his senses now. Now he's all right because he's got a fish, you see. One moment he's bloody angry with me, now he wants me to help him, desperately. I said, 'You tell me where to pull in and I'll pull in,' whereas I would have normally went into a place that was easy for landing. So I pulled in where he told me, and we landed the fish. He says, 'That's the second fish I've caught there today.' I said, 'So Mr Frost took you out to fish?! Why were you grumbling so?!' He said, 'It irritates me when you say you're going to meet me and you don't.' I said, 'I didn't tell you I was going to meet you!' I said, 'A lot of people you would frighten. Especially a young ghillie. Right,' I said, 'we'll go back now and I'll take Mr Frost down.' So I took Mr Frost down and *he* got a fish. I said, 'Mr Robins has had two fish so, if you like to stay here, I'll boat you once more.' And I did, and he gets his second fish. So that's four fish have been caught — three with me and one, four.

·   We came back and I said, 'Well, I'm going home now.' 'Oh,' said Mr Robins, 'you're not going home,' he said. 'I want to catch another fish.' I said, 'All right. I'll give you half an hour,' because now, you see, it's coming on for seven o'clock. So I took him down in the boat again, and he was into *another* fish! We took a considerable time playing this fish, but eventually we got him in. Mr Robins wanted to go on fishing then. I said, 'No. It's Mr Frost's turn. I'm going to give Mr Frost one more trip and then I'm off home.' So we came back, I picked Mr Frost up, took him down, and he gets another fish! So that's six fish — five with me, and one before I arrived. Mr Frost said, 'Right. We'll pack it now.' So I rowed him back, and there's Mr Robins waiting, rod in hand. He said, 'I'll have one more trip.' I said, 'You won't! I'm going home!' He said, 'What do you mean you're going home?!' He said, 'I'm dictating you to take me down in the boat!' I said, 'Well, I'm not bothered about what you'm dictating me! We've had six fish, we've had an enjoyable evening, and I'm leaving of it to that!' I said, 'It's coming eight o'clock now. Your dinner is served at the house at eight, and we're off home!' So Mr Robins puts his rod on top of his car and, although they'd got individual cars, all the fish went into his boot. And he'd some drink there so Mr Frost said, 'Right then, Willie. Pour a sup of whisky each!' 'Oh,' said Mr Robins, 'you buggers ain't going to have none of *my* drink!' and he jumps

15

in the car and he's gone, leaving his net and tailer on the bank.

Mr Frost'd got a drink so I stopped and had a drink with him. He said, 'Willie's on the bloody ball again!' meaning he was being temperamental, moody. Six fish! And all the way up the river probably there hadn't been another fish caught! It was only because we'd come in where there was a shoal of taking fish. It's a lot of luck. I said, 'What about the net and tailer?' He said, 'Let them stay there! Let the bugger come back and fetch them!' So Mr Frost jumped into his car, I jumped into the Land Rover, and he arrived back in the yard just in front of me, and Mr Robins was already there. I said to Mr Robins, 'Have you put the fish away?' He said, 'No. They're still in the car.' I said, 'Right. I'll put them in the freezer.' 'First,' he said, 'have you got my net and tailer?' I said, 'No.' He said, 'Why?!' I said, 'Well, *I* didn't leave them behind!' And then he tore me off a strip, he said, 'That's *cheek*!' 'Well,' I said, 'you were very cheeky to me and Mr Frost said leave them where they are, that it's up to you to get them!' I said, 'It's like this, Mr Robins. As you've been so rude to me and wouldn't even give me a drink after I've done my best, your net and tailer must stay down there all night!' and I drove off home, leaving him still out there, stamping around.

Now, you see, a young man, or any person that come and took my job, if they had somebody like that, they'd put their notice in right away, they couldn't stick it — manners have declined on the part of the workers *and* their employers, though Mr Robins isn't actually a member of the Syndicate. But you've got to be patient when people lose all understanding. It always amuses me. It gives you the temperament of a person, what he *can* be like if he turns a little bit nasty. And Mr Robins, when he's in good form, you couldn't wish to have a better person. Everybody's human; everybody's got different little fads, different ways. This is what I've got used to, and this is what the youngsters don't like.

I've only got one child — a daughter called Jill. Preferably I wanted a daughter but, after a daughter, it would have been nice to have a son as company for her, for family life, and he *might* have followed in my footsteps, though there are so many other interests in the world today and they're more easy to come by if you like to go out and search for them. I've sometimes imagined I was taking a lad of eleven or twelve on to the river to teach him to fish for a salmon.

We'd come in through Greystone Gate, down through one field, and I'd see a fish rise. 'Yes, there he is! Did you see that fish?!' We're standing on the bank now, or on a croy. Probably it's easier on a croy to start a person because, if he makes a bad cast, it falls into the fast water and the line's straightened out. 'Come on, then. Pull four or five yards off your reel and leave it loose on the ground.' I'm assuming he's right-handed. 'Right. Now hold the rod with your right hand at the top end of the butt, and hold the line on the butt by your right forefinger. You've got it. Catch it hold there. Now, release your fly — your fly is caught just above your reel. Release the fly so the fly's dangling. Now flick the fly out into the water and, as you do that, release your finger and all your loose line will fly out into the river, we hope. But if it doesn't, it doesn't matter.

'Now, strip in your line. *I* call it "stripping in". Some people call it "pulling in" or "hand lining". That's right. Keep pulling the line in with your left hand. Now pull another couple of yards off your reel. You're not going to cast right across the stream, you're going to cast out as much as you can. You can't run before you can walk. Now up with your rod. Good. Cast forward. When you send your line forward, that's called "shooting the line". Don't use your body, just use your forearm and your wrist. And don't move your foot because, if you move your foot, you'll step on the line.' He should be holding the line in his hand but, nine times out of ten, it's on the ground beside his feet. 'Right. All your line's gone. Strip in again and pull off some more line. Out again. We'll keep stripping in and pulling off more line, and when I find that you can't cast any further, we're really fishing properly and I'll keep you to that amount of line.' A normal cast for the boy would be eight to ten yards. I cast thirty, but he'd have to be a good caster to cast twenty. After he's caught his first fish or he's fished for a day or two, I'd gradually work him up to fifteen, eighteen, twenty yards. With ten yards at first, he's doing well. But you never know a person. When *I* started it was much harder because the rods were heavy and the reels were heavy: today they're light as vanity... And, whenever he's casting, I'm telling him not to go back with the rod beyond one o'clock. To be a good caster you *shouldn't* go back beyond one o'clock. It's only a little technicality, but nine times out of ten the beginner goes right back to four and hits the bank or bushes or whatnot behind him. What I say is, 'Up with the rod! Stop at twelve, one o'clock!' and, to give the rhythm, 'One, two, three, *out!*' and then the fly goes out across the stream. A lot of people like learning in a field or on a lawn, but I like to take someone straight on to the river.

So I've taken this boy along the river, you see, imaginary, and I've got him fishing, and then I've said, 'Oh! Did you see that?!' 'See what?' I say, 'You *must* be watching the *water* when you're fishing! A fish *came* to you! OK, then. Take a pace back upstream and bang your fly across again. Now then, strip in a little bit faster. There he is! You've got him! Well done! Now, keep the point of the rod up. Keep the point of the rod right up, playing him. You've got to let the rod *bend*. The more the rod bend the better, the less pressure there is on the fish. We've only got nylon on, which has a breaking strain of eight pound so, if you point the rod at the fish, it could break you. Stick the butt of the rod into your tummy and keep the rod up. And if the fish wants to run, don't touch the line, just let him run. That's right. Let the rod bend, really bend. Only, if the fish jumps… There! … As soon as he jumps, you must drop the point of your rod so there's no tension, so you won't pull the fly from his mouth… Now the fish have gone upstream, so keep your rod up. Let him go. Now then, as soon as the fish turns, you must put a bit of a strain on him. OK? OK. Now he's coming back downstream. Reel in! Reel in! What you've got to do is try to get the fish on to the surface. Try to keep a slight strain on him. Get your rod well up. On we come. Bring him in. Bring him in. I'll go down the bank with the net. Bring him in. That's right. Keep him up on the surface. Bring him in over the net. Right. I've got him. He's about seven pound. That's your first fish, isn't it? Well done, boy! Well done! Get me the scales. Yes, this salmon is seven and a half pound. Well done!'

And then, while we're walking to another pool, I explain to him that when you go fishing it's not just catching a fish, it can be the sound of the river running over a stick or down a little rapid, one day like the tinkling of bells and another like the sighing of the wind amongst dry leaves. It can be the sight of a grey squirrel trying to get hold of the nuts on a hazel branch hanging over the water, and the branch is bobbing up and down, and the squirrel's right on the end, getting partly wet but not unbalancing. Or, it's all the birds. 'There's a dipper! And there goes a kingfisher, look! The kingfisher's the pretty bird and the danger bird. He builds his nest with fish bones, but he's so showy. It's lovely to see blue coming up the river when everybody's down in the dumps. And there's

18

the old cormorant! Look! Two of them, flying over high. They'll devour their weight in fish in a day... That bird up there? That's a buzzard. We get a wonderful lot of buzzards here. What bird's that? That's a grey wagtail. Endsleigh's a damn good place for birds...

'Yes, you *are* lucky to be here, but a lot of people don't appreciate it. Hey, look! Look! There's a mink there. See him? Two. See two mink? Devils! Their sport is killing fish just for fun. They don't eat a lot, but they kill a lot, especially the baby fish. What's that? Where? Well, that's a dragonfly, so delicate in colour and also in itself. This is what I was telling you — it's not just catching fish, it's enjoying the life of the river. There's a tremendous lot of things to see. We used to get a lot of dragonflies years ago, but we don't see so many now. Same with the butterflies. You got hundreds of Peacocks, Red Admirals, Small Coppers, Meadow Browns ... but today it's mostly the Large White, the one that causes me work in the garden, laying eggs on the cabbages. You know, the sad part of the Tamar Valley now is the farmers with the sprays, they're killing everything — the butterflies, the wild flowers... Before they kill *us*, we'd betterway keep moving on down the river! OK?...

Two

I'll now tell you something about my family and my early days before I came here.

I was born in Hardicott Valley on the 2nd of June, 1913, in an isolated cottage called Cott, a quarter of a mile from Hardicott Farm and about a mile and a half from Milton Abbot. Milton Abbot was a village then of about forty families, two mile from Endsleigh and, with Endsleigh, part of a fourteen thousand acre estate belonging to the 11th Duke of Bedford. My father, George, was a general labourer on the estate — he'd been that for most of his working life. In 1913, he was forty-three and my mother, Dorothy, was forty.

Cott was a matter of four dilapidated rooms on the level — they'd call it a 'bungalow' today. We pulled out of there when I was two and came to the village to live in Ivy Cottage which I can't remember and which no longer exists. The Duke's plan was to turn Milton Abbot into one of the most modern villages in the country but this was knocked into a cocked hat by the First World War, though some of the work was completed afterwards. Any rate, when I was four we moved to the edge of the village, to No.1 Milton Green, a two up and two down semi-detached, a mile from Endsleigh Gates on Barton Road, the main road from Milton Abbot to Horsebridge. Our front porch was bang opposite the village school where I was first taken at the age of five by a girl in the Juniors called Freda Dawe. She lived below us on the Launceston to Tavistock Road at Coombe Lodge, one of the entrances to Endsleigh. Her father, like mine and like most of the men around, had some job on the estate. No.1 Milton Green was also one of the Duke's cottages and my father held it at the weekly rate of two shillings. It was thatched. There were a lot of thatched cottages in they days but, as the roofs burned down, they were replaced by cedar shingles which looked a bit thatchy from a distance. Now, when the shingles have rotted away, they put on slate.

Before she met my father, Mother was a dressmaker in her mother's house in the village of Chillaton, three mile out from Milton Abbot — probably in they days they called theirselves dressmakers if they were only stitching up a blouse. Her maiden name was Maker — Dorothy Ann Maker. Everybody called her Nance. She had a cousin, a big sheep farmer, in New Zealand. I remember in the mid-Thirties my father saw an advert in the *Western Morning News*. Anyone called Maker was to get in touch with some solicitors in London because this cousin hadn't made a Will and they were looking for the next of kins. So my mother got in touch. But, by the time the money was allocated out, I think the relatives got about three quid each. My mother, come to it, never knew she had so many relations in Devon and Cornwall! There were Makers everywhere! Makers, Makers, Makers…

The only grandparent I ever saw was my grandmother on my mother's side — I saw her three times when she came to stay with us, but I can't even remember what she looked like. As regards uncles and aunts, my father had one brother who drove a horse and trap for a doctor in Lifton. My mother had three sisters and one brother. The sisters moved from Chillaton to Bristol, Reading and London; they all lost touch. Her brother moved to Reading as a valet. His employer, a bachelor, came wearing a pink carnation to meet him at Reading Station. He left him all his money when he died, so he went into the antiques business. When *he* died, at ninety-two, he left three hundred and ninety somewhat thousand. So he was the rich one of the family. When I was about twelve, he came with a motorbike and side-car to stay at the Bedford Hotel in Tavistock. He'd already been left this money, set himself up in business and married a rich girl — money makes money. He arrived one day at No.1 Milton Green during the school lunch-hour, and seemed quite pleased with me. After taking me for a ride on the back of his bike, he said, 'Well, here you are. Here's something for you.' It was a pound note. I thought it was a fortune. About six year after, he came to visit in a motorcar with his wife and his son, Reg, a pansy sort of boy. Reg fell down outside Endsleigh Lodge and scratched his knee, and you'd have thought he'd broke his neck the way he was carrying on. In 1958, when my daughter, Jill, was three, the wife and I took her to see this uncle in Reading. When we were walking out of his showroom, he said, 'I'd better give Jill something.' By now he was a very rich man indeed.

He put his hand in his pocket and he went down and down and down and he brought her out a shilling.

My parents had three children of which I was the third. My brother, Ernest, was born in 1900, so he was thirteen year older than me; he'd already left school when I went there; he was running around with the roughs when I was going with the toddlers. Then there was a girl born between us in 1905. She died of meningitis when she was two or three, so I never knew her. I don't even know her name.

Ernest put his age forward when he was sixteen, and joined the Navy. Before then, he'd drifted away to work as a general on a farm in Somerset. After the Navy, he done a bit of butchering here in Milton Abbot before drifting away again, this time working on a farm in Hampshire where he met up with an Irish girl which'd plenty of money. Next he joined the Army short term — the butchering department at Catterick in Yorkshire — and, when he came out, he married this Irish girl and they bought a smallholding in Hampshire. The smallholding was doing well, but they'd been married only about four or five years when she had an illness and it killed her. Health before wealth. He was alone.

When the Second World War came along, he joined the Army again and landed up in Northern Ireland. There he picked up with another Irish girl, again with plenty of money, and he married her for life ever after. They've been married for thirty years, but they've got no children. At first he worked on her parents' farm somewhere. When her parents died, they sold the farm and went to live in Portadown. Ernest have said to me and the wife hundreds of times, 'Why don't you come over to ireland to see us?' Though next door's been blasted by the IRA, he says we don't want to be afraid; we've only got to keep our heads low and they won't blow our brains out. I wouldn't mind going personally, but the wife hates water and she hates flying. So I haven't met my brother for around twenty-three years.

I never liked going to school. As you got older, you looked at the boys and girls that had left and were doing a little job and you thought they'd got freedom. You didn't realize what was involved in work. You imagined *anything* would be better than going to school. Of course, when you left, you found that life wasn't going to be so easy. The Depression was on —

the same as it is now, though, in the Twenties and Thirties, the unemployed didn't have houses, they didn't have Unemployment Benefit: they were walking the roads from one workhouse to another. Milton Abbot was the half-way mark between Launceston and Tavistock, so they'd call in to Mr Pethwick's bakery, the official calling-house, and collect their allocated bread and cheese, and fill a can with cold water which they'd boil on the roadside for making tea after picking a few sticks and lighting them.

At school we were about forty kids. Same as at home we'd bucket lavatories, no running water, and only oil lamps. It sounds stupid, doesn't it?, but there were two playgrounds — a Boys' Yard and a Girls' Yard — though, in a classroom, boys might be sat between girls. There were two classrooms, one for the Infants, taught by Miss Tory Davey, and the Big Room for the others who were taught by the schoolmistress, Miss Smith, and, before her, the schoolmaster, Mr Nicholson. You worked up from Standard One to Standard Seven and left at the age of fourteen. After tests at the end of each year, you might have to stay on for another year in the same Standard. I was in Standard Seven when I left, but you were graded within each Standard into Grade One, Two and Three, and I was in Grade Two, average or above average, not what you'd call brilliant. Marks were done in ten — two out of ten, three out of ten... Arithmetic I was quite good at, and I used to get ten for handwriting, and ten for drawing or sketching — sailors getting off a ship, a duck flying off a pond in the middle of a wood... I was a good little sketcher. I wouldn't have minded being an artist, but that's always easy to say after the event; you've got to put a lot of work into it to *be* an artist. I was very interested in woodwork, and Miss Smith showed me how to use a fretsaw. I'm sure she tried her best, but I'd have preferred a man. *None* of the boys wanted to be in there being taught by a woman. Miss Smith was very strait-laced and very pale, with a white blouse and a race of beads, and a black skirt down to her ankles. To start with, her hair was in a bun, and then she had it bobbed. I can't remember anything about being with Miss Davey in the Infants, except wanting to be away from her in the Big Room with Mr Nicholson, the schoolmaster. Schoolmasters then were like little squires, totally different from today. I can see Mr Nicholson now — grey beard, a bit baldheaded, stiff collar, dark coat and breeches, stockings with a tassel. But, by the time I reached the Big Room, Miss Smith had taken over.

Miss Smith was very, very hard. If you grinned, she'd say, 'Get that idiotic grin off your face or I'll *knock* it off your face!' She was inclined to hit you with the flat of her hand up against your ear, or else she hit you across the back of the hand with a ruler. If you whipped your hand away, you might have it across your face. The girls got the same — no preferential treatment. If she seen you nudge a girl or pinch a girl or catch her hold by the knee, you'd have a couple of strokes and be moved to another desk. Even if you'd met Miss Smith in the street and hadn't said, 'Good-evening, Miss,' you might get a stroke for that. If you couldn't do the right spelling, you were taken out and put in the corner as the dunce. One punishment was writing lines. I was always being kept behind at lunch-time, or after four, writing 'I've been a naughty boy' fifty or a hundred times as neat as possible. Another punishment was to be sent out to the lobby where you hung your bag and cloth cap. For instance, nibs were split in the middle and you could 'cross-nib' and do queer writing. You might be sent out for doing that or for having a blob on your paper. Two or three of us boys would take it in turn to go out to the lobby pretty regular.

It's quite embarrassing talking about this, but then kids will be kids and a boy will be a boy and, if a boy is not a boy when he's young, he never makes a man. It's as simple as that. We were afraid, but we weren't unhappy. Boys in the country were tough. If you wanted a scrap in the yard, you had a scrap, knuckles to knuckles. If you went home with a black eye, you might have a crack from the buckle-strap around your father's waist, and be sent to bed on the strength of it. You'd think nothing of scratching your legs in the brambles bird-nesting, and I bird-nested from the age of six. You were told *not* to *rob* the nests, but you did: you made a collection of eggs and you labelled them. See?! We talk about this day and age how the poison is killing off the birds and whatnot. But we children were killing the birds off: we robbed the nests of *all* the eggs! Thrush, partridge, pheasant, moorhen, mallard, owl, rook... You'd climb a tree to get at a jackdaw or a rook's nest, and not be afraid. A town boy would say, 'Ooh, you can't get up there!' You'd think you were on top of St Paul's Cathedral! See my right eyebrow? It was nearly knocked off when I was seven, eight year old. I'd a home-made trolley, a long piece of wood with four wheels and a back axle and a front axle, and a piece of rope for holding while you steered with your feet. I was going down the hill on Ramsdown Road and the thing turned over: instead of going down the hill on the trolley, I was going down on my face, skinning my right eyebrow as I went. But in they days you didn't have no doctor or stitches; you just said your eyebrow was hanging and your mother pushed it back and held it with a little bit of plaster. I've been half albino with one white eyebrow and one brown one ever since. Three years later, a boy said to me, 'Is my knife sharp?' and I tried it and cut an inch of my right thumb open — you can still see the damn great mark. This day and age you'd have about eight stitches. Then you just bound it together with your handkerchief and didn't even *tell* your mother. It was hard days in every way. Many of the children were in rags and tatters. In some families there was eight and nine kids so, if it was girls, their dresses was passed down and almost worn out. Boys thought a patch on their trousers was a bit disgrading, whereas today they love to *have* patches. I was on my own and my mother always managed to make me some new trousers out of a bit of old whatnot, so *I* was all right. I wore short grey tweed trousers with black stockings going right up underneath, and a grey tweed jacket with leather buttons and a tweed belt, and lace-ups, leather-soled boots.

The School was Church of England, and the vicar of the village church, St Constantine's, was a school governor. He was the Reverend Henry but we called him Parson Henry. You could always hear Parson Henry coming from a long way off because he had a habit of humming Sunday's tunes. I'd often be in the lobby doing sums with Arnold Croote, a pal of mine — his sister, Mabel Littlejohns, has worked at Endsleigh as a chambermaid since 1968 — and Parson Henry would come in the door and look at us under his tremendous eyebrows and say, 'Really! Really! Out here again, boys?!' He was so nice. Gerry Masters — a cousin on my father's side — and myself, we went down pinching apples from the vicarage orchard one evening after school. We were up in the apple tree and he came out and he said, 'Really! Really! You boys come down from there! Come *down*!' We wouldn't come down, so he said, 'I'll get the policeman!' I just threw an apple at him, so he went to get the policeman. The policeman came and said, 'Come on, you devils! Down from there or you'll get a kick up the behind!' We then threw apples at the bobby and, as he ducked, we jumped and were gone like flying hell. The parson and the policeman were the real McCoys in they days and, although in a certain section, and I belonged to that section, we were just as daredevil, you didn't have the trouble that you've got today. We never tore people's property to pieces with flick-knives. We pinched an apple. But what's an apple? Right up to today, that's the worst thing I've ever done: steal an apple from Parson Henry. I remember the first car in the village was old Parson Henry's — in about 1926 he bought a Morris Cowley Bullnose. The second car in the village was a Ford T, a Tin Lizzie owned by the landlord of the Edgcumbe Arms. Until about 1920, the post was brought from Tavistock by horse and cart. Unbelievable!

It's sad really I was so mischievous at school because I could have learned a lot more, although we never had the facilities as they have today. The school's even got a computer room now. But, of course, everybody gets so highbrow that they don't want to do an ordinary job later. My mother knew I was bored and she didn't mind if I mitched. In blackberry time she'd say, 'You can stay home today, Boysie,' — her always used to call me Boysie — 'and us'll go blackberry picking!' and, afterwards, she just told the old attendance officer the truth. Very often a gang of us would be late back from lunch after playing 'Fox and Hounds'. A couple of foxes would go off before us, and the huntsman with his pack of hounds would try to find them in the fields and culverts. We'd creep into class late with our legs filthy. Some girls joined in, but not the prim and proper ones like the farmer's daughter who thought herself above the ordinary worker's child, the same as it is today.

Though my father was Church of England and a good-living man, he didn't bother about going to church, he preferred to sit in front of the fire. My mother, on the other hand, was very 'chapely' — Methodist it is now, but it was Wesleyan in they days. She went to chapel twice on Sundays and, as she was a good alto singer, she sang in the chapel choir. She was the chapel's Sunday School 'caretaker'. The Sunday School — and the Wesley Guild — was at the back of the chapel, and I was made to go there every Sunday afternoon from when I was five year old. Walter Frise, who looked after the greenhouses here at Endsleigh, was in charge. He came dressed in boots and bowler hat and a navy blue suit — most of the men seemed to be dressed in navy blue in they days — and told us stories from the Bible. At the end of each year little prizes were given for good attendance. Well, as I *had* to attend, I received little books about Jesus Christ, then *Pilgrim's Progress*.

Everyone who went to Sunday School was called a Sunday School Scholar and, in the summer, we went with the grown-ups on a Sunday School trip to seaside places like Exmouth, Bude, Polperro and Polzeath. My mother would come home from a Chapel Meeting, and probably I'd gone to bed and I'd call out, 'Well, where are we going, Mother?!' 'Oh, we're going to Exmouth.' Now, Exmouth is quite a nice beach, you see, so I'd be some pleased. 'When is it?!' 'In about three weeks' time.' Those three weeks felt like three years. The night before the trip I had to have a wash, standing up in the galvanized bath. You made sure you washed your knees and your feet, never mind about the rest of your body because you were only going to paddle. No one swam in they days. No one even bathed. For the women in their petticoats it would take a hell of a lot of undressing. Even the men, because of their longjohns, only turned up their trousers and went into the water up to their ankles. And everyone was scared of the sea because they only went there once a year. They're in the sea now all the time, country people, aren't they? The modern trend. I *still* can't swim.

Any rate, the night before this Sunday School trip, I couldn't sleep, I was tossing and turning. You'm up early and your mother is packing sandwiches and putting cold tea in a bottle, and it's ages before the solid-tyred charabanc with screens like Perspex fitted in the sides come from Matthews' in Tavistock. You get in this charabanc, all open, and, if it starts to rain, there's a hell of a scramble to get the canvas hood up. And, when you get to the beach, you take your stockings and your shoes off, though you'm almost afraid to go into the old sea in front of you, and you paddle, and you climb over the rocks collecting shells and seaweed and you build castles and you run about on the sand while the grown-ups mostly gossip. Then, soon after you've picnicked, you've got to leave for home. You've got to leave early because you're not coming a hundred and one down a motorway: there's only narrow roads and you're probably only doing twenty-five, jugging along, singing a song, with a stop somewhere like Ivybridge for something to eat, before getting home dog-tired.

My first Sunday School trip was when I was about eight. We went to Bere Ferrers by horse and wagonette, a large covered carriage that could take twelve or fifteen. At Bere Ferrers, I was on a swing in the shape of a boat, and Freda Dawe passed me and I kicked her in the head and put her on her back. Freda, the girl who used to take me to school, was now fifteen and the *last* person I wanted to knock out. Someone shouted, 'My God!' and I was off the swing and down to her. There was pandemonium for five minutes till she came round.

I'm afraid that going to Sunday School didn't affect my general mischief. Some evenings me and Arnold Croote used to tie a reel of strong thread to the knockers of people's doors, get back the other side of the road in the pitch black, and pull the thread. The knocker would knock and some old man would come to the door with a lamp or a candle in his hand, and you'd see him looking round till, as there was nobody there, he'd go back inside. Or if we knew an old couple were a bit cantankerous, we might tap on their window, and the husband might come outside and crack his horsewhip. Miss Tory Davey lived in the village and I was threatened with Remand School by Miss Smith for getting two or three younger kids to throw tobs of mud at her as she was walking in the road.

One of my few really *happy* memories of school is Miss Smith and Miss Davey taking us in a charabanc, when I was about thirteen, to a pantomime at the Palace in Plymouth as a school treat. Before the pantomime they escorted us into Woolworth's where the bright lights almost blinded you and I bought my mother a comb and my father a shaving mug for threepence each. I enjoyed the whole occasion greatly. The school had never *been* anywhere before.

Out of school, you made your own entertainment. When I was eight, nine, I mostly played by myself at the table in my bedroom, making my own toys. For instance, I might make a little wooden truck, using cotton reels I cut in half with a tenon- or fretsaw for wheels, and wooden skewers for axles. Or I'd cut out little bits of wood and fix them into cotton reels for telephone poles, and have a bit of cotton running along from one pole to another. The boys next door — Fernley, Stanley and Clifford Cox — sometimes came in to play with me. Their father, John, was a carpenter, which included being the village wheelwright and undertaker. Clifford, the youngest, has been working here at Endsleigh as a general for the last three or four years. He's called 'the old boy' but he's six years younger than me. He still lives at No.2 Milton Green. Mind you, it's all changed, because he's now got a bath and electric light. In my day there was a pump at the back between the two adjoining cottages and you'd to go outside and pump water up from a well into a bucket or a pitcher or a can with a spout. To wash, you poured a bucket of water into a galvanized basin on the slate slab let knee-high into a wall of the back porch. As a kid, I never used a flannel, just soaped my bare hands. I usually washed when I was dressed, so there was a watermark around my neck. Clifford had a scar in the centre of his top lip for sixty-three years. My mother left an empty peach tin on the slab in the back porch, and Clifford, when he was two and a half, picked it up and fell on the jagged edge of the lid.

My father couldn't afford to give me pocket money as such, but he taught me how to trap and skin a mole. I'd put traps down at night in a farmer's field and, in the morning, say before going to school, I'd put the moles in my bag, and in the evening I'd skin them in our outhouse and make a penny to sixpence from each by posting them to Horace Friend in Wisbech in Cambridgeshire. Another way to get spending money as a kid was to shout, 'Coppers! Coppers!' to Tavistock and Plymouth people as they passed through the village on a summer trip. There might be five or six charabancs with pink and green streamers hung out at the back, and us kids would shout, 'Coppers! Coppers!' and the trippers would throw handfuls of farthings, halfpennies and pennies at you, and you'd scramble to pick them up. That would happen year after year: as you got older — up to ten, twelve, thirteen — you'd be still shouting, 'Coppers! Coppers!' You could also get spending money off the old hawkers who came around shouting, 'Rags, bones and rabbit skins! Any old rags to sell?!' and you ran and got the dozen or so rabbit skins you'd stuffed with paper and hung up to dry, and you sold them for a farthing or a halfpenny each. I skinned rabbits myself from when I was eight or nine. Later, when I was thirteen, fourteen, as my father always had a ferret, I went out ferreting and sold rabbits to the local 'regulator', Mr Prout of Launceston, for 3d., 4d. each. I've always had a sweet tooth, so such money was for sweeties, which you could buy for a halfpenny an ounce or I bought tuppenny comics — *Rainbow, Boys' Own* or *Tiger Tim* — which came out on Fridays.

Every year a horse and trap used to come round, selling cherries for a penny, tuppence a pound, and I always remember being asked by the owner of a cherry orchard if I would come over one Saturday and earn sixpence by helping to pick cherries. I went up a twenty-bar ladder with a basket, and I'd picked five, six pounds of cherries, and the damned ladder slipped and the whole basketful went crashing to the ground. Labour in vain. The lady of the house told me to put the bruised cherries in another basket and, instead of getting sixpence, I was allowed to take these home.

One event I looked forward to was the visit of the Travelling Bazaar which was a horse and wagon with a frame hung on each side with pots and pans and cups for sale — all the women would rush out to buy. You'd also have visits from Dixie Parker. Quite a nice name, isn't it? Dixie Parker was the scissor-grinder and he'd come from Stoke Climsland with his donkey and little trap and a little grinding stone, and he'd sharpen your knife or a pair of scissors just for a few pennies. Marvellous.

Then, in summer, there was always the haymaking, when the boys and girls helped the farmers turn the hay with a long-handled prong and then put it into mounds. During that time, there'd be a little bit of frolics or, as they used to say, 'making the hay sweet'. You'd chase a girl and roll her in the hay and kiss her through a bit of hay twisted into a ring. I did that from the age I could run, right on till after I'd left school. By the time I was at Endsleigh, I was *still* helping in the hayfield, though making the hay sweet with older girls.

Early that year when the whole school was taken to the pantomime, my parents thought I had the flu and called Dr Musgrave of Lifton who ran a surgery in Milton. He took my temperature and said, 'Bed! You've got double pneumonia!' Oh, it was pretty grim. I was ill for four to five weeks. To begin with, Dr Musgrave visited me every day. I was wrapped in a cotton wool jacket and only allowed a basin of Oxo or Bovril for nourishment till a certain day after which I would improve or deteriorate. I'll always remember my mother coming up and saying, 'You'm going to be all right,' because I'd passed the turning point.

The same year, I hurt my left foot. Of an evening, I often used to bat a ball or play football or rounders in the rough field of a tenant farmer — for rounders you'd hit the ball with your fist, and run around some stones. Any rate, I pulled the tendons in my left foot, kicking a football, and I've had a gammy foot ever since: a terrible foot I've got. I've lived with it from thirteen. With nothing being done, it's all hammer-toes and shrivelled up and shorter than the other foot. I limp sometimes, and sometimes when I'm wading and I'm putting all the pressure on my right foot, if I stand on an odd stone and it overbalances me, my bad foot haven't got the strength to pick me up. At one time they was talking about having my left foot off. When I say that to some people, what do they do?! They burst out *laughing*! They sort would laugh to see their granny's backside on fire. I take it as a joke. I'm still walking and I can go down and come up these stairs [our sessions took place in my attic bedroom] quicker than you probably.

But you, I suppose, don't have cramp. Because of my gammy foot, the cramp in my left leg and thigh has got me terrible for years and years. As long ago as when I was courting and newly married, I've been in the cinema and the cramp have taken me and I've had to stand up. People say, 'Sit down!', 'Sit down!' and you can't and you feel terribly embarrassed, so I always try to get a seat on the alleyways so I can stand up out there. Down at Plymouth Argyll at the football I sit in the grandstand tensed up and crammed for three parts of an hour in each half and, all of a sudden, the cramp'll take me. And if I go to stretch in bed I've to jump clean out as it gets me in my muscle right away. Just as well I sleep on my own or I'd kick the wife out with me. Very often I've to hobble into the bathroom and run a drop of cold water in the bath and stick my foot in that and press on the heel. I used to take tablets for it before I went to bed, but my present doctor says the fewer tablets you take the better. I sometimes use a special spray that footballers use. One night I jumped out of bed, making a hell of a noise and waking the wife. I said, 'I've got' the cramp!' She said, 'Well, why don't you spray your leg?!' I said, 'How the hell *can* I?! I can't walk, and the spray's in the bathroom!' The old remedy to stop you from having cramp is to have a cork in bed. I have two or three. They're blooming uncomfortable because you lie on them when you roll over. A doctor who came here fishing said he was called out late one night to see someone and, when he pulled back the clothes to examine him, his bed was full of corks. He thought, 'Well, here's an alcoholic.' But, instead of that, *he* suffered from cramp.

I shouldn't complain. In my job you meet people with worse deformities than a gammy foot. Either their hands are deformed or they've only got one leg or they've only got one arm. There's a gentleman that belongs to the Syndicate, Major Smyth-Osborne, and he's only got one arm. One arm! So he wears a false arm. And he's a marvellous fisherman! When he hooks a fish, he drops his rod into the hook that's on his false arm, plays the fish beautiful, brings it in and tails it. Yet you and me, we've got two arms and we're always grumbling. I've got a *blind* gentleman — Colonel Ansell, the great horseman. Totally blind, yet he's a superb fisher and never grumbles! You take him down on to the bank or on to a piece of staging or on to the shingle or into the river — he'll wade the river — and he'll just say, 'Am I square to the flow?' The first time he ever came here, only a couple of years ago, I met him downstream and he said, 'Well, Horace,' he said, 'the bluebells here are beautiful!' His seeing those bluebells through the eyes of his housekeeper hurt me tremendous. There's a lot in life and you've got to count your blessings and name them one by one.

Life wasn't easy for my parents. When I was a kid, my father — he never served in the Great War as he was classed as 'agricultural' — was only earning fifteen bob a week as a general labourer and, by the time he was pensioned off in 1940, he was only earning thirty. As a general, he helped to make rides and build croys and dig drains. The drains were open wall drains. Skilful but slow. Today, someone comes in with a damn JCB with a great spade behind and puts a pipe in and covers it the same day. That's the trouble: it's the machine doing the work. The only way you'll get full employment is to have a war and kill off half the population... Sometimes he was loaned to a farmer. Sometimes for extra money in his spare time of a Saturday afternoon he might muckspread or cut thistles. I know that for cutting thistles with a scythe he earned sixpence an acre.

One of the great arts in they days was stone hedging — a layer of stones, a thin layer of turf, a layer of stones and so on, ending with a thin layer of turf on top — and my father was a great stone hedger, though he did turf hedging too. Every year at Lifton they had agricultural competitions for stone hedging, turf hedging, and spearmaking for thatch. My father entered for the stone hedging and was always champion. The farmers' boundary hedges were always having to be kept in trim by the Duke's men when they got tore down by the cattle or the rabbits. In they days there were rabbits, rabbits everywhere and, if the water rose, they would all come out from their ground buries along by the river and go up into the fields to make ground buries again or buries in the hedges, even boring out the stones. And people ferreting did a lot of damage. They'd take out a stone or two, if the ferret laid up, and listen to find out where the old rabbit and the ferret was, and then they'd dig out the hedge. An under-keeper at Endsleigh once saw what he thought was a rabbit bolt out on top of a hedge, and he banged at it, and it was his own son's head: he killed him dead as a rag there and then.

Though he was a teetotaller, my father smoked heavily — Black Jack in the old clay pipe. He spoke very broad: there's an old Devon expression 'fell down head', and he used to say 'vildernayed'. He had a bushy moustache — most men had moustaches then: bushy, drooped or handlebar. He was well built, big boned, pretty tough. If you wanted a rough house, he could give you one, so nobody fell out with him. He was a very strict parent. You had to do what you were told; little boys had to be seen and not heard. If I misbehaved I knew his buckle-strap and, rather than have a crack with that, I whipped up the stairs pretty smart and was gone to bed. Otherwise he was gentler than I am. Mother and Father were both very gentle, placid people, and rather reserved. They never got in a flummox like I do. They wouldn't be fussed like I am this minute talking to you. He was six foot tall — I'm five foot ten — and, even at ninety, he didn't have a big tummy like I've got from riding around on four wheels; it was melted down from hard work and walking. For years he couldn't even afford a second-hand boneshaker. Today the workers are saying that they'm so badly off. They've never been *better* off! With my State pension and £45 a week take-home pay, *I'm* better off! My father could hardly afford a wheelbarrow, where I've got a private car and a coloured television. I can buy a mac, where they, poor devils, only had hessian sacks to wear across their shoulders if it was raining. They worked a half day Saturday. I remember one Saturday, while I was still at school, Father walked to Smale's in Launceston, seven and a half miles away, for a new pair of hobnail boots which cost him fifteen and six. So that's fifteen miles, there and back, for a pair of boots which cost him sixpence more than his weekly wages!

Because he didn't know any different, all he was interested in was work, hard work, on the estate and in our garden. We had an enormous garden with plenty of produce — I had my *own* little flower and vegetable patches — and we kept poultry and a couple of pigs. The butcher would come and kill the pigs on the spot at Christmas time. We'd sell one to the butcher and keep one ourself. My mother would clean the pig's belly at the pump outside, and some of the pork would be minced up for hog's puddings — they'd hang in the pantry for weeks and weeks and weeks, tied up in a little bow. She'd salt the bacon, and have sides, wrapped in muslin, up on the laths stretched from beam to beam of the kitchen ceiling. She'd smoke the ham — that's the shoulder or thigh — over the fire, salt it for so long, hang it in muslin, and cut off pieces for boiling when required.

My mother was five foot five, and a good-looking woman though she carried a high colour. Even if they wanted to, humble folk couldn't afford to powder down their rosy cheeks, like they do today. Though she was willing to help other people, she wasn't interested in their affairs as such and, though she might go next door to have a yarn, she didn't go gossiping from cottage to cottage. Once they used to say the ladies were the talkers but, now the ladies has taken over the men's jobs and the men does the washing of the dishes and the ladies is out in the garden, men probably are becoming talkers in their place.

Apart from her involvement with the chapel, and apart from doing a bit of washing for the farmers in their furnace houses and helping in the kitchen at Endsleigh when the Duke and Duchess were in residence, my mother's time was taken up with drudgery in the home. Night after night she'd be on one end of a saw and my father on the other cutting logs to keep the fire burning. The thick slate floors downstairs, the 'blue flags', had to be scrubbed; the stove had to be black-leaded; the little diamond window-panes had to be kept clean. She baked the bread, made the soup, skinned the rabbits for the rabbit pie, cleaned the herrings… Now they can't even comb their hair. Then everything was slow: now, with technology, everything's going so fast that people pass their *selves*. And there was seasons then without the freezer. As a kid you looked forward to going out in the garden in summer picking the peas; you was eating peas as fast as you was picking of them — they're very windy, aren't they?! Apples was stored, but they'd only last till just after Christmas. Now you can even have a *salmon* all the year round! I know a man who's got a piece of fish in the freezer which was caught ten months ago! I've lived in two completely different generations.

If my father was working in the actual grounds of Endsleigh — then about a hundred acres, now about seventy-five — he'd to be inside the gates by half past seven and he'd work till half past five (barring Saturdays when it was one o'clock), with a quarter of an hour's break for crib during the morning and an hour for lunch. If he was working anywhere else on the estate, he was allowed a half hour's walking time there and back. Workers weren't allowed to smoke in the *grounds*: they'd to knock their pipe out or throw their cigarette end away before they walked inside. Instead of smoking, many of them went round with an empty pipe or a twig or a piece of grass in their mouth. In they days most men seemed to smoke. I've never had the inclination. On the river bank you get offered a cigar. Well, I don't accept it even though I could give it to somebody else. If a person gives you a thing, it's a gift to *you*, and it's rude to pass it on...

There's people living in Milton Abbot village now that have never been inside the Endsleigh Gates but, from when I was a boy of about twelve, I used to meet my father down the drive when he was leaving work. They was very strict about letting anybody inside, but I was known — everybody knew everybody then: we was one big happy family — and I'd be allowed to enter the side gate past Endsleigh Lodge because I was my father's son. I could meet him, of course, anywhere and any time outside on the *estate*, say, take a pasty to him for my mother while he was trimming hedges along Barton's where the Duchess landed her plane or while he was working on the river. Shortly after I left school, my mother gave me a box camera, a Kodak Brownie No.2, and, in the summer of '28 when I was fifteen, I cut down across the fields to Beera and photographed my father and his mate, Fred Alford, dismantling a croy on the Cornwall side with a bar iron and a sledgehammer. I know it was summer because in the photo, though my father is wearing a cap, Alford is wearing a straw hat. Underneath their waders, they'd be wearing corduroy trousers. In they days, workers often wore corduroys tied below the knees. You called them yorkers. They usually tied them in with binder twine or with hay — make do and mend. Alford used straps... That's one of the first photos I ever took. All my life, since then, I've been taking photos. Of all the cameras I've used — the Brownie Box, the Halina Super, the Kodak Instamatic and, my latest, the Konica — I recommend the Konica. But it's been one or two photos a month probably, not click, click, click, like so many people do today.

There was never any mention of my working at Endsleigh or on the Bedford Estate when I left school. It's *true*! You're sat there in the armchair and you hold your hands to your head and look at me dead serious and then smirky, and I think to myself, 'I wonder is he believing me?' You've got to be on my side a *wee* bit! You're scraping my mind, you're pulling it to pieces, and it's making me all dizzy. But you see, I didn't discuss things with my father, he kept his own counsel — fathers were harder to get at than they are today. When I said to him, 'Did you have a good day?' it was just 'Oh, nothing special. Have you chopped up the wood for the morning? Have you fed the ferret? Have you fed the pigs? Have you dumped the manure in the ash pit?' Any rate, I wanted a cushier job than general labourer and, probably, at that particular time, that's all I'd have been given. No, I was more interested in gentleman's service. I had my rich uncle in the back of my mind: as a boy of fourteen, I thought that way I might get rich quick.

For six months I was roaming around with nothing much to do. Then I was lucky. A job came up in the *Tavistock Gazette* or the *Tavistock Times* for a boy on the estate of a gentleman called Mr Ward who lived at Bourneville, Brentor, that's seven miles from Milton Abbot. I applied for the job and got it. For half a crown a week, I cleaned the shoes and helped the between-maid in the dairy and the poultry man in the pens. I didn't live in the main house: I lived in the Farm House with Mr Medland, the hind, and his wife. But I ate in the Servants' Hall with the cook at one end of the table and the butler at the other. Mr Medland gave me extras to make me keen — tuppence for every dozen eggs I collected, and tuppence a tail for trapping rats and moles — as well as a working suit. Mrs Ward, who gave me my wages, not weekly but ten bob a month, said that, for every ten bob I put in the Post Office, she would double it. But I hardly ever saved ten bob to *put* in the Post Office. My father had given me his second-hand boneshaker, and I cycled home, all winds and weather, every Sunday. By the time I'd bought cream for my mother and sweets and, say, a tin of boot polish or an orange for myself, and paid for my photography, I might only be left with about two and fivepence. In the eighteen months I was at Bourneville, I think I only put a couple of ten bobs in the Post Office for Mrs Ward to double.

After about twelve months Mr Ward wanted me to be his valet, and I said I'd be delighted. Apart from brushing his clothes and so on, I'd to harness his horse and bring it to the side entrance either in the carriage or the jingle. I worked for him personally for three months. During those three months he fell ill, and I had to sit beside his bed and read to him from the London dailies and the *Tavistock Gazette*, though some of the words stumped me. Then he died and I became a general again for the Family Trust. One day I was working in the poultry pen when one of Mr Ward's nephews came along and said, 'I've got a little surprise for you. Uncle left you this,' and he handed me six pound notes. I was thrilled: I was over the moon. You know, £6! I put them in my right-hand pocket and then I took them out and counted them and put them in the other pocket; I kept on changing pockets with them, thinking they would grow! The legacies went from £6 to those working at my level to £500 to the butler. I suppose Mr Ward took to me in the short time he knew me because I was brought up the right way. I'd been taught at home to do what I was told and not to answer back. I'd had my fling at school and, in my first job in the world, I wanted to make an impression, especially on a man I liked so much.

When I showed my mother the money, she said, 'You ought to put that away in the Post Office.' But I didn't put it away in the Post Office, I spent it. There was a Women's Institute trip to Ilfracombe. My mother and father was going, and I went too. And, with six quid, I'm the richest boy on board the charabanc so, when we got to Ilfracombe, I start lashing out. I thought, 'Well, I've been lucky and I'm going to share my luck.' I said to my father, 'Here's a bob. Have a game of hoopla!' I said to the old girls, 'Come on, Mrs So and So! I'll take you on the bumpers!' … I got rid of quite a portion of my £6 that day. The rest I spent a fortnight to three weeks after when the new brooms at Bourneville gave me notice. While at home, wandering around for a week or two, I bought anything I wanted — films for my camera, a cricket bat (I was now going out occasionally on the Green for a knock), a pair of trousers, a flashy Tootal

37

tie to go with my working suit, a tennis ball, rat tails... Rat tails were little thin sticks of liquorice covered with white, pink, green or yellow sugar-coating. You'd chew 'em up and then you could stick out your black tongue at the girls.

Today you see boys and girls coming out of the Comprehensive in Tavistock arm in arm. I didn't become really interested in girls till I was nineteen, twenty and had started at Endsleigh. When I left school, all my pals were boys more or less my age and boys kept to boys and girls kept to girls. There was Tom Bray, who became my closest friend, Stan Cox, Arnold Croote, Walter Alford, Horace Branch — who all went to school with me — and Gerry Rooke from Ashwater. Tom Bray worked as a general on the estate. Then, during the war, he went and joined the electricity people. In later life he had a girlfriend or two but, early on, he wasn't interested in women; he preferred going to the pub, and he was as happy as a sandboy. Stan Cox helped his father in the carpentry trade. Arnold Croote was a gardener on the estate. After the war he moved on to Taunton as a mason's labourer. He was mad about motor-cycles. Walter Alford, who worked on the estate as a mason's labourer, could imitate almost any person, any animal. He'd get behind a tree and do the cuckoo, and everyone would say they heard the cuckoo. Immediately after the war, he was walking up Lamerton Down with his push-bike, and a bus came along and ran over him. I was a bearer at his funeral. Horace Branch was a general on the estate. After the war, he became a baker's roundsman in Launceston. He was a wonderful sketcher. Gerry Rooke worked at Leigh Farm which is part of Leigh Barton where Philip Tuckett, one of the Syndicate directors, lives now. That was our little gang. They're all dead now but Arnold Croote and me.

On Sundays — I was now a member of the Wesley Guild and went to Prayer Meetings, and Sankey Evenings which had hymns that went with a swing — if one of the gang wanted to go to church, we'd all go to church and if one of them wanted to go to chapel, we'd all go to chapel. Then we'd walk the two miles out to Pridham's Garage in Lamerton and back, no girls attached to it. You know, just to kill time, nothing else to do. We even went to *chapel* or to *church* for something to do! I'd already lost any faith I may have had. The wife is Church of England. After we married in '42 she didn't go to church, she came to chapel with me at

Christmas, Easter and anniversaries such as Harvest Festival. Now we don't go to chapel or church ever. The older you get and the more you think about these things, you picture that people have just sat down and made them all up. Perhaps there's a sort of power, but I don't believe in details such as the afterlife. Milton Abbot is still very Methodist but, in all the little hamlets around, the chapels have closed down and the flock is inclined to go to church if they don't go by the seaside. There ain't so much religion now. Until mechanization, the majority went to church or chapel because they'd no way of getting anywhere else...

After Bourneville, I went from one extreme to another — you had to grab what you could because there was so much unemployment. Perriton's Bakery, Pym Street, Tavistock, advertised for a youngster to learn Confectionery. I applied in writing, and I had an answer come back by return asking to see me in person. So I push-biked in to Tavistock, and I suppose the old boy that interviewed me, Mr Perriton Senior — one of the two brothers that owned the place — thought to himself, 'He's a trier, push-biking six miles in from Milton Abbot. He must be better than a town boy.' Any rate, he gave me the job — a three year apprenticeship learning Confectionery from the raw stage at 10s. 6d. a week. It seems a big jump from half a crown, but don't forget at Bourneville I had food and lodging and a working suit supplied. At Perriton's I'd to pay sixpence for my lunch in one of their cafeés in the town.

I learned how to make icing and how to decorate. I learned how to make Congress and jam tarts. I learned how to make sponge and saffron cakes. Perriton's was a great firm for saffron cakes. This day and age, saffron is classed as a poison; you never get the true saffron cakes as they only put in a colouring. I became quite professional at making them. You had great big wooden tubs that took a hundredweight of flour and so much lard and so much yeast, and then you scalded your stringy saffron, put that in and mixed everything up, and left it to set as your last job of the afternoon at about two o'clock. Then you had to be back at three o'clock in the morning by when the yeast would have risen and the cake would be at the top of the tubs, and you'd take it out and put it in pound and two-pound tins which another man would put into the oven. I'd cop it if I didn't grease the bottom of the tins properly; the cake would have to go into the pigswill with the bad bread and whatnot for the old farmer to collect. I wore a white apron and, if I was over the tub, a white cap.

After about five months, I helped out generally. Someone would say to me, 'Knock up a few Congress tarts!' or 'Knock up a few saffron buns!' or 'Knock up a few Christmas puddings!' and by 'a few' I mean four or five hundred. If all the Christmas puddings wasn't sold, they put them back on the rack; they were so good that they could keep indefinite. Same with the Christmas cakes, though the icing was knocked off for making up again. Easter was yellow-iced cakes with little chicks stuck on top. Good Friday morning, you had to be in mighty early because hot cross buns had to be out on the streets at six o'clock for the old Ford vans to take to the shops and door-to-door out in the country.

I loved the work for a time but, after about two years, I was thinking of chucking my hand in. Firstly, Mr Perriton Senior's son, 'the young boss' as we called him, was tempery and dictatorial. Secondly, the Confectionery floor was a bit stuffy because it was over where the bread was made and, when you take a couple of hundred loaves out from the ovens, there's a hell of a lot of steam rising. Things came to a head quite by chance. The young boss was very interested in pistol shooting and at the top of the building he had a target gallery. One day he was going upstairs when one of the boys who worked with me in Confectionery passed him. That was bad enough. You were never allowed to meet in the stairs. The superstition was that if you met one another in the stairs you'd never meet one another in heaven. Say one of the old Perriton brothers was coming up from the bakery and you were coming down from Confectionery, you'd be expected to go back. So the young boss was annoyed at this boy meeting him in the stairs. He asked him where he was going. The boy said he was whipping outside to buy something in the town. 'Well, you're *not* to go!' 'I'm going!' ... One word brought another and, in the end, the boy was *stopped* going, and the young boss brought him up to Confectionery and gave us *all* a dressing-down. Three of us took off our aprons there and then. We said, 'Right! We're off! You can have your bloody job!' and we walked out, just like that. I copped hell when I got home. By now I was earning twenty-one shillings a week, and my parents thought I'd thrown away a chance in life. In they days, confectioners was looked up to.

40

So, in 1932, at the age of nineteen, I'd packed up a good career by choice. It was a choice I've never regretted. I wouldn't be doing the work I'm doing now, would I? Also, I was on and off the dole for a year and, during that time, I loosened up a bit as a person, doing odd jobs and entering more into the life of the village and the villages around. I remember I did some corn harvesting, and I dug foundations and made some drive-ways for a builder. I even helped out on a lime-spray stall at the Devon County Show. I was a member of the Play Group of the Wesley Guild, and we performed in Milton Village Hall and at places like Bere Alston, Gunnislake and Chilsworthy where I'd have to go on the back of someone's motorbike. I think it was at this period that I played Septimus Quirke, a Cambridge tutor, in a play called *Three Half-Crowns*, and in comic sketches for two called 'Tit for Tat' and 'Hawkins v. Hawkins' with my cousin, Gerry Masters. Before the curtain raised, I was very nervous but, oh, once I'd started, I wasn't bothered about anybody. Milton Abbot have always had a dramatic group — the Milton Abbot Players — but I've never belonged. My daughter, Jill, is quite a good little actress. She was President one year. Now she's Secretary. I dropped drama from the war on, the same time pretty well as I stopped going to church. Reg Brown, one of the nicest gentlemen that ever lived in the village, he's one of the top men in the Milton Abbot Players still, and he's gone eighty. You should interview *him*. He can remember every-thing, quick as lightning.

There was never no Scouts or Guides in Milton Abbot, but there was The Milton Abbot Reading Room where for sixpence a year you played skittles, darts, shove-halfpenny and whist, or read a paper or a book if you wanted. It was attached to the Village Hall, and run by a committee that paid a small annual rent to the Duke. And there were now a few buses. The last bus back from Tavistock was ten o'clock so, Saturday night, you might go in to Tavistock to the pictures or to walk around the streets. And, from the age of eighteen, when I was old enough to go into a pub, I took a drink — I'd ask for scrumpy or a Mackeson or a port and lemon. But what one's got to remember is you couldn't *afford* many things, so it was mostly Reading Room, Reading Room, Reading Room.

I wasn't up to scratch for the local football team because of my bad foot, though after the war I travelled round with them as linesman for two or three years till the club disbanded. But I *did* belong to the cricket team. There wasn't any speciality about me; I was just there to make the number. We played all the villages around. The captain was a local farmer called Guest. He kept the team together, and the Duke, or his agent, took an interest — he had a pitch made with a pavilion in a field of this Mr Guest, being as he was one of his tenant farmers. So Milton Abbot was one of the first local cricket teams to have a pavilion with a changing room for the visitors and a changing room for the home team *and* a refreshment room, although the water had to be carried over in milk churns from the village. The Guests had a small dairy and the away teams always looked forward to visiting Milton Abbot because Mrs Guest laid on real Devonshire teas. Farmer Guest and his wife were dedicated. I used to travel to away matches in the dickie seat of my neighbour Fernley Cox's old Jowett, a 1927 model that cost him a hundred and thirty-two quid. The tax on a Jowett was £7 per annum. Just fancy! £7 per annum tax! I pay £90 somewhat on my Vauxhall Chevette now!

I belonged to the Milton Abbot Cricket Club from as soon as I came away from Bourneville right up to the war, and I still follow cricket in the paper. They've made a hash of it, but I support Yorkshire. I never fancied Somerset. From a kid, in the days of Verity and Sutcliffe, it always stood out a mile, Yorkshire did. It was great fun following our local team, which was a good social mix. You might go to Tetcott, then, after the match, come in to Launceston for fish and chips, and then do one or two caterwauls in the Bell Inn. Bats and pads were provided, but not the white trousers and the cream shirt the girls liked to chase. I didn't wear a cap. Except in the Services, I've never worn a cap or a hat in my life. I can't *stick* a hat! I'm hot blooded, I perspire a lot and I get a bit of an itchy head. A lot of people say it's safer to wear a hat. When you make a cast and come forward with the heavy flies, the fly can give you a hell of a crack on the back of the head. But that's your fault; you shouldn't make the mistake. Then the weaklings say that, without a hat, you'll be bitten. This time of year in particular there's a tremendous lot of wasps about, and there's always a lot of horseflies and greyflies. But they'll bite you in any case! If you've got a hat on they'll bite you on the arms. Without a hat, they won't bite you in your hair. I've a good head of it and they're not going to go into *that* which *is* a hat, a white one, in itself!

Then people talk about sunstroke. Well, I've never been sunstruck and I've been in the sun all day! In the mind a lot of it is! In the mind! Admittedly I can't *lie* in the sun and sunbathe, because I was fair-haired when I was young, and fair-haired people is inclined to peel, really burn. Same with glasses. In the last ten years or so I've worn reading glasses and distant glasses, but I wear them because I have to for my sight. Some people say you should wear goggles or glasses for safety when you fish! Again, it's all in the mind. One of the American ambassadors got a fly caught in a tree, trout fishing somewhere in Scotland. He was looking up at it and tugged and the fly came down into his eye and it blinded him. But that's just a stroke of bad luck. It's the same as if you go down and walk across the yard and there's somebody come down on a motor-bike and they can't stop and they kill you. All this 'It's advisable to wear glasses', 'It's advisable to wear a hat', 'It's advisable to do this', 'It's advisable to do that'! They'm getting weak not only in the body but in the mind! Major Smyth-Osborne, he's only got one arm and so he hasn't got his balance, but very often *he's* not wearing a hat, and he's *never* wearing glasses! ...

It's not raining, is it? I want it to rain heavy.

I'm not used to sitting so long. I'll whip downstairs and get some biscuits. That'll give me a break...

As well as cricketing, I started going to dances. There was a lot of dances in our Village Hall — we called them 'hops', the 'local hop'. We went to an occasional dance in Tavistock, what they used to hold in the Market Hall, but that was very rare. Where we went mostly was to villages such as Mary Tavy, Peter Tavy, Lydford, Brentor... The dance would start about eight and go on till two. We'd have to push-bike. I wasn't much of a dancer — I'm a real old country jan, you know — and I picked the steps up so much as I could: the waltz, the foxtrot, the two-step, the valeta. The bands were made up of local boys. Brentor had a very good one — Georgie Gale and His Band. You weren't really serious about girls, you were just out for an evening's enjoyment. All around the hall was chairs or long forms you sat on. You'd have the Milton Abbot boys one side and the Brentor girls opposite, the Brentor boys opposite the Lydford girls and so on. You always stayed round in a batch. There was no drink in the halls so eventually you'd say, 'There's a couple of girls there gone out. They've probably gone down to the pub. Let's follow them.' You'd buy a pint of scrumpy for tuppence and have a swig of that, and that would put the devil in you, you didn't care a damn whether it was Christmas or Easter, and you might say to the girls, 'We'll meet you next Sunday.' But next Sunday might be streams of rain and we weren't going to cycle in streams of rain to see something in skirts.

Jumping the gun a bit, I was well in my twenties and I'd been at Endsleigh for some time when seven of us went to a dance at Bere Alston in the butcher's motorcar. At this dance there was a 'draw', the same as it is today, and my name was drawn out of the hat, so everybody shouted 'Hooray!', especially the Milton boys. The prize was a little coffee set, china on a china tray. As it was presented to me, I said, 'Look. We'll take the coffee set off the tray and give the tray back.' And then — we'd had a drop of drink — one of our seven took the china tray and shoved it right up to the other end of the hall where it smashed to smithereens; the caretaker with brush and pan was brushing of it up. The Milton Abbot boys were looked down on for ten minutes, and the girls we were making up to shunned us for the rest of the evening. Yet I was the innocent party.

The first girl I got really serious about was shortly after I'd started at Endsleigh in '33. Her name was Sybil Puttick. She'd jet black hair and a very pale complexion. She was quite pretty and she was about five foot eight, almost as tall as me. She lived in Launceston and worked there in a grocer's shop called The International. Launceston, like Bere Alston, was quite a cycle ride. I just got chatting of her up after going to the pictures with some of our gang — after the pictures you'd buy cod and chips wrapped in paper and take it out on the streets and eat it, wandering around; you enjoyed coming in to Launceston from the wilds because it was all lit up and so many girls were wandering around, too. I said, 'I might meet you again,' casual, just like that, and, when I was next in Launceston wandering along the street, I saw her so I wolf-called and, there you are, Bob's your uncle, we got more friendly.

I was running around with Sybil, very serious, for about twelve months. I was invited to her home and eventually I brought her back to mine. One morning, her brother-in-law was giving her a lift to work on the back of his motorbike and a car hit them for a six. He wasn't injured, but she broke her leg. She was rushed to Launceston Hospital and her leg was set, and I remember I went to see her the next day. Then she was taken to Plymouth Hospital and from Plymouth Hospital she was taken to Moorhaven Hospital near South Brent. Moorhaven is a mental hospital now but then it was a tuberculosis unit and Sybil had tuberculosis, brought on by shock. I don't know the details. It could have been in the family because tuberculosis was the main killer in that age. Arnold Croote used to take me down Saturday afternoons on his motorbike and, it was sad, every girl that was in that hospital was like the girls you saw in those days on boxes of chocolates. And there was so *many* girls there! I can remember a girl in the next bed to Sybil. She'd been ill for a long, long time and was on the mend and on the point of going out, and she was allowed out in the grounds and she tripped and fell and she was dead within five days.

Eventually *my* girl died. I'd got engaged to her in the hospital, and I was told that she was dead. It was a terrible thing. I remember it as though it was yesterday. The body was brought back to her home and I was informed would I like to come to see her. I went to see her and her mother said to me, 'Now look. Here's her engagement ring. It's been taken off.' But I put the engagement ring back on to her finger. It's as simple as that.

Probably we would have got married. One doesn't know. I grieved for a short time, but life goes on and I went on with my work. I wore a black armband to the funeral, and then for a while I had a little black diamond on a sleeve of my coat. Everybody was terrible for mourning then. White shirts, black ties. Six or seven year ago I went to the funeral of a prim and proper old lady and the main mourners was each in a different coloured anorak. If she'd been alive she would have shot them.

Three

Mr McNicol, with two ghillies under him, Ross and Teague, was the man in charge of the fishing at Endsleigh — the hatchery, the seven artificial trout ponds and the fishing rights for the fourteen mile of river from Greystone Bridge to Gunnislake. His Grace, the 11th Duke, brought him down from Scotland about 1901. At first he lived in Endsleigh Lodge at the entrance gates. Then he got friendly with a girl who lived at Trecombe near Stoke Climsland in Cornwall on the other side of the river. It'll give you an idea of the authority Mr McNicol held from the word go if I tell you he had a pair of steps built down by Leigh Wood Gate and a boat tied up there so that when he went courting he could cross the river and walk up through the wood to this girl's home. Fishery Cottage was specially built for them in 1907 when he married her. There was a lot of *little* dukes about in they days, and Mr McNicol was one of them.

My father for two or three years had been loaned on and off to help Mr McNicol by feeding the fish and by trimming and cleaning the ponds in the grounds and in the hatchery, and he came home one evening in 1933 — I think it was July — and he said, 'Mr McNicol says that, seeing you're unemployed, would you like to come down to Endsleigh and talk to him?' I thought, 'I don't know if I *want* a job to do with fishing!' I'd never bothered about fishing. I'd never had the *chance* to bother about fishing — fishing in they days was something private. I'd never even had a fishing rod in my *hand*. But I said to my father I'd go down to McNicol, and I was taken on, starting September/October, at fifteen bob a week. I said I'd try it, and that was the beginning of where I am now. Probably my father had a little bit of pull. You see, my father was a straightforward, clean-living man who did everything he was told, everything, and McNicol liked and trusted him.

The Endsleigh hatchery was a hut where McNicol hatched out

brown, golden and rainbow trout before placing them in little ponds outside to bring them on to different sizes. Later they were sent up to the Zoological Gardens in London, or dumped in the river, or dumped in the seven large ponds about the estate. A few salmon from ova brought down from the River Thurso had been hatched out that January, but they was the last lot of salmon we reared before the hatchery was disposed of to the River Authority after the war. Every morning and every evening I'd to feed the fish and see that the gratings were clear in Coombe Pond, Hardicott Ponds No.1 and No.2 down in the valley where I was born, and Edgcumbe Pond and Dairy Dell Pond — a four mile trip. Two ponds, at Inny Mere on the Cornwall side, were left wild and I'd only to clear the gratings there. Maybe three times a week I'd to skull a boat over and back with a paddle in the stern.

To begin with I didn't make the food myself: McNicol made it. It was dog biscuits crushed up and soaked in water and mixed with minced offal, and it was handed to me in a can and I went round on my bike and dished it out to the fish with an enamel spoon. I wasn't yet allowed to feed the baby fish in the hatchery hut or even in the hatchery ponds. I'm raw, I don't know anything about fish, I don't know one end of a fish to the other, so I'm the lop being sent out where nothing really can go wrong. These fish were all climatized. They'd been put there over a period of time, mostly for ornamental purposes, and them's sizeable fish from half a pound to two pound in weight. Each pond had a special iron bar with a crook that I'd to push in and fore and back between the bars of the grating, releasing the leaves to go downstream. On my travels I might meet a gardener and have a chat for five minutes. I might meet a forester or a general labourer. I never met my father. Sometimes a member of the public might be watching me. The public could get a ticket from the agent's office in Tavistock to come in. It was all gracious: it was all free. Now it's all money, money, money. Then it was all give, give, give.

One day I was riding to Dairy Dell below the house and I nearly knocked Mr Fitt, the head gardener, for six as he came out of a greenhouse. The head gardener! — very prim and proper, and dressed to kill with his little knickerbockers and his brogues and his long stockings with a red or green tassel and his tweed trilby. He came out, and stepped back pretty quick. He reported me to my boss and my boss

47

defended me, said I'd to ride because I'd so much to do. Mind you, when the Duke was in residence — for three weeks between mid-May and mid-June — you'd be more careful: even if you was walking you'd make a detour.

The ponds in the hatchery had wires around them to keep back the kingfisher who especially liked to eat the little golden trout. On top of the posts you had tiny traps and, as the kingfisher pitched down on the tiller, he was caught by the leg. Sometimes the leg was cut off and the bird escaped, but usually you could finish him off by cracking his head against the post or a stone, or with your hand against your knee. Later, wire was also put around the big ponds out on the estate, not because of the heron, though he likes fish — the gamekeeper was supposed to take care of *him* — but to keep away the otter. Before then (and sometimes after, at Dairy Dell in particular), I'd trap an otter by driving two stakes sideways, two to three inches under water, at where I saw his tracks. On these stakes I'd place a slate and on the slate I'd set a rabbit gin on a long chain I'd peg to the bank and, when the otter came along next time, he'd step into the trap and try to swim away, struggling and in pain. He'd be drowned by morning. Cruel, isn't it? But this was the cruel age — the age of 'trap and shoot', the age of gaffing. I'd take the otter back to Fishery Cottage, skin him and leave him on a board to dry. McNicol would give me a bob and probably sell him to Horace Friend for thirty bob or forty. Skinning an otter isn't the same as skinning a rabbit — the flesh sticks to him; you've to trim, trim, trim. But, skinning a rabbit, skinning an otter, gutting a fish ... there's nothing to it. It's common sense. You're brought up to do it from the cradle. That's the difference between a town lad and a country lad. I'd know how to gut *you*...

I was allowed to use a gun. When I went to the hatchery, I'd an old double-barrelled hammer gun. My father gave it to me and it was given to *him* by the old farmer at Sherrill Farm for shooting rooks and rabbits. McNicol supplied me with cartridges to shoot herons, cormorants and otters for the protection of the fish.

Camouflaged, near the hatchery, was a shed where McNicol kept the containers for moving fish. I'd hang up rabbit carcasses in there in a wire-netted cage. Under the carcasses were biscuit tins and, the more blowflies got into a carcass, the more maggots would drop down into the biscuit tins for feeding the fish in the hatchery as a weekend treat. The stench in that shed was *terrible*. Arnold Croote and myself rabbited with a ferret and nets. I'd ride pillion on his motorbike into Launceston some Saturdays with so many as fourteen rabbits round my waist. We sold them to Tonkin, the regulator, for sixpence each.

Just as there were seven trout ponds on the estate, there were seven small ones down at the hatchery, each a different depth for different sizes of fish. I've kept some of the metal signs we hung on stakes to show when the fish were hatched out. For instance, I've one for the first lot of trout — golden pink-eyed trout — I helped hatch out in March, 1934, and so on right up to April, '39. In 1937 we tried cross-breeding golden pink-eyed trout and rainbow trout. I never saw the end of that experiment — maybe the otter or the heron had them.

In January, 1934, the year after I was taken on, I went with McNicol to the redds above Dairy Dell and he showed me how to strip a trout — take the ova from the female and the milt from the male. You'd hold the fish by the gills, run your finger and thumb over their tummies and, by this motion, release the ova and milt into a can, then stir it all around and leave it to stand for five or ten minutes. In they days after stripping a fish we took it by its tail, held it with its head upstream and, as soon as it started to wriggle and pull away, let it go. Today they just throw it back — they say that hitting the water knocks out the air.

Then you'd take the fertilized eggs back to the hatchery hut and lay them in glass, grooved trays clipped in launders inside tanks separated by fine gauze gratings. The tanks were in the centre of the hut and around the walls, with spring water running through. You left the eggs in total darkness till they showed a little black spot, 'eyed up', in twenty to twenty-five days. If meantime on inspection a *white* spot appeared, this meant the egg was bad and you removed it with a tweezers. By the thirty-ninth to the forty-second day (it would take ninety to a hundred days in the river) they'd developed little heads and little bodies with yolk sacs that kept them alive for five or six weeks more after which you removed the grooved trays and fed them with a little spoon containing Spratt's fishmeal. You'd to keep an eye on the level of the water in each launder, else they'd overflow into one another and you'd have a mix-up. Then, in another five to six months, they'd be transferred to the shallowest pond outside and after so many years might be carried, say, by horse and cart to ponds around the estate.

I remember in the spring of '34 a horse and cart was loaned by a farmer, and my pal Gerry Masters was supposed to arrive with them at eight o'clock in the morning after which the fish could be netted and put in appropriate cans. He didn't arrive till twenty past eight and McNicol said, 'Well, cancel today! Come back again at eight o'clock tomorrow!' This was how you were spoken to. If you were detailed to do a job, you had to be there rain or shine and on time. I can still see McNicol taking his watch out before sending Gerry away.

I was introduced to His Grace and Her Grace in '34, and that was the only encounter I ever had with them. They came to the hatchery and McNicol just said, 'This young man is my assistant and I'm hoping to train him.' They nodded and said, 'How do you do.' I probably curtsied! — they was like royalty so far as Milton Abbot was concerned. As a kid I used to run down into the fields to watch their toot-tooting convoy of beautiful cars arriving by Coombe Lodge about seven o'clock at night at the end of their road journey from Tavistock or Exeter Station. And, even in the era of the car, I sometimes saw them coming to church — which no doubt was good for the collection — each one in a separate landau, with a driver and footman in livery. His Grace would be in his high top hat and long-tailed coat, and she'd be wearing a large hat with a damn great bunch of flowers or a bunch of cherries or a great bowl of fruit on it. We'd stand opposite the church gate to watch, and everyone was pushing over and saying, 'There's the Duke!' and 'There's the Duchess!', and probably they'd get them wrong because it was just the butler and the lady's maid, as they might come too, very classy, a little duke and a little duchess theirselves. Some mornings, roughly half past six, I'd hear the carriage and pairs being exercised for Sunday. The horses came, clip-clap, clip-clap, as far as the school.

His Grace was medium built, very militarified, with a large moustache. Like his son, Hastings, the 12th Duke, *my* duke, he wore knickerbockers and a cloth cap. I think he was reserved and of a shy disposition.

It was Mr Rundle the agent's idea that he was stand-offish and so the ordinary worker was told to avoid him at all costs, even hide behind a tree if he was in the locality. Well, if he was with the Duchess, you always knew he was in the locality because she was deaf as a post and he'd be shouting, 'Yes, my darling! ... No, my darling! ... Three bags full.' Whoever was around would be brushing himself down and making everything just right. Though he did two things wrong as far as Endsleigh was concerned — he introduced the bamboo and the grey squirrel — he was a good employer. After walking or motoring around on his own or with the agent, he's always put on more work: the men would be put on overtime immediately he left.

The Duke only fished occasionally. The Duchess was the real fisher; when the fishing was right she'd fish whenever she could, always accompanied by a chauffeur and perhaps McNicol or Ross or Teague. She liked canoeing, shooting the rapids with people like the Miss Russells. And she liked birdwatching. Before my day, she used to ride — sidesaddle. My father once saw her coming and he opened a gate for her and bowed, and she arranged for him to be given a shilling. She was known as the 'flying duchess' because she was so keen on flying. From 1928 till 1937 when she vanished over the North Sea, she always came to Endsleigh by plane, first as a co-pilot, then solo. They buried the telephone wires by Barton Road so she wouldn't get hung up, and three fields were knocked into one with a hangar and the sausage flying. You'd see this Gypsy Moth, a little black patch in the sky, getting larger and larger and larger and larger, and a smoke bomb would go up, and she'd circle down around Endsleigh, and get out wearing one of those leather helmets and goggles and a long leather coat and top boots. A Rolls would be standing by to pick her up. She'd jump in and drive it to the house herself. His Grace was said to hate planes — *and* telephones.

There was a great gloom cast over Endsleigh in 1937 when Her Grace disappeared, because she was a great sporting character, game for anything. It was stated at that period that she was out to complete her two hundred hours of solo flying, that she had another eighty-odd miles to go and her pilot had drawn up a route for her. She was seventy-one. It was a beautiful afternoon when she set out from Woburn, and then a snowstorm sprung up and that was the last of her — March the 22nd, 1937. We thought it might be the end of the road for us at Endsleigh, but His Grace returned the following year.

51

Endsleigh was the Duke and Duchess's fun place, their big plaything for three weeks of the year. The 'cottage' was originally built and its grounds landscaped, for the pleasure of the 6th Duke and his wife, Georgiana, back in 1810 on the part of the Bedford Estate which once belonged to the Abbots of Tavistock. But the 11th Duke, what I call the Grandfather Duke, spent a tremendous lot of money on the place. Right up to his death in 1940 he improved it all the time and, with the help of McNicol, he *made* the fishing, there's no mistake about it. In my time, there were about a hundred workers here — thirty foresters on the Devon and Cornwall sides, twenty-five groundsmen or gardeners, three masons, three carpenters, gangs of general labourers (my father's gang was twelve)... Before Their Graces' arrival they'd be working overtime, perhaps till eight o'clock, cleaning, cutting, trimming, repairing, and for that they'd get a bob an evening on top of their wages.

The Duke's convoy included three Rolls, a Daimler, three Fords for fishing, and two luggage vans, one of which was used as a transport van for fetching provisions and taking the staff, say, into Tavistock or to a dance in Milton Abbot Village Hall on their day out. He brought thirty or so indoor staff, and as many women from the village as wanted gave them part-time help. Bachelors lived over the stables in the stables yard — in my day there was no horseriding, but there was once stabling for about seventeen horses. The cook or the head butler or one of the lady's maids might have slept in this room we're talking in. They ate in a room at the back of the house we now use for lumber. Eleven chauffeurs lived over the great big garages at Harragrove, the walled garden, now a private nursery. A couple of women from the village cooked their food, did their char-ing. No, no, no. They didn't have their wives with them. No wives running round with you in they days! Their uniform was similar to what it is today — the navy blue suit with the peaked cap and white shirt and black tie and black boots. But nearly all of them came with a walking stick and behaved like little dukes to us common people up at the Edgcumbe Arms in the evenings. I say, 'chauffeurs', though some were footmen. The footman would go around in the car with the chauffeur, and get out and open the door; and it was the footman's job to clean the car every time it was used. You see? Ten men doing one man's job. It may seem extravagant, but His Grace was making employment. If Mrs Thatcher could sort that out — have ten men doing *my* job — well, it would help the economy. The trouble is I got in touch with a bloke to train him recently and he wanted a hundred and thirty pound a week to start with, and not knowing anything about it!

At each lodge when His Grace was in residence — Endsleigh Lodge, Bedford Lodge, Coombe Lodge — there was a little pillbox like an old sentry box, and *in theory* the lodgekeeper's wife would be sat there from nine o'clock in the morning until seven o'clock in the evening in a long red dress and a white pinafore and a white cap, ready to open and shut the gates. But the chauffeur would blow his hooter well in advance to put them on the alert. Lodgekeepers, usually a gardener, had a tweed suit provided, and they usually thought themselves a little bit above the likes of my father in his corduroy trousers. There was always a little bit of difference and jealousy between the different sections that worked here. I suppose some were jealous of *me*. I wore nail boots, a tweed jacket, plain shirt, a pair of corduroy breeches buttoned below the knee, with long grey socks pulled over; occasionally a tie. Don't forget, you could buy a jacket then in Tavistock or Launceston for twelve and six...

When His Grace drove in, mid-May, everything was at perfection. You had the rhododendrons. You had the azaleas. There was camellias everywhere, especially along the Higher and the Lower Georgies, wood walks named after the 10th Duke's wife who is said to have inspired some of the planting. There's a tremendous lot of oak, ash, chestnut and beech at Endsleigh, and a lot of ornamental and foreign trees. In the arboretum up by Edgcumbe pond there's a famous Weeping Beech, and a Wellingtonia about a hundred and fifty-two feet high, supposed to be the tallest Wellingtonia in the British Isles.

Once, one of the focal points at Endsleigh was a foreign conifer planted in a special greenhouse built beside the greenhouses above Dairy Dell. The Flying Duchess, she'd been off on a yacht trip somewhere and was presented with a tiny foreign fir. She brought it back to Woburn and it was transported down here to Endsleigh in a large flowerpot, and planted in this special greenhouse built to a certain height. But, year after year, year after year, the tree kept on increasing and another tier had to be put on the greenhouse. The tree still grew and grew, and this greenhouse went up, oh, fifty feet high, and the tree was still going up, still going up. Then it got out of control: you see, it went to sixty feet and they couldn't build much higher. So they started trimming of it, and by trimming they killed it. But this greenhouse was built purpose in eight foot sections for that foreign conifer. At Endsleigh it didn't matter the expense. Right by the dilapidated greenhouse we're left with today, Derek Bradbury, the Manager, has some tomatoes growing inside the base of where the greenhouse for this conifer used to be.

Unlike today, the drives, the rides, the walks were spotless. All the grass, all the rubbish was picked up by the estate horse and cart and brought to the ashwell by Dairy Dell Pond to be burned. In the stables yard and the back yard, men would go on their hands and knees with a piece of wood with a nail drove through it and get the weeds out by scraping — no poison. You could put your bread and butter on the steps going down from the greenhouse to Dairy Dell. A hundred-odd steps, and there wasn't a weed! And wherever there was steps there was different coloured, long-legged primulas, even beside the hundred and eighty-nine steps leading to what is called Swiss Cottage... I'm doing my *best* to explain! ... You'm one of these sophisticated schoolmasters come from London... I'm not being sarcastic at all! You've got to remember it's two different types of person that's trying to talk to one another! ... Swiss Cottage was built, back, I think, at the time the house was built. It's a three-storeyed thing, two hundred and fifty feet above the Tamar, where one of the gardeners lived on the downstairs floor and the top floor. On the between floor was two rooms, the ducal rooms, with valuables, antique stuff, and, if the Grandfather Duke had guests, they'd go up there and the gardener's wife would make them a cup of tea. The view is terrific. You can look upstream, and you've got the river weaving up the valley with Endsleigh, on the right, nestled amongst the trees. Swiss Cottage is sold now to the Landmark Trust for the use of holiday-makers. So is Dairy Dell Cottage and Dairy Dell Pond. They've also bought the Dairy which they may restore. Water circulated there round jars of cream and butter placed in little lead tanks.

Another gardener lived in Dairy Dell Cottage. When His Grace wasn't in residence and the general public came in with their permits from the Bedford Office in Tavistock — I've seen forty or more wandering here in one day — the gardeners' wives at Swiss Cottage and Dairy Dell Cottage would provide tea and bread and butter for a penny. The gardener's wife at Dairy Dell put out trestle tables and long forms. Near the pond there's a Holy Well, once used for baptizing people and moved from the old Tavistock Abbey at Leigh Barton and, after the visitors had had their tea and bread and butter, she'd say, 'You'd betterway go over and make a wish,' and they'd throw in a halfpenny or a penny, and probably her'd come over early in the evening with a little trout net or a little butterfly net and take the coins out. I've since thrown in a halfpenny, hoping I was going to have some luck with the football pools. If I'd had any, I mightn't be sat here talking to you...

Further on from Dairy Dell was the Bathing Pool, where children trout fish today. Built purpose for the Duchess, it was shallow one end and deep the other and surrounded by rhododendrons and bamboo. The expense for this was colossal because the water was piped two and a half miles underground from the River Inny. The old cast-iron pipe, about nine inches in circumference, is now blocked up, and we use the stream water from Dairy Dell.

Just upstream from the Bathing Pool, but on the Cornish side, there was an empty boatman's cottage — it's there no longer. When the Grandfather Duke was in residence — his son continued the custom — it was instructed that a fire was to be lit there at nine o'clock every morning so that from his bedroom or when he came out from breakfast and went on to the terrace he could see the chimney smoke and it would look romantic. That cottage was a wonderful place for bats. After the war I took somebody interested in bats over there. There was hundreds. I'm not up in the bat world but there's bats here in the clock tower of the stables and in the roof of what's called the 'nursery end' of the house. They're protected, you can be fined for destroying them, yet you can destroy a human person and be fined nothing, sometimes not even be locked up. The Law has gone crazy... By 1960, the boatman's cottage was all in disarray and falling down and I caught the son of a former employee with a bag of lead. He'd waded over and stolen it. The agent in Tavistock was informed and he was sent to prison...

At Endsleigh before the war the grass was always cut by scythe. You'd see seven men with scythes — one swath, then another — going up the terrace and along the lawns. The grass was patterned beautiful, better than any lawnmower could do it — those scythes had to be sharpened and they were treated with pride! Again the work of the general labourer. We call it today 'Jack of all trades and master of none'. *Then* they were a master of everything they touched. The yew walk above the herbaceous border on the terrace was trimmed with pruning knives — not clippers. In the yew walk, in the rose walk below it, everywhere you went, there was oak-framed seats made by the estate carpenters. In the Grotto at the end of the terrace there was spring water: it hadn't dried up out of neglect. Spring water, in they days, was everywhere. Pity there isn't more springs now — there'd be no water shortage. Luckily Endsleigh House is on a spring. It's about a quarter of a mile up the drive in a field and the water's piped down into a tank over the trough and foundation tablet in the stables yard. Because there was bits of shell from people's travels with the bits of local rock on the Grotto walls, the Syndicate have called it the Shell House. Names seem to keep changing. We don't know where we'm to. In '81 or '82 the Shell House was renovated. Visitors was whipping the shells and rocks as souvenirs. They was also pulling up the sheep knucklebones on the veranda outside the small dining-room. These things wouldn't have happened in the Grandfather and my Duke's days.

In the Grandfather Duke's days you could drive a car, even a Rolls, along rides three and a half miles out through the fields. And these rides and every inch of the fourteen mile by the river from Greystone Bridge to Gunnislake was steamrolled and cleared of cow and horse manure, and the gates posted open, while he was here — in other words farmers had to remove their cattle. You could ford over to the woods on the Cornish side and even the rides through the woods over the river were kept clear of leaves and twigs and sticks. Immaculate! In Wareham Wood there was a siren. You turned a handle and it would make a hell of a noise; you could hear it for miles. If the Duke with his chauffeur and footman needed help, another chauffeur and footman would have to rush across. If they was very far away, the car hooters, with the knob you pressed down that went oooaaaaargh, or the horns with the bag that went burp-burp-burp, they'd do instead. Don't forget everything in they days was dead still — no lorries, no chain-saws.

Dotted around the estate were little tea-houses. There was one at Castle Head, that's right at the top of Dunterton Wood; there was one at Hardicott; there was one on Carthamartha Island (that was sectional and put up each year in case the river flooded and took it away); and there was one at Duchess Pool on the Lower Reaches. Cups, saucers, plates, that sort of thing, was kept there and the fireplaces laid with a

Horace aged nine outside Milton Abbot Day School, 1922

Horace and his mother (centre back of charabanc) on a Sunday School trip, 1924

Endsleigh Fish Hatchery, 1937

Nesta on Black Rock,
5.5.40. She became
engaged to Horace the
following December

Workmen rest from birch-brooming Endsleigh's main drive, a mile long, 1938

Horace on
one of the high
'stagings', originally
placed to make
fishing easier for 'the
Flying Duchess', 1940

Leading Aircraftmen Horace Adams (left) and Jack Tuck, 1941

Mr Peter Stockbridge with the twelve salmon he and a friend caught during one afternoon at Leigh Wood Waterfall Pool, 1954

Horace with a 16 lb. salmon caught for Hastings, 12th Duke of Bedford, May, 1952

Beginners' luck. Robin, Marquess of Tavistock, son of John, 13th Duke of Bedford, with his stepbrother, Gavin Lyle (left), on their first visit to Endsleigh, 21.7.54

Horace (left) with John, 13th Duke of Bedford, 17.5.60

Horace's workmate, Mr Bert Moore, crossing Hardstone Pool in 1963. The ice
had frozen to a depth of nine inches

Horace with Mr Herbie Symons (right), 1977

basket of logs beside them. The message would go out to have So and So tea-house ready and the fire would be lit if necessary by a woodman, ready for the picnic. The insides were panelled with pinewood and the outsides made of cut-back fir tree planks, bark side out. There's only the one tea-house — at Duchess — left. Rodney Hill, my son-in-law, have just fitted of it up.

For her birdwatching the Duchess had a hut built in Wareham Wood by the Inny Mere ponds. It was round and, instead of having glass panes, it had shutters. It fell down after the war. She didn't shoot game down here as it was the wrong time of year, but I believe she was a good shot. Game was raised here for the Duke's friends. But not much — just some pheasants and partridge. The gamekeepers' job was mostly to keep down vermin. There were two of them — the head keeper, Buckingham, who lived on the Cornish side on top of Carthamartha Rock, approximately a hundred feet above the river, and the under-keeper, Westlake, who lived bang opposite him on the Devon side.

Though the Duchess, in particular, was interested in fishing, the fishing wasn't taken then quite as seriously as it was by my Duke or as it is in this present age. When a bridge was slung over Edgcumbe Pond it was as much for decoration and so Her Grace could *feed* the trout as for actual fishing. Even the thirteen rowing boats on the river were for decoration as much as anything, same as the ten to fifteen canoes tied to a platform at Endsleigh Ham — here bang in front of the house, opposite where my gauge-board is now. There was a floating dock specially made at Leigh Wood and, during her stay, Her Grace might only fish there for half an hour. And every day the Duke and the Duchess was in residence *all* the boats were washed and *all* the stagings washed and sanded! And at every one of the twenty to twenty-five pools there was a white stake to hold a net and a priest and a trestle for the rod which might never be used! But it all provided *work* for people, didn't it? It was bread and butter for the families. It's as simple as that. I've often heard people say, 'Why should others have money? Why haven't *I* got money?' My answer to that have always been, 'Well, *you* would keep the money for yourself. The other person is spending of it and employing others.' The Bedford family in they days were marvellous, wonderful employers — even your house was painted on the outside and repaired in and out every five years. And, though I was concentrating on my own side of things with McNicol, I was wandering round an estate which, in *they* days, was absolutely beautiful.

McNicol was five foot nine, medium built. He was well turned out, not really dressed to do any work, in knickerbockers, gay tartan stockings, and a tweed trilby like the head gardener. He was very straightforward, very abrupt, and everything had to be done as he wanted it. A fish was a lump of gold with McNicol. My God! If anything went wrong, it was blue murder! Officially you worked five and a half days, with Saturday afternoons and Sundays off, and officially you weren't working after half past five. But you had your responsibility. My parents would be quite worried about me because I often didn't get home till half past eight, nine o'clock. One Saturday night I'd been to the pictures with my pal Arnold Croote, and a storm was blowing up. We had fish and chips pretty smart, and come back here on his motorbike. By now there's a hell of a storm on, the streams are roaring and we're dripping wet and by the light of my little pocket torch we're clearing the gratings of the ponds so they won't overflow. And all night I'm turning and twisting in bed, and on Sunday morning the storm is only just abating so I've a job coming down here on my push-bike to see that everything's all right. You know what happens if you've got storms. It brings down branches, it brings down leaves. These had to be cleared, and you could adjust the flow of water because the ponds had a bypass.

I said McNicol was abrupt. I should have said he was very, *very* abrupt. If I looked down when he was talking to me, he'd say, 'Horace, mun, I'm bloody talking to you and I want you to look at me!' He was also very thorough. I was taking instructions from him one morning at Fishery Cottage because he was ill in bed and Fred Coombe, a mason, arrived and said, 'There's a dead salmon on the rocks down at Underhill.' 'Well, Fred, mun, why didn't you bring it so Horace could cut it open and see what's wrong with it? You'd better go and get it. Horace can wait here and do a job for Mother,' — McNicol always called his wife 'Mother', and she called him 'Dad'. So I broke some wood till Fred come back in about half an hour. He said, 'Well, it's like this, sir,' he said. 'I can't find the fish.' 'Dammit, mun!' said McNicol. 'Half an hour ago you said there was a fish down there. The otter doesn't go for dead fish. What have happened to it?!' 'Well, sir, it's like this,' said Fred. 'I never saw the fish. I was *told* there was a fish.' 'Ah, mun,' said McNicol, 'now let this be a lesson to you! Never repeat what you've been told unless you're doubly sure it's true!' It's a good story and it's a true story, and that's how thorough McNicol would be.

Provided you did everything you were told, McNicol was very friendly. He'd often say, 'Would you like a drink after work?' and it was always whisky. His wife would say, 'Dad, you shouldn't *do* that!' and he'd say, 'It's no business of yours, Mother!' He himself was a hell of a drinker. Every Friday he'd go in to Tavistock for the offal — at first he'd a jerks-and-stops motorbike and side-car, then a Climo with a dickie. While in Tavistock he'd visit The Newmarket pub. Well, when I met him at Fishery Cottage to collect the offal, he often didn't know why I was there. Talk about drinking and driving — he'd have lost his licence before he got half way back! Mrs McNicol would usually ask me to stay to supper. They was lucky as regards food. Venison was sent down regular from Woburn and, if it was winter, you'd have a bit of pheasant from Keeper Buckingham. Mrs McNicol liked to make great big apple dumplings. McNicol sat in the carving chair, but she had to do everything else. If I got up and said, 'I'll take the plates out,' he said, 'Sit still, mun!' She was very humble. He was a bit aloft.

Ross helped now and then in the hatchery, so McNicol sometimes invited him to Fishery Cottage too. Ross, under McNicol, looked after the river from Horsebridge downstream to Latchley Weir. Teague, under McNicol, looked after Latchley Weir down to Cotehele. Teague was assisted by a Tamar and Plym bailiff called Mr Percy Abbot. In other words, Ross, and Teague assisted by Abbot, looked after the seven mile Lower Stretch, and I was being trained to look after the seven mile Upper Stretch which runs from Greystone Bridge downstream to Horsebridge.

Every day the Duke was in residence, bar Sunday or if the river wasn't troutable, McNicol had to provide eight trout, all the same size, for breakfast at the house. Endsleigh Waterfall was a damn good trout place. He and Ross would have to stand there on the jetty almost all day, fishing for trout with March Browns. Potatoes had to be the same size, too. They were grown in large flowerpots in the greenhouses.

When McNicol knew that the Duke or the Duchess were going to be salmon fishing, tomorrow or the next day, he and Ross and Teague would fish in advance with the barbs broken off their flies, just to rise the fish so he could say, 'There's a fish in Such and Such Pool.' That always seemed a bit of a gimmick to me because the fish might move on.

I remember once the Duke instructing Teague to catch him a salmon. Well, the old boy took a salmon up to the house, and the Duke invited him in. (So, you see, the Grandfather Duke was quite human though he was classed otherwise.) The butler showed Teague into the drawing-room and they had a drink together. 'Well, Teague,' said the Duke, 'I'm very pleased you were able to get me a fish. What did you catch it on?' Teague had a stammer. He said, 'Y-y-your G-g-g-grace, I, I, I, c-c-caught it on a T-t-t-t-t-tory Fly,' meaning, in his mind, a bunch of red, white and blue wool. His Grace said nothing — he didn't know what a Tory Fly *was*. In fact, Teague had caught the salmon with a wire basket in the fish pass of Gunnislake Weir!

McNicol took me fishing in 1934, the season after I arrived at the hatchery. Don't forget I was a complete greenhorn. First he showed me how to cast, out at Coombe and Edgcumbe Ponds — you mustn't run before you can walk. With trout everything is much lighter — a lighter rod, a lighter reel, a lighter line, a lighter cast. And with trout you try to imitate a real fly, so he chose a March Brown. I've always stuck to a March Brown; it's very popular down here in the West Country. I'm talking about wet fly fishing... You've really got to teach yourself. Of course, today, there's a lot of money in teaching others. I often wonder who taught McNicol. He taught himself, I expect. I dare say, though, he taught me how to tie a fly, how you whipped the thread on to the hook. You had to pick up whatever you could, and build from there. No theory: everything practical...

Any rate, early May time, he took me down to Leigh Wood and, after pointing out the lies, showed me how to fish for salmon. First of all I'd to watch him splice the three parts of his old Greenheart rod together with leather thongs, then see how he put the big brass reel on, threaded the line, and tied the line to the cast with a figure of eight. He showed me how to tie on a Silver Doctor fly. He told me to lean up with him against a tree. They had a great habit then of hiding theirselves or keeping their back up against a tree so that the fish wouldn't see them.

An old fad as I call it. Shadow, yes, but I don't believe that they can see *you*. In fact, I'm sure they can't.

He started fishing and, woe betide, he was into a fish. Now it was quite exciting because I'd never seen a salmon hooked before. He asked me to hold the net and he took a long time to bring the fish around to me. It was between eight and nine pound, an average size, and he caught it between the croys at Leigh Wood. There's a double set of two croys at Leigh Wood, with a distance of fifty yards between them. It's marvellous to think that McNicol had so many croys built, starting in 1910 — Leigh Wood Croys, Woodtown Croy, Inny Croy, Joel's Corner Croy, Southcombe Croy... — with only ropes and pulleys, and fifteen or sixteen men, very often including my father, rolling enormous rocks into position. And they're still standing today! Now, if Clive Murphy and Horace Adams started building of a croy, even with the help of a JCB, the first spate that came down he'd be washed away. It's as simple as that. For to help build croys, roads, drives and steps, general labourers till the war used to raise stone with sticks of dynamite from little tiny quarries all over the estate...

In June I was sent up to Bush Pool on my own, and I caught my first fish. I was sent there in the morning because McNicol said it was better fished before noon while it was nice and shady. Today people fish all day long, sunshine, rain, it doesn't matter a damn, and I don't think it *does* matter a damn. At Bush Pool you'd to do a bit of wading, so I fished in Wellington boots. I used a Jock Scott fly, about a 3/0, and within a matter of ten minutes I was into a fish! I was panic-stricken, trembling all over. The fish is on before you realize what's happened. The salmon strikes hisself, he comes up and takes the fly, whereas the trout is feeding and you've got to strike *him*. Even now if I'm fishing off a high bank and the water's fairly clear and it's a still pool and I see a salmon come round to my fly and take it, I'm like a lump of jelly.

Up till then I'd only *watched* McNicol. Catching a fish on your own is very different. It's your wits against the fish's. You can hardly control yourself but you *have* to control yourself. You look around for help and there's no help there. You don't know where you're going to land the fish. You've got a net but you haven't probably been sensible enough to take it down the bank with you. I got this fish in somehow — eleven pound. It took me eleven and a half minutes. They always say you should be able to land a fish a pound a minute, so that wasn't bad, I felt quite proud. But a fish can have his best boots on and jump around the pool or get under a snag, so there's no hard and fast rule.

When I brought the fish back to McNicol I had in the back of my mind that I might be given it, but I really knew it would be sent to the Estate Office and turned into money because the more money the agent got outside of his allocation, the more he could do on the estate. Maybe McNicol kept the fish himself. He might have given it to a farmer. I was so thrilled, you know, that I went home and told my mother, and probably *she* was looking to see if there was a fillet given to me. But no luck. Not very much given away! No money, let alone any fish! Things were tough. In they days to have a piece of salmon, well, you would think you was God yourself. You were the *poor* man. The poor man never had salmon. The poor man had rabbit.

So I wasn't bothered about not being given the fish. I was the servant of the Duke and even more the servant of McNicol and I was just thankful that I'd got a job and that I'd experienced the joy of fishing — the concentration involved, the forgetting. You're concentrating all the time when you're fishing but, when you've *hooked* a fish, you've got to concentrate more than ever. Nine times out of ten the fish is lost because you've lost concentration.

When you fish, you forget about all your worries and the rat race. That's why so many people take to it. Once they start fishing they forget their wife's just run away with their best friend or there's a bill unpaid. And when they *hook* a fish ... well ... I still get the same feeling I did fifty year ago. It's undescribable the kick you get out of it. It's a *tremendous* sensation. It's like your tummy turns right over. I've caught up to seventy-two in a season. But I don't want to give the impression that salmon fishing is easy. I've had the privilege of being able to pick and choose where to fish, while the ordinary fisherman have only been able to pick and choose, say, on a beat where I know there's no fish at all. And, now especially, I only go to places where I think there's a fish and I think I might catch a fish. And, when I *think* I'm going to catch a fish, a fish usually comes to me because I've got that second sense. I can't afford time out on the river and spending hours, flog, flog, flog. So I think to myself, 'Everything's right. I'll go up and concentrate on Such and Such Pool as nobody's fishing it.' — for instance, there's been a flood

62

and the water's just clearing and I know there's some fish moving up. And, if I haven't got a fish in half an hour, I'll pack it in.

I'll stick my neck out and say I've caught far more fish than my predecessor. But since '62, in spite of pollution and the poacher, there's been more fish coming up to spawn. You see, under the Grandfather Duke, the agent was allowed to net, from mid-April right up to the end of August, a thousand salmon in Weir Pool and at a place called Netstakes (now Impham Meadows) in the tidal stretch of Gunnislake. Ross was one of the netsmen. I'd often have to push-bike down from here to help. Eight mile! All winds and weathers! There'd be four of us — two on the bank or the shingle, holding the net taut, two in a boat (one rowing, one shooting out the net). Circling, you'd row three-quarters of the way across the river, leaving a passage for salmon to go upstream, then head back to shore. Once on the shingle, all four of you would pull the net in, two kneeling, pulling the leaded bottom line, and two standing, pulling the corked top line. There might be nothing in the net; there might be three fish; there might be twenty. The most ever caught with me down there was fifty-nine. Ross had a Baby Austin 7. We began to pack these fifty-nine fish into the Baby Austin on a tarpaulin on the back seat for Ross to take them to the fishmonger in Tavistock. The car started going into the ground! Fifty-nine fish, average weight eight pound, is a hell of a weight! Ross had to go into Tavistock two or three times. The fishmonger had to pack them in lumps of ice — cold storage in they days weren't refrigerators or deep freezers. Of course the Duke, by allowing this netting was killing the goose that lays the golden egg, killing many of the spring-run salmon he'd been introducing from the Thurso and the Tay. And this netting went on with his son, the 12th Duke, till he saw the red light and stopped it in 1952, the year before his death, because the public netsmen thought he was greedy in his privileged position below the weir and they threatened to destroy his nets. After his death, the Bedford Trustees allowed the netting again but, in 1962, when they sold up, the River Authority disallowed it.

Before the war I dealt mostly with trout but, through helping with the netting and watching and listening to McNicol and being his ghillie and fishing on my own with a second-hand rod I picked up for five or six quid, I got more and more interested in salmon.

To put it roughly, I learned that salmon — sea trout or peel worked on the same principle — came up the Tamar from the sea in spring and autumn runs. And they didn't run up the river for people like McNicol and Horace Adams to catch them: they run to make their redds and spawn up in the shallows of the Inny, the Lyd, the little tributaries coming into the parent river, by the end of November. There's some that talk of 'an autumn run' when spring-run fish have got stuck in the deeper pools and then start to move because of an autumn flood, but what I call autumn-run fish is autumn fish straight from the sea with sea lice on them.

The bulk of salmon spawn from November to early December. Hatching of the eggs, or ova, takes about ninety days. When the baby fish are three or four inches long they are called parr. After about two year of river life they start losing their grey covering and become silvery and begin their journey to the sea when they're called smolts. The smolts drop back tail-first in shoals of twenty, thirty fish. You'll see this happening in May. You might be sat having lunch on the river bank and all of a sudden you, who is inexperienced, will say, 'Cor, look, Adams! See all those trout bubbling!' Well it's not trout: it's smolts. And then they're gone, dropping back to sea. And those that come back to spawn the following year are called grilse as distinct from salmon which may not return for two years or three. So, if I took you down the river today and I caught what we'll presume was an eighteen pound salmon, that fish would have probably had three years' river life and three years' sea life and, on its return from the sea, it hasn't fed, it's lived on the fat of its own body: it's only fed while at sea.

A salmon after it's spawned is called a kelt and goes from a lovely-looking fish to almost like an eel, black and flabby. Most kelts die but some drop back to sea and return the following year or the next. If you catch a kelt you must unhook it and return it to the river — it's unclean and not edible. An unspawned female is called a bagget and an un-spawned male is called a rawner...

You see? I'd to learn they sort of things from scratch. I'd to be shown the pools and the lies — at Carthamartha Pool there was a ridge of rock and the fish usually lied against that ridge, their tails back to it. I'd to be taught how to use a tailer, a net and a gaff. I'd even to be taught how to use a priest. In they days priests were lengths of wood with a lump of metal at the end. The modern priests are metal. In fact mine's usually a stone. If I'm fishing by myself, I just tail or net the fish and give him a crack with a stone across the head. So there you are. But I've still got a priest I made out of a piece of fir about ten year ago. I drew some flies on it — a Jock Scott, a Thunder and Lightning and a Yellow Torrish. McNicol was all for winged flies. I now carry around a job lot but I like to use the cheap ordinary plain brass tube and a wee bit of black and yellow bucktail. I've learned from experience it doesn't matter a damn what you put on if there's fish in a pool and they're inclined to take. It's as simple as that. *He* fished with a bright fly like a Silver Grey or a Silver Doctor on a bright day and a dark fly like a Jock Scott on a dull day and he always said that if fish come to a medium fly drop down in size, and if the water's warm start with a small fly — the higher the temperature the smaller the fly.

I shouldn't tell you this really — it's one of the little bits you keep under your hat — but he taught me that the best fishing is when the river is anything from eleven inches to one foot three. He also used to say, 'Where there's one taking fish there's nine others.' And he said, 'Fishing is eighty-five per cent skill and fifteen per cent luck.' *I* say it's five per cent skill and ninety-five per cent luck, though it helps to be a person like I am with that inner sense of when you've got a damn good chance of catching a fish. You've also got to have patience: you've to keep on keeping on and fish a pool down, then go back and fish it down again. Today, the age of the motorcar, people go from pool to pool too quickly. And if people are fishing a pool down and a fish rise behind them, they've the tendency to reel in and go back to behind where that fish rose and to fish down over him. That's where you judge the sportsman. If I'm around I always say, 'I'm sorry, sir. You've passed that fish. You must fish the pool down, then come back and, if nobody else is going to fish the pool right away, well, you may fish it down again.' Any rate, it's probably a running fish. If he leaps or heads and tails behind you, then does the same three or four yards further on, he's not going to take because he's moving up.

To go back to fish lies for a moment, McNicol told me some may alter from one year to another, so you should study the water you intend to fish before putting your tackle up or you can tire yourself out with unnecessary casting. For instance, if you see a fish move, study that movement. If he moves again and isn't going forward, then he's coming in to settle. Also, fish will lie in a pool where they've cover (depth) and room to swim around or get away. They'll lie in sunlight but it's no good fishing them there because, as you cast, they'll see the flash of the rod, the flash of the line, every movement; and if the light's behind you and a fish in front and you just move your hand, nine times out of ten he'll pull away. Fish are very alert: they'm all there and half way back. In the summer, fish up till half past eleven, then from half past five, six o'clock, when the light's getting off the water. In Scotland, there are fishing rivers with no trees at all but down here, McNicol told me, if you fell a tree on the bank, if you open up too much, fish will move on. I've proved that. About twelve year ago I counted with the Chairman of the Syndicate twenty-three salmon lying right under a bank where they'd plenty of depth of water and five or six trees. And then those trees were taken down to open up the bank for fishing. Fish stopped lying there: there's never been a fish caught there since.

I once asked McNicol was hooking a fish cruel. He said they don't feel anything at all. They might be frightened but they don't *feel* anything. I think it was a Professor Jones, some scientist, he put fish into a tank and pierced them with a needle and there was no reaction at all when the fish couldn't see the movement. What *is* cruel is netting fish at sea and pulling in the net and just dropping them in the hold one on top of the other and letting them die of suffocation. But by fly fishing, which isn't cruel, we're conserving by balancing Nature. Otherwise there'd be too many fish and if you've got too many of anything it destroys itself — if there was fifty men had to live in this room they'd kill one another off. With thousands of fish in the river there'd be smell, there'd be disease. No, the river fishermen ain't doing any harm.

As well as the tickets to members of the public looking at the Endsleigh grounds, the agent in Tavistock issued two buckshee passes a day, bar Sunday, to anyone wanting to fish for trout on the Devon bank from Greystone Bridge down to the junction of the Tamar and the Lowley. Now, to begin with, I wasn't allowed to go up to a stranger I saw fishing and say, 'Good-morning (or good-afternoon), sir. May I see your pass and may I see your licence?' He could say to me, 'First show me your warrant!' because I could be anybody, I could be a rogue. But on the 5th of August, 1937, the year the Duchess went missing, I was issued with a private Water Bailiff's Warrant. It was signed by Mr Rundle, the Duke's agent, on behalf of the Conservators for the Tamar and Plym Fishery District which later became part of the Cornwall River Board and then the South West Water Authority. My daughter always says to me I should have it framed. Not that the warrant brought me an increase in wages. My take-home pay remained at the level they started, fifteen bob a week, till 1940 when they was bumped up to one pound five.

Having a warrant meant I'd to check the passes and the licences once, twice a week, and one morning in '38 I was cycling up river on a flam new bike I'd bought for £7.15s. when I noticed a gentleman fishing well below the boundary. He told me his pass was in the inside pocket of his jacket which was in his car back at Greystone Gate — the gate was locked and people had to climb over because no strangers' cars were allowed along the drive. So, after asking him to move up to the boundary, I went back at his suggestion, opened the car door, searched his pocket and came across his pass among fifty quid in notes.

When later I reported what happened to McNicol at the hatchery, he said, 'Did this gentleman accompany you to get the pass?' I said, 'No. He told me I could help myself.' He said, 'You're telling me you went and opened his car door, you searched his jacket and you found his pass in a wallet full of money?!! Well, you're damn foolish, mun! What if a tramp had already been to his car, or went there later, and pinched his wallet?! You could have been accused of theft! The gentleman should have known better than to ask you to do such a thing! I'll arrange for his name to be crossed off the fishing list!' And although the gentleman was a colonel and we were only working men, the colonel was never allowed to fish here again, not even after the war under the next Duke. That's how very, very strict things were at Endsleigh.

Four

War was being mentioned in the papers day after day. The Duke, a military type, said that those of his workers who joined the Services would have their Service pay made up to what they earned from him for the duration. The plan never materialized because he died in August, 1940, and his son was anti-war.

Meanwhile, after the death of Sybil, I'd got friendly with a girl called Win Daniells in Tavistock where she cooked for Dr Watt. I first met her at a dance in Lydford. She was short and plump and, like Sybil, she was dark and pretty — I always went for the *pretty* girls. In June, '39, I asked her would she like to come to Endsleigh one afternoon, so she push-biked out and I showed her round. She was accompanied by her cousin, Nesta Daniells. Nesta was short, well turned out, rather shy, very prim and proper, pretty with corn coloured hair and she wasn't yet eighteen. I fell for her immediately; she swept me clean off my legs; it was what they call 'love at first sight'. She was a real bundle of charm. She was living in service in a vicarage at Launceston — her boss was Canon Rigg. Her parents lived about eight mile north of Launceston in a cottage at North Hill.

I was at the Horse Show at Launceston a few weeks later, and who should I spot but this girl! I approached her right away and took her on the swingboats and dodgems to get acquainted with her — this was the first time we'd been on our own. She kept looking at her watch and finally she said, 'I've got to be in by nine o'clock.' I said, 'Can I come with you?' She hesitated, then she said, 'All right,' but she didn't allow me to take her within a gunshot of the vicarage because of the house-keeper, and I just said 'Good-night. I hope we'll meet again,' and I didn't even kiss her. When I found out from Win that her eighteenth birthday was on the 21st of July I only sent her a card signed 'Guess Who?'

Then, the next Saturday, I was in at Launceston — I never made no appointment for meeting of her — and I spotted her *again*. She was out shopping and window-gazing around the town, and we got chatting and we made a date and it went from there till eventually I was invited to her home. I thought, 'She's only eighteen and I'm twenty-six. What's Mother and Father going to think of their daughter bringing home an old man?!' Her father had been a farrier in the 1914 war and he was now working as a blacksmith for a father and son called Harris in Bathpool. Her mother seemed very dominating and she looked at me a bit cross-eyed over her glasses. Nesta had a twin brother and an elder brother and she was their only daughter. But I got on well with everyone. Probably I romanced a bit, said I'd got a good job at Endsleigh and that, if I kept my nose clean, my bread was buttered for life. I must say this about her mother: she knew how to cook a damn good meal *and* eat it, and she still does at ninety-three — she'd eat the horse and chase the rider. At North Hill, there was always plenty of grub — everything fresh from the garden; their own poultry; plenty of butter and jam and cream and pastries and cakes. When I invited Nesta over to milton Green for my parents to inspect, my father wasn't bothered, but my mother fell for her right away which was the main thing.

I always remember that the 3rd of September, 1939, was Nesta's Sunday morning off and I went on my push-bike to meet her, and we were walking through Launceston Square and we heard Chamberlain's voice coming from a radio in the White Hart Hotel saying war was being declared. We gripped hands and she said, 'My God! What are we going to do?!' I said, 'I'll have to join up, but we'll be all right!' I think I was quite excited. I didn't know the meaning of war, the seriousness of it. It didn't occur to me that one of us might be killed. At least my daughter, Jill, and Rodney, her husband, they understand the danger of *nuclear* war. They haven't got any family and I'm sure it's because they don't want to bring children into the world to be destroyed.

Coming up to late September, a school was evacuated to Endsleigh — Seafield Park, a boys' prep school in Hampshire. They had their sports field down in Endsleigh Ham. And, because McNicol was going to be on his own, except for Ross and Teague, my father along with three other men started clearing out Edgcumbe Pond so we could put in fish from the hatchery. In fact we put in two hundred and seventy golden trout mid-February. Two hundred golden trout went into Dairy Dell Pond, three hundred and fifty rainbow trout went into the river... Putting rainbow trout in the river was stupid. Once rainbow trout get into the river most of them just disappears.

In January I volunteered for the RAF at the Recruiting Centre in Plymouth. A couple of weeks after, they asked me to come for a medical which I failed. They didn't mind about my deformed foot — they just hit you on the knee and if your leg didn't jump, well, probably it was false — but they found a spot on my lung. I reported to Dr Lee in the village and he said I'd never be fit for the Services. I thought to myself, 'Am I TB?' Then I heard from the RAF again. They asked me to have an X-ray in the hospital in Torquay. So I went there, and this X-ray passed me, Grade 2 — if you were Grade 4 the next stop was the grave. Then I was taken ill. At Christmas, Nesta and I went to a dance at Bere Alston and we got really wet push-biking home.

I was away from work for several weeks on the borders of having pleurisy. When I went back to work I received a notice from the RAF saying I was to report to Padgate in Lancashire. Dr Lee wouldn't sign the necessary certificate. I was very upset. I was keen to join up for the adventure. I didn't want to be left behind at Endsleigh doing agricultural or felling timber. I don't think Dr Lee wanted *anyone* to be enlisted — he'd a religious kink. I took the bull by the horns and went to see Dr Davie of Tavistock for second advice. He took me on his panel and by June I was on my way by train to Padgate. I was kitted out and, after a few days' square bashing, I was sent to Bridlington on the coast. I'd never been away from home before, but I was enjoying myself. I was a good mixer in they days. I call myself now a bit of a loner. That have come on to me in the last ten years. When you become older you'm *inclined* to go into the shell. Also, there's so much poaching done that, if you mix, people's bound to ask, 'Had any fish?' and you can say the wrong thing.

We were met at Bridlington Station and marched to our billets, beautiful hotels on the sea front. I stayed at Bridlington for about eight weeks. The food was wonderful and, in the evenings, you might play darts, gamble on the cards, drink. On my evenings off I liked to go to the amusement arcades or dancing in the town. As a rookie my wages was 4s. 6d. a day and, out of that, a bob was kept back compulsory for what they called 'gratuities'. As I allocated a bob a day to my mother, I personally was only having half a crown a day.

My main impressions of Bridlington are drilling and physical exercise. We'd to do physical exercises in shorts and singlet on the grounds, on the beach, everywhere. Copying a corporal. Arms up in the air and seeing how far your hand would go down your side when you're stiff as a damned crutch. You'd to run, jump over hurdles, leapfrog. Some would fall by the wayside near to collapse and they'd be caught by the scruff of the neck and pulled back without mercy. The sergeants were devils. They'd say, 'You might have broken your mothers' hearts, but you won't break mine!' Then you'd have to march up and down the streets and the promenade. Once we were marching at the back of Woolworth's and, this is the type of corporal we had, he said, 'Eyes *right!*' and saluted, then 'Eyes front!' when we passed a pretty girl. I could always march quite good although I'd a gammy foot. They say people were more human in the RAF, but there was all this marching and you'd to polish your buttons and your badge: there was still a lot of bullshit.

My first little bit of action was when there was an imaginary scare and we were sent marching up and down everywhere in twos. There was two girls coming up the promenade so me and a mate said, 'Halt!' and asked them to show us their identification cards. They couldn't do so and we said, 'You're under arrest!' and we marched them back to the cookhouse, our headquarters for the day. The sergeant there was a little bit frustrated, he thought we'd gone a bit over the mark as he knew these girls — they worked in an amusement arcade. We'd done it for a joke. Everything at that time was a joke in a sense.

Next I was sent down to Cosford, an enormous camp just off Wolverhampton, where you were picked out and trained for whatever trade in the RAF you wanted. Mechanics, batmen, cooks — you name it, they had it. There was fourteen or fifteen football pitches, so many rugby pitches... I didn't join in any of the sports because of my foot. My foot was sometimes useful, you see! You were in Nissen huts and the bloody bugle would blow to get you out of bed at half past six, and you'd to rush to the wash houses. There was no privacy, now; you was washing and cleaning your teeth with the toilets right behind you. Somebody'd got false teeth and they'd drop out in the basin. Revolting. Early on, about forty of us were taken into a Nissen hut and issued with gas masks

71

and capes, and a sergeant gave us a demonstration how to fold the cape and put it on top of your haversack. Then he picked out a short little bloke called Bennett. 'Right, Bennett!' he said. 'I want you to show us how to fold a gas cape!' Bennett just sat tight. 'Bennett, I'm speaking to you! I want you to fold the gas cape!' You're back at school, you see. You're bigger boys but you're back at school. Bennett still just stuck there. 'Bennett, are you going to fold that cape?!' 'No, sir! I'm not interested in the gas cape, in the war, in you or in anyone else!' *He* wasn't going to say, 'Yes, sir. Three bags full,' so he was sent straight back on spud-bashing which he loved because he never had to do no exercises, no drills.

I put in for Flight Mechanic and was taken into the Works and shown the ins and outs of a plane. There was a lot of climbing around to do and after a few days I was complaining about my foot. They realized I wouldn't be any good and immediately downgraded me to the cook-house because it showed on my records that I'd done a little bit of confectionery. It was tremendous hard work in the cookhouse. I take my hat off to cooks who've to cater for hundreds. I'd to start from the bottom of the ladder, cutting up potatoes, frying bacon, making porridge but I didn't climb any higher in catering because a mate of mine, Jack Tuck from Wantage, said, 'Why not train as a batman like me?' So I put in for batman and I was transferred to Squadron Leader Rose, cleaning his shoes, pressing his clothes, polishing his buttons and his sandbelt, under supervision. I'd a proper little holder for the buttons, and I wore gloves so I wouldn't get Duraglit on my hands. You see? Getting a bit of a pansy! For pressing, I'd an iron, a piece of cloth and a basin of water. Don't forget everything was more crude in they days. You'd press the water out of the cloth and lay it on, say, the leg of the trousers. Mind you, there was always a crease there: you was only smartening of it up. But you'd to make sure you didn't get a double crease. And, as for the shoes, it really *was* spit and polish. You'd put on your polish, then really spit, then shine on and on and on, and then rub with a piece of newspaper. When I came out of the Services, I was a little bit of a dabster, I was. My wife never had to clean my shoes or anything like that. I took *that* weight off her.

I got engaged on December the 13th, 1940, when I came home for a short leave. My mother was so pleased to see me. You know, you walk in the door dressed up in blue knowing nothing and you'm the cat's whiskers, you'm winning the war! The war was a gimmick so far as I was concerned, and it's sad to say that, because some of my poor old pals was knocked over... Right. Now then. The first thing I did was go over to North Hill and bring Nesta back with me on the bus for a few days, during which we went into Tavistock to Mr Gribble's jeweller's shop, 11 Duke Street, and I bought her a diamond ring. Her father was an old-timer, full of discipline, so I'd asked his permission for her hand. People's only human and I was afraid that otherwise somebody else might whip her away while I was in the Services.

Probably the old Commanding Officer had spotted Squadron Leader Rose was looking prim and proper because, when I got back to Cosford, I was asked to report to the Adjutant's Office. I was that little bit nervous because the glasshouse was only just around the corner and you'm in there for nothing. But I was told I'd been recommended to look after Wing Commander Hope at RAF HQ at Exeter, and given a form to write out an application. A fortnight, three weeks after, I was posted to Exeter. Just like that.

In January, '42, I came down to Tavistock to see Nesta — we were getting married in about a fortnight, on the 18th. I was on French leave — I'd got forty-eight hours off from duty so I bolted, thumbed a lift. We went to see *Marco Polo* at the Carlton. We done a bit of talking about the wedding. The 18th was a Saturday and I was to be allowed home on the Wednesday. On about the 10th, I didn't feel very well and my neck was swollen so, the next morning, I reported sick to the MO, Flying Officer Cummings. He said, 'Oh, there are five or six teeth here that have got to be pulled out,' and the dental surgeon pulled three out on the top and three out on the bottom, leaving me like a rabbit — within eighteen months of discharge I had all the others taken out and got false teeth. I was then put in dock at Broad Clyst. The next morning the dental surgeon came round with the Senior MO. The Senior MO looked in my mouth and said, 'You've got the mumps. Twenty-one days' isolation.' I said, 'I'm going home on Wednesday and getting married on Saturday!' He said, and this is the very words he used, 'It don't matter a bugger, Adams, if you're getting *buried*! You've got to stay here for twenty-one days!' and I was put in a cubicle in a room for infectious complaints. I reckon I caught the mumps at the Carlton in Tavistock. I could have put two thousand five hundred men at risk, but there was

73

nobody else connected with the camp at Exeter who caught the mumps at any period.

Oh, I was heartbroken! I wrote to Nesta's home to say the wedding would have to be cancelled and she didn't receive the bloody letter till the Thursday. There was pandemonium. The flowers all had to be cancelled and the I-don't-know-how-many chickens they'd killed for the fifty guests had to be sold to the butcher. I can remember looking out of the window as I lay in dock on the day I was supposed to be married and seeing it snowing like hell outside.

I was actually in dock for twenty-three days and then I was given ten days' sick leave, so I came home. I was in a critical state for getting married, it could have killed me, but we made a quick arrangement and got married on the 7th of February, a day of snow showers, hail showers, rain and sunshine. We had a C. of E. service. I wore my uniform and Nesta wore a white veil and a long white dress. A cousin of mine, Claude Masters, a gardener at Endsleigh, was the best man. At the reception he made a bit of a speech. The wife's people were teetotallers so there wasn't a lot to drink — just tea and coffee and a drop of bubbly for the toast. The local bread roundsman was a confectioner himself and he always promised the wife because he was a great friend of the family that he'd ice her a wedding cake and ice it he did. There was *supposed* to be rationing but you could always get anything you wanted in the country if you had your hat on the right way. After the reception a local garage proprietor drove me, the bride, the bridesmaids and the best man in to a studio in Launceston to have our photos taken. After that we came home and had a bit of a dish-up again in the evening. Then, at about ten o'clock, my mother and father and Nesta and me come home to Milton Green in the car of a pal of mine, and there, in our little cottage, we spent our seven day honeymoon. Then it was back to camp for me and on as usual.

After the Wing Commander, I was made batman to Group Captain Loel Guinness, the CO. I'd to meet him in all his gold braid at West Hill House, his private billet near Ottery St Mary — the camp at Exeter was quite dispersed now because, as Flight Command, it was taking quite a bashing. The curiosity was that his *wife* was present — Isobel, one of the

Manners girls from Belvoir in Rutland. First of all it was all formality. You know, I came in and saluted them. Then I was told to sit down, to be at ease. Inwardly I was shaking like a jellyfish. The Group Captain *and* Lady Guinness would be my bosses. I'd be a valet-cum-handyman, the lot. I'd live in the house and have my own bedroom. There was also in the house a cook, an in-between maid, a gardener, and a nanny and a nanny's maid for their two little kiddies, Belinda and Billy. I was asked if I thought I'd be happy. I said, 'Yes.' It was home from home; I'd be living with rich people again.

Group Captain Guinness had about twenty pairs of shoes I'd to polish and God knows how many suits I'd to press. I'd to take him up a cup of tea every morning and, when he came off duty in the evening, I might have to go up and get his smoking jacket or make him a pink gin. I might have to wait at dinner, do some housework for Lady Guinness... I was their personal servant. I don't want to talk too much about it because, for the time I was with them, I didn't do anything as such for the country. I suppose, though, I was that little cog in the wheel. The Commander-in-Chief is watched by everybody. If he's turned out smart they've all got to smarten theirselves. And he *was* smart.

Bomber Harris stayed once for two or three days. When he was going away I made sure that *he* walked out of West Hill looking smart. That morning I took him up a cup of tea in bed and he said, 'There you are. Have a drink,' and he gave me five quid. You did well that way but you weren't allowed to talk about it because it might be deducted from your wages — mine were now up by half a crown a week. Lady Guinness's brother, John Manners, also came to stay. He was in the Army. I'd have to pack his suitcases when he was leaving and he'd say, 'You don't have to fold it, Adams! Just throw it in!' He was a young lad and he didn't care whether it was Christmas or Easter.

When I went on leave a boy would be sent from the camp to take my place. Once when I come back the Group Captain called me in the morning to his bedroom. He'd just had a bath and he rang the bell job which sounded in the passageway leading to the kitchen. He said, 'About my shoes. They're not clean!' I said, 'I've been away on seven days' leave!' He said, 'That's no excuse. you could have done them as soon as you got back last night!' Before I went I'd left six pairs polished ready. There you are. Going back to the younger generation again, can they

75

take that? But in balance the Guinnesses were very good to me and, till we found a place in a cottage near by belonging to someone who hadn't been called up, they let Nesta stay at West Hill House for long weekends.

We'd stay in this little cottage together. There'd be me, Nesta, the owner and his wife and their baby. One night me and Nesta got back quite late from the pictures when a bombing raid began over Exeter. We were in bed and the couple called to us, 'Come on! We're going downstairs to get under the kitchen table!' I wouldn't get out of bed. I said, 'If I'm going to die, I'll die here!' But the wife went down with them and the baby and got under the table. So if a bomb had come through the house they'd have had me as well as all the rubble on top of them.

There was a raid on three occasions that the wife came up. Fighter Command, you see. They would follow them in. And there was not just bombing but all this here machine-gunning. They were after anybody, anything, not just Service personnel. There was a hell of a lot of casualties at that period. But you couldn't let it frighten *you* too much, especially when you had a young bride. You're her protection, her bodyguard, so you've got to throw your chest out a wee bit. You got one or two that panicked because the bombers dropped flares to light their targets up and it would be like daylight. There were boys in the camp who'd get up in their pyjamas and run like hell and they didn't know where they was running. And Plymouth got knocked about terrible, night after night, week after week. I could see the great big glow from Milton Abbot if I stood on Ramsdown or a part of Barton Road when I was on leave. But I didn't like watching. I'd seen enough burning at Exeter.

A bomb dropped quite near a WAAF in Exeter. It frightened the hell out of her and she had a streak of white right back over through her hair from shock. It made her so attractive! Which can't be said about the behaviour of a lot of the WAAFs every year at the Christmas Day Party in the Officers' Mess. You were sat around the tables, airman, airwoman, airman, airwoman, and the women would go on drinking though they could take no more. One and then another, I can see them now, falling off the forms like skittles. Then they'd bring everything up and more or less creep about in it. Otherwise everybody had a really good do. I never wanted to take my leave at Christmas. All the officers were serving *us*, it was our day out. I've a menu card for '44. It says 'The

Commanding Officers and Senior NCOs join in wishing you all a very happy Christmas'. We had roast Norfolk turkey and chestnut stuffing or roast pork and apple sauce, followed by Christmas pudding with brandy sauce, followed by beer...

A mother's a mother and you can never have another. In '44, on February the 28th, mine died. I came home on French leave that afternoon to see her because the wife, who was living at Milton Green, had written to say she wasn't very well. I brought her some chocolate biscuits — in Exeter they let the Service boys have anything under the counter, and without coupons. As I walked up the garden path, Nesta came running down to me. She said, 'You've been quick, darling!' I asked her what she meant. She said, 'I sent a telegram to you via Station Headquarters this morning to say your mother had just passed away!' She'd been lying down in bed and, when Nesta propped her up, she flopped over in her arms. I was knocked for a six. I went straight upstairs to her bedroom. She was covered up, all but her face which was very pale. The curtains was drawn and everything in the house was still — you don't have the wireless on. I could have broke down and cried, but you've got to be brave. My father, who'd retired in 1940, was now seventy-three. I wondered what was going to happen to the wife, now she'd an old man to look after. He was frightened because Mother was only seventy-one and the strongest of the family, and he thought she was going to live for ever. I'd never known her from the day that I was born ever to have an illness.

My mind was in a turmoil. I wasn't even supposed to be home. I went to the telephone kiosk in the village, and I rang Station Headquarters. The orderly at the other end, a WAAF corporal, knew me. She said, 'Where *are* you?!' I said, 'I'm at Milton Abbot and I'm on French leave and', I said, 'my mother's passed away and there's a telegram been sent to SHQ!' She said, 'Well, the telegram's sat right in front of me on the table.' I said, 'What am I going to *do*?!!' She said, 'I'll put it in my pocket.' I said, 'Good! I'll catch a train right back.' She said, 'I shouldn't. Just turn up in camp tomorrow.' So I decided to stay the night to try to sort things out a bit. The wife was a little bit frustrated, and her mother arrived and was being dictatorial. But we were lucky because Mr Cox, the next door neighbour, was the undertaker, so everything was taken out of my hands and organized.

I went back to Exeter the next day, the telegram was produced and I was granted nine days' compassionate leave. I returned to No.1 Milton Green where my mother was now in a coffin, though still in the bedroom. I took a last look at her. A lot of people seem a little bit happier when they'm dead because all their strife and their worries is taken away from them, and that was so with her. On the burial day, we walked the eighth of a mile from Milton Green to Milton Abbot Church. The Wesleyan Chapel wasn't registered for funerals so we did it C. of E. — any rate, there's no cemetery attached to the chapel. There was six men carrying the coffin. The wife and myself were chief mourners and we walked behind. My father didn't go, and by brother was in Ireland. I wore my uniform. I saluted when the coffin was lowered. I was upset inwardly, but you mustn't show that. The wreath from the wife and myself and my father was arum lilies.

The funeral was after lunch, about half past two. Then there was the usual bunfeast for the mourners, which is terrible to my mind. At the funeral everybody's sad and then there they are having a drink of sherry or a cup of tea and talking as though nothing has happened.

My discharge date was the 2nd of June, 1945. Group Captain Guinness had been posted overseas. I put in an application for overseas service but they said I wasn't fit. There was a lot of us sent out. We were fit enough to go in, but we weren't fit enough to carry on. The war in Europe was over and, like we'd unloaded the fish at Endsleigh, they were unloading us. Before that you were just a little bit of gun fodder and luckily I didn't come in the way of the guns. It's as simple as that. 'Rank: Leading Aircraftman. Cause of Discharge: Ceasing to fulfil Royal Air Force physical requirements although fit for employment in civil life. General Character During Service: VG. On Discharge: VG. Degree of Trade Proficiency: Superior. Has always proved a willing worker who has taken a great pride in his work. Has been employed on batman's duties which he has carried out in an exemplary way. Absolutely honest and always cheerful.' Always happy, always gay,/Chummy at work, chummy at play./Laugh away your worries/And don't be sad and glum/And everyone will know that you're a chum, chum, chum... Goodbye. No more, 'Sir! 575!'

On the 4th or 5th of April, crowds of us from different branches of service at Exeter were sent up by train to Uxbridge in Surrey. We arrived about lunch-time. After lunch we were allowed out of camp till midnight. Some of us caught an Underground train into London. We roamed around sizing of it up. I'd never been in London before and I thought, 'I've cousins here. When I've settled down, I'm going to come back and call on them' I remember as well as yesterday standing under Big Ben as it was striking nine. Early next morning we were kitted out. I was issued with a shirt, tie, shoes, socks, a grey three-piece pinstripe suit and a trilby. Eventually I caught the train at Waterloo for Tavistock North, and the wife was there to meet me. I gave the trilby away to a passer-by before we caught the bus to Milton Green.

During my leave, I did a little fishing on the Lynher and I went with the wife for four or five days to her parents' home. She wasn't expecting a baby yet. I thought we'd have a child so soon as nine months after we were married. We were both fond of children and we were disappointed. A person that doesn't want a child will have children like shelling peas.

Any rate, as June approached, it dawned on me 'What work are you going to do? Everything on the estate looks dilapidated and overgrown. McNicol is coming up to pensionable age and is depressed because the new Duke never visited Endsleigh during the war and the hatchery was no longer in operation. If the new Duke *is* going to take any interest in Endsleigh, what are his intentions as regards the fishing?' I went to see the agent, now a Mr Bliss, who found me various jobs, take-home pay £1.12s.6d. till things was sorted out. I was planting tree seedlings in the forestry nursery behind Bedford Lodge. I was mixing cement and plastering and painting for the estate masons, and making and installing doors and window frames for the estate carpenters in the village. Sometimes I was on the river with a slasher. Sometimes I was netting down at Gunnislake. On VJ Day I got down to Gunnislake on my push-bike about 6 a.m. At seven we were sitting in Teague's kitchen and he switched on the radio and peace was announced. He said, 'Right! We're not fishing today!' and I cycled all the way home again and went drinking in the Edgcumbe Arms with my cousin, Bill Masters, and Dick Dodge, a tenant farmer.

That was in August. In November, Teague and Ross retired, and

79

Herbie Symons, who'd been a trapper at Endsleigh till '36 and then been loaned to the Tamar and Plym Fishery people before going into the Navy, took over the seven mile lower stretch from Horsebridge to Gunnislake in their place.

In January, '46, I was Water Bailiff back on the river in earnest again, checking licences and passes for the free trout fishing. And Mr Bliss presented me with a new double-barrelled shotgun — a Cogswell and Harrison — for killing vermin. I was after cormorants mainly. You'd see, as now, as many as twenty cormorants in flight. I'd stand under a tree by Carthamartha Pool, and seven at a time would land on an oak branch on the Cornish side. Bang, you'd get one. You'd stay twenty minutes, half an hour, and in they'd come again. Another bang! ...

We come on now to February, '47. McNicol is retiring and I've been called to Mr Bliss's office. He said, 'Mr McNicol thinks you're capable of taking charge of the Endsleigh Stretch.' That was the seven mile upper stretch of river from Greystone Bridge to Horsebridge. 'He is retiring in March and he and his wife are moving to a semi-detached house in Milton Abbot. He has recommended that you succeed him and that you and your wife come to live at Fishery Cottage. Your wages will go up by ten shillings a fortnight.' This meant I'd be taking home £2 a week. 'We hope that you want the job and that you will look after His Grace when he visits us on May the 19th. Pending repairs to Endsleigh House which the school's left in turmoil, he'll be staying in Keeper Buckingham's house at Carthamartha.' I said, 'I'd love the job, and Fishery Cottage is the most beautiful cottage on the estate, but it's in a lonely place. I'll have to consult the wife.' Next day, I rang him to accept. He said, 'Call on Mr McNicol before you go on the river this morning. Tell him you're the next man on.'

On the 7th of March, Tommy Peters, the estate driver, helped me load the McNicols' furniture on to a lorry and place it in their new home, and, again with Tommy's help, we moved into Fishery Cottage on the 11th. No.1 Milton Green was let to people called Edgcumbe, farm labourers not on the estate. Gone already the days of one big happy Miltonian family working for the Bedfords.

Fishery Cottage seemed like a palace after our little place at Milton Green with its sloping ceilings, and where you were all cramped up and you could only have your bed one way, and you'd no running water and only a bucket lavatory. Now, instead of being two down and two up, we were three down and three up, with a kitchen, a nice sized dining-room, a nice sitting-room, a hallway, a larder, three bedrooms and a bathroom — one lavatory in the bathroom and one outside, both flush. We were highly honoured, we were over the moon, apart from me fussing would I be able to hold the job. The roof was thatch but, after two or three years, the thatch was ripped off and replaced by cedar shingles, as were all the cottages on the estate, including Milton — there'd been fires at Coombe and Bedford Lodges.

So there we were in this beautiful cottage, with me taking home £4 fortnightly, and with no rent, no rates to pay, and ten ton of wood given us a year. There was no electricity, though mains to replace the dynamo were laid on at the house in 1938, so we still used oil table-lamps, and cooking was by Rayburn stove. There was a telephone through to the house but no ordinary telephone. We were still in the dark ages. Now everybody's got one. They don't sit down and write letters any more because they can just pick the telephone up and say, 'Hallo, darling. How are you?'

Mr Bliss visited us when we were settled to check if the wife still thought she'd be happy in spite of the loneliness of the situation. There's a crossroad about a quarter of a mile up the drive from the house. If you bear left you come to Harragrove Gardens. If you bear right, you come to a road that drops down to the hatchery, but you go an eighth of a mile straight up in front of you and you come to Fishery Cottage and Swiss Cottage. Though you couldn't see them, we were three hundred feet above the river at a point between Black Rock Pool and Wood Gate Pool, surrounded on three sides by woods and at the bottom of a thirty-two acre field. Our only neighbours were Mr Russell Percy, a gardener, and his wife, in Swiss Cottage about two hundred yards away. That had its own set of one hundred and eighty-nine steps down to the river. Fifty or sixty yards from us was another set — three or four steps and then a run, then three or four steps and another run... It was quite something living up there. If a gale was on, you'd hear the trees roaring. Right outside the dining-room windows there was trees that could have crashed onto the house. Thunderstorms, especially, were a bit frightening. One night — we hadn't been there more than three years — we

81

heard a tremendous crash or, rather, the wife and me did (my father was in the other room sound asleep). I thought, 'My God! Burglars! They've smashed a window in!' I picked up my gun which I used to take to bed with me, and we crept downstairs. The wife always says that I pushed her in front of me, but that's not true. The dining-room door was a little ajar. She whispered, 'Well, what are you going to do?!' I said, 'If anyone moves I shall shoot them for certain!' — I was really edged up. Then I pushed the door open with my foot and I was action stations. But it was only part of the ceiling had collapsed. It had made a hell of a mess and dented our MacMichael radio. I'd to take out a wheelbarrow and a half of plaster.

The only thing that *really* frightened the wife about Fishery Cottage was the bats. If a bat came in the bedroom window she'd be panic-stricken, scared stiff it was going to get into her hair. There she was, flopping and jumping around. Well, that was just *enticing* the bat to go into her hair. She should have got into bed and pulled the sheet over her head. Any rate, once you put the light out, a bat's gone.

I took a gun to bed with me only because we'd a lot of trouble with the pigeons eating the green stuff in the garden. I propped it in the corner of the room and kept two or three cartridges on the dressing-table. The garden was in direct line with the window and within firing distance. I'd creep over to the open window and, if I saw a pigeon, I'd creep back, load the gun, creep over again, and Bang! Vermin. We growed all our own vegetables — potatoes, Brussels sprouts, cabbage, you name it. My father helped me with these while the wife weeded the flower beds. We'd a tremendous lot of grass and he cut this with a scythe. And we still kept a pig as well as eighty-odd head of poultry, half of them running wild.

The wife was, and is, very, very houseproud. She thought Mr and Mrs Cox, who'd been the Adams's neighbours at Milton Green for thirty years, would like to see our beautiful new cottage. She used a lot of elbow grease, set everything out nicely, and invited them to tea. I was home when they arrived, and she'd got the sitting-room and the dining-room doors wide open as they came in the front door. She said, 'Now this is our sitting-room.' And, as she took them in the door of the sitting-room, there, sat on the back of one of the armchairs, was a mouse! So that was disgrading right away! When the Coxes were gone, we pulled the chairs into the middle of the room, got the cat from the kitchen and put it in and shut the door. Yes, we brought the cat with us from Milton Green — a ginger tom. I've never been without a cat until recently — he suffered so much from a kidney infection that we had to put him down. I've never had a dog — they're too much trouble to keep under control. This ginger tom we brought to Fishery Cottage thought he was in Wonderland with no main road to cross and so much freedom. I always believed in having a male cat because it saved drowning the kittens in a bucket or cracking them at the back of the head. In '37/'38, one of the gardeners' wives put a cat with a stone in a bag and dumped it in the river at Endsleigh Ham, but the bag bursted and the cat climbed up the bank and ran away.

Talking of dumping, I saw on the television tonight [Saturday, July 28] that they've got all the five million pounds worth of silver which was whipped recently from Woburn Abbey. It was found dumped in a waterworks. The Marquess was interviewed. He was at Ascot when he was informed. He didn't do very well at the race meeting — his horse was well back the list — but he was over the moon about the silver. That's the words he used — 'over the moon'. The wife won't be over the moon. She was out at bingo when I came out tonight [approx. 10 p.m.] and she doesn't know I'm here. She'll be worried; she'll think I've foolishly gone on the river and I've runned up against a poacher and, poor old bugger, I've been knocked in the water. It could often be a lonely life for her if she didn't find her own entertainment. She plays bingo at the Carlton in Tavistock two evenings a week (Thursdays and Saturdays) — there's been a bus laid on from Launceston. She also plays sometimes in Plymouth, and she plays at Paignton when we go there on holiday. She's very lucky.

Going back instead of forward I was now preparing for the visit of the new Duke. I'd to see that the stakes and nets were by the pools and that the boats were repaired and painted. I tied up a few salmon flies as I was told salmon fishing was what interested His Grace most. I concentrated on the Jock Scott and the Silver Doctor till I was told his favourite fly was a Silver Grey, so then I tied up a few Silver Greys. I'd also to instruct Kidd, the head forester, to get his men to clear the scrub along my stretch, including the three miles up the Inny to Wooda Bridge should His Grace want to go sea trout fishing in the evenings. I can't speak for what Herbie Symons was doing on the Lower Stretch. We didn't socialize much. He was of a different make-up from me — a little bit sophisticated, not a Joe Blunt; well turned-out whereas I've always been rather scruffy. I don't wear a hat and I never put a fly in my lapel but he was a typical fisherman with stacks of flies in his hat and lapel which I always called 'showmanship'.

Ten o'clock, Tuesday the 20th of May, 1947, I was waiting on the Devon side at Inny Foot, about to meet Hastings, 12th Duke of Bedford, for the first time. This was the King of Endsleigh, make no mistake about that! And I knew he was an exceptionally good fisherman — the Bedfords had an estate in Scotland where he'd fished a lot. I was very, very nervous. Mr Pratt, a taxi-driver from Rezare brought him down, with his two secretaries, Miss Houseman and Miss Dix, and Keeper Buckingham, from Carthamartha House to the Cornish bank. Buckingham, when he'd crossed over His Grace and the secretaries, did the introductions, then left me to take the three of them downstream to Inny Croy. These two girls hanging on to His Grace's tail weren't fishing yet, they were watching only. You see? A duke and his secretaries staying with his gamekeeper! The war was the turning point. The war brought people together. In fact, Winston Churchill, he'd to bring in different parts of the community — Liberals, Labours — as a Coalition Government. You were beginning to rub shoulder to shoulder.

His Grace said, 'I'd like for you to put on a Silver Grey,' so I tied one on to the cast and he proceeded to fish on the croy. Then he wanted me to take him out in the boat at Inny Croy Pool. He's six foot one, six foot two, and it's a flat-bottomed boat and he's stood up in the stern fishing away and I'm trying to keep out of the fast current. I'm shaking because I don't want to put him overboard our first encounter. Later, we wandered down to Bush Pool and waded. I wore black Wellingtons — they like green now, but colours didn't come in till the Fifties. He wore canvas waders and a cap with earflaps with tapes he tied under his chin — he suffered a wee bit from ear trouble. Luckily we didn't catch any fish that morning or it probably would have been pandemonium with me, not knowing his reaction. Finally we walked back to where Buckingham had promised to skull them back at one o'clock. As we walked, His Grace was casually talking, asking me if I'd enjoyed my time in the Services and the previous time I'd been here with McNicol and if I was interested in the river, and if I thought I would be able to carry on which he hoped I would. He was very shy and I was a bit shy, so it was two shy persons. But he was very, very friendly, a real old toff. Before leaving, he said, 'Thank you *very* much, Mr Adams. I'll be meeting you here at the same time tomorrow morning.' I didn't yet realize it, but he was a devil for people being on time.

Next day it was raining quite hard, and there'd been quite a drop of rain during the night. Ten o'clock. Same procedure. He was on his own and we were both in oilskins. We wandered downstream to Inny Croy and I took him out in the boat and he was into a fish immediately — nine and a half pounds. I was more at ease now because there were no lookers-on. When he hooked it, I took the net off the post and went down to the river. He said, 'Hold on! I shall take a considerable time to bring it in!' He took about five and twenty minutes, and I netted the fish first time round, then killed it. His Grace shook my hand and said, 'Well done, Mr Adams!' Then I said to him, I said, 'The river's rising so we'd better move downstream again pretty smart to keep in front of the rise.' We got to Bush Pool, but the river was really rising rapidly. It had risen a foot or one foot three, with dirty water coming from down the Inny off Bodmin Moor where it had been teeming. So I said, 'The river is out of order. I don't think it's worth fishing,' and we went back. Now I was panic-stricken because the gamekeeper wouldn't be there yet to take His Grace back to the Cornish side. But, thank God, when we got above where the Inny enters the Tamar, the water was gin clear and only up an inch or two. So I got him into the boat on the Devon side and safely crossed him myself. I said, 'I'll come back with you to Carthamartha if you like,' but he wouldn't hear of it. He just plugged on, carrying the fish and his tackle, on his own. He was very independent.

The third morning, which was the Thursday, His Grace didn't turn up, it was just the secretaries. His Grace had been taken down to the Lower Reaches with Herbie Symons. I'd to take the girls down to Bush and Gravel where we caught nothing. I'd to pay a lot of attention to Miss Dix who'd never fished before. Miss Houseman, the Senior Secretary, had been with His Grace for a considerable time. She looked very matronly, a real old spinster type, I'd say in her late forties. Miss Dix was in her late twenties, a vicar's daughter, very prim and proper with a very high-pitched voice.

I wasn't needed on the Friday, except to go to tell Kidd that His Grace wanted an oak tree felled at Leigh Wood Croys. Then, on Saturday, I'd to meet him and Miss Houseman at Endsleigh House and go down with them to Leigh Wood Croys in Mr Pratt's taxi. Four foresters had just felled the tree, and it was bang across the drive. We got out of the taxi and climbed over the stock. His Grace said to me, 'Mr Adams, are these my foresters?' I said, 'Yes, Your Grace.' I knew them all — the foreman was called Reed and one was called Northy; one was an Irishman, a funny sort of bloke, called Paddy and I'm not too sure of the name of the fourth. They were jumping to attention and saying, 'Good-morning, Your Grace!' 'Good-morning, sir!', a little bit frustrated to see us arrive and the road blocked, the very first time His Grace had proceeded down that way.

We were fishing for about a quarter of an hour when, bang, His Grace was into a fish. He usually played a fish so it was on its side, played out when he brought it to the net. In this case, any child, a fool, could have netted the fish for him, though it was a really big one. I cracked it across the head, took it up the steps, weighed it immediately. It was seventeen pound! You know, marvellous! And then, all out of the blue, His Grace said, 'Mr Adams,' he said, 'you say those men are my foresters.' He said, 'I would like for you to divide this fish into four and give them a portion each.' Now, when he said that, I almost went through the bank because, all the years I'd been here, I'd never been offered a piece of fish *myself*, and here's His Grace offering some to four woodmen! I was getting a bit brassy now, a little bit wayward, so I said, 'It's all very well, You Grace, giving them a portion each, but I shan't know which portion to give!' He said, 'They're lucky to be getting a portion at all!' Any rate, the foresters couldn't *believe* it when I said, 'This fish is for you.' I tossed a coin for the best portion which I'd always been told was behind the shoulder, and — it was so damn funny — Reed, the foreman, won it. I was playing cricket that afternoon, so I strapped the salmon to the carrier of my bike in a bass, push-biked home, cut the fish into portions, wrapped them in greaseproof paper, washed, had my lunch, changed into my white flannels and cricket boots, rushed around on my bike distributing

86

the portions, then off I went for the game of cricket. I was probably out for a duck, so I had a duck instead of a piece of fish. But on the Monday I took His Grace out again and caught an eight pound fish and he gave it all to me. I thought, 'Adams, boy, he've taken to you! You're home and dry. Your future looks secure.'

I've been lucky in life. Even in the Air Force I went right into the hornets' nest, I met 'society' right away, and I've always found it easier to get on with that type of person. What's 'society' more than you? Often not more than their money. They're all human and, if you have that in your head and keep your place, they're easy to get along with. There's a Mrs Bailey comes here, the wife of Captain Bailey, Lord Trenchard's brother-in-law. To begin with I was a wee bit shy of her — you sometimes think they're a little bit above you, for why I don't know. But she's turned out to be a wonderful, down-to-earth person. I'd a bilious attack up the river one Sunday morning — of course, the 11th and 12th Dukes never allowed fishing on a Sunday — and I'd to keep my back into the wood, and Mrs Bailey, who was fishing Thompson's Pool, kept on shouting, 'Are you all right, Mr Adams?' I said, 'Yes, I'm all right.' Finally she said, 'Well, you don't seem right to me. I'm going to reel in and drive you home.'

Any rate, His Grace was here in '47 for approximately a month, and him and the secretaries between them caught thirty-nine salmon. I'd to take one up to McNicol who was pleased as Punch that I got on with His Grace from the word go.

Before returning to Woburn, His Grace instructed Mr Bliss to let the river for salmon fishing when he wasn't here. He'd to choose carefully and inform me of his choices. Till then, apart from the trout fishermen, we'd only had élite guests such as Sir Thomas Russell. Dear old Sir Thomas was a great character and a great fisherman. Back in the Grandfather Duke's days, he caught a thirty-two pound salmon at Leigh Wood Croys — still the record for Endsleigh. He called the Tamar 'the dirtiest river outside of China'. He was known as Russell Pasha. As a young man he helped to form the Sudanese Camel Corps Police. Then he spent about forty years trying to break the drug traffic and bring about law and order in Egypt. He'd an officer there who stubbed his cigarette out on a darkie's head. 'We all had a good laugh,' he told me, 'but I had to reprimand him.' Her Ladyship was a little bit dictatorial; she'd push you till you got your back to the wall and couldn't go any further, but Sir Thomas, he was always full of humour. Once, when he was staying at Carthamartha House, we got a fish, about ten, twelve pound, and I was walking with him back to the boat and we met a tenant farmer, Mr Vigars, with his daughter, Doreen. Mr Vigars, of course, was delighted to meet a cousin of the Duke. He said, 'I see you've had a bit of luck then, sir!' 'Yes,' said Sir Thomas. 'We caught him about five minutes ago up at Lowley Run. Would you like a look at him?' So I emptied the fish out of the bass. Doreen put her hand down, touched the fish and said, 'It's cold already!' This amused Sir Thomas *very* much.

Five

As regards these new people coming here in '47, one of the first I can remember was Major Lionel Marsden, a BBC newsreader, a very pleasant person with a real cockney wife. One morning about half past eight I was push-biking up river and I saw him wading Gravel Pool. As I approached, so he slipped. I said, 'Are you wet, sir?' He said, 'What the hell do you *think* I am?! I'll have to strip off.' He'd a rope in the car and we tied it from bush to bush, and he hung up everything except his underpants which he put on over another pair of trousers from the car as a way to dry them. But then he slid down over the bank and sat in the sand, so *again* he'd a wet arse and no fish as they say. He was in a *hell* of a mess. And, right out of the blue, a car was approaching and this was his wife with their friend, Mrs Preedy of Bradstone Manor, an oldish lady that used to wear a felt hat with two damn great feathers from the tail of a pheasant stuck up in it. We all had quite a laugh. That was my first meeting with Mrs Marsden. She was a good-looker, though I could never figure out what she was saying. The major asked me to give her a little tuition but she didn't take to fishing, wasn't keen.

The following week, on the Monday, I invited the Marsdens to tea at Fishery Cottage. I went ahead on the push-bike and told the wife they were calling and she was running around with the duster — she's always been terrible houseproud. So we all sat in the dining-room having home-made cake and cups of tea, and Mrs Marsden was so difficult to understand the wife was quite confused and didn't know whether to say yes or no. At one point, Major Marsden was rolling on with me about the Football Pools and Mrs Marsden said to the wife, 'Have *you* tried them?' and the wife thought she was talking about drying the washing and said, 'Yes, I was lucky. I dried it before lunch.' Roars of laughter. But, you see, there you are — friends already. And that's been one of the beauties of my job at Endsleigh, making friends, and, if you don't make a friend, that person rarely comes back. There was a colonel here a few years ago. He *called* himself colonel: probably he was in the Home Guard. He was fishing Dunterue Pool and I explained the difficulties. To start with, it's a very tricky wading pool, it's got one of the slimiest bottoms on the Tamar. Secondly, the stream goes right down the middle and, if you're not careful, as you cast your fly across the stream, it's inclined to belly, so you've really got to mend your line. He turned right around and said, 'How would *you* know? How long have you been here? Three years?' I said, 'No. Fifty!' He thought he was going to step on me, but he found I was stepping on him. He hasn't come back, and probably he'll never come back.

Any rate, Major Marsden said if ever we were in London we were to get in touch with him and we said we might do so in mid-October because we'd written to my cousin, Frank Bevan and his wife, Flo, at 12 Purbright Road, Southfields near Wandsworth, and they'd invited us for a fortnight. Before the war workers on the estate had only been given Saturday afternoons, Sundays and Bank Holidays. After the war, the new Duke gave everybody at least a fortnight's holiday, and he gave me three weeks in the close season as I worked so many Bank Holidays. During that three weeks, usually from mid-October, the wife and I went to London and Father went to the wife's parents, for thirteen years in succession. We'd come home to Fishery Cottage and we'd have to go around with dustpan and brush collecting dead flies. You'd go away. You'd leave your house spotlessly clean in case anything happened. All the windows is shut. Yet you'd always find thousands upon thousands of dead flies. In the bedrooms especially it was *terrible*.

My first memory of our stay in '47 is coming in one evening and saying we'd been to the Whispering Gallery of St Paul's Cathedral. Frank said, 'What do you mean "Whispering Gallery"?' He'd lived in London for thirty years and he'd never bothered to go to St Paul's! Yet that was one of the first things we wanted to see. *And* Westminster Abbey. I went to watch Fulham play at Craven Cottage. Frank said, 'Don't take your wallet. You'll feel a nudge on your back and you won't take any notice. Then you'll put your hand in your pocket and your wallet will be gone and that nudge on your back will have done it. So simple.' But I kept my wallet on me. The wife says I'm obstinate and a know-all but, for those thirteen years, all over London I went, including Petticoat Lane, and I never lost it. Of course, I kept my money in my *jacket* pocket. You see people now with their cheque-books hanging out of their hip pockets. They *deserve* to lose them... A lady from London was fishing here once with her husband and she says to me, she said, 'Where do you go, Adams, for your holiday?' I said, 'London.' She said, 'You must be crackers!' I said, 'You come down into the West Country. I can say the same thing. *You* must be crackers!' She said, 'We come here for the quiet.' I said, 'We go to get *away* from the quiet. We're stuck too *much* in the quiet.'

Later on during that first holiday we received a telegram at South-fields telling us to meet Major Marsden at the BBC Studios, the Paris Cinema, Lower Regent Street. We arrived just before midday to find a queue of people waiting to go in to a recording of *Saturday Night Music Hall.* One of the attendants at the door spotted us. He said, 'Excuse me, but I think you must be looking for Lionel Marsden.' We said, 'Yes.' He said, 'You're Mr and Mrs Adams from the West Country, aren't you? Step inside.' And there was Major Marsden. He gave the wife a kiss and shook hands with me and patted me on the back. He said, 'Right. I want you to come in here,' and he put us into the front row of the studio and left us. As I've told you, I've always been of a shy disposition, so I said to Nesta, 'Let's slip back,' so we moved back into the third row. Now, here's the fun. After a person had shown us the signals for laughter, for clapping and for 'oooh!', Rob Wilton, the comedian, came in to get us in the mood — the show included him, Evelyn Laye, Victor King and Harry Mooney. He stepped off the stage, got straight on to the knees of a man in the front row, put his arm around him and started a lot of nonsense, ending with a story about fishing, which went a wee bit flat as the person he was talking to wasn't me as arranged. I can see, now, Rob Wilton getting off that lap and strolling up to the stage a little bit disappointed.

Another day, Major Marsden showed us round Broadcasting House; so we could see London all lit up he even took us onto the roof against rules and regulations. In the cafeteria, where we had something with piccalilli which I hate, Alvar Lidell was at the next table with a lady. The lady said rather loudly, 'There's one other BBC announcer I'd love to meet and that's Lionel Marsden,' and Alvar Lidell gave her a dig in the ribs and glanced at our table. Lionel Marsden winked at us and said, 'The trouble is everybody wants to meet you. You're treated as something

91

very special although you're only reading something off a piece of paper.' Then he took us to see him reading the *Nine O'Clock News*. He was sat behind a glass panel and we were in another room. We thought it a strange coincidence that the main item of news that evening was about a West Country sailor whose wife had produced quads. Afterwards he introduced us to Frank Phillips, a senior newsreader who'd once been a singer. He eventually brought him down to Endsleigh fishing. I netted a fish for him at Duchess Pool in Gunnislake. I didn't like him. He lacked patience and he was stuck up, fancied his weight a bit.

By '49 Mrs Preedy was a widow and married to her husband's best friend, Sir Percy Simner. Her first husband was a KC and her second husband was a KC, retired, with a house at Queen's Gate Gardens. So we called on *them*. The parlourmaid who opened the door called Sir Percy who ushered us into the lounge where Her Ladyship welcomed us and was soon out with some photographs. I'm right at home because she's a down-to-earth sort of person, but the wife's afraid to move in her armchair, don't know whether to cross her legs or what. When the girls came in with the tray of tea I said to Her Ladyship, 'I hope you haven't put out the best china for me. Being an old country jan, I'm liable to break the handles.' The wife was so upset with me for saying this, she gave me a punch. One year, though, *I* was the one that was embarrassed. Mr George Cansdale, the Superintendent of the London Zoological Gardens, took us around the Gardens and then says, 'What about some lunch?' We had roast beef which was a little bit on the tough side and my chewing wasn't up to scratch because of my new dentures. It was one thing having Mr Cansdale down on the river where he could let his hair down, but now he was in his best bib and tucker, and I was making a hash of it.

The wife and I was always struck how in so big a place as London you would meet *by chance* people with whom you was somehow connected. One year we stood with a group of Scotch, Welsh and others at the Opening of Parliament. When the group started to disperse, a middle-aged man turned to us and said, 'You're from the West Country, aren't you?' I said, 'Yes, we live in a little village called Milton Abbot which is six miles beyond Tavistock going towards Cornwall.' And the wife said, 'And I was brought up near Liskeard in the district of North Hill.' He said, 'Do you know Bathpool?!' She said, 'Yes. That's where my parents live now. My maiden name is Daniells.' 'Nothing to do with Sid Daniells, the blacksmith, by any chance?' Just like that! So she said, 'Yes. Sid Daniells is my father!' and he told us that he and his parents lived next door to her parents for a time at a place called Cocklesrest. Unbelievable, really. He was a journalist and he took us to lunch at a Lyons'. On another occasion I went to Chelsea to watch them play Blackpool. It was a record crowd, over seventy thousand. Some were shouting for Stanley Matthews: I was shouting for Bowie. I know the score finished up three all but, in the interval, a man touched my elbow. He said, 'West Country?' I said, 'Yes. From near Tavistock.' He said, 'I'm from St Austell.' And there we were stood shoulder to shoulder and yet if I went up to London *looking* for someone from St Austell I'd still be up there looking!

One year we went to see the Reverend Arrowsmith, Prebendary of St Luke's, Chelsea, and another Endsleigh visitor. We decided to attend the eleven o'clock service on a Sunday but arrived a little late. We were shown into our seats by one of the stewards and immediately after the service which we thoroughly enjoyed I had a tap on my shoulder. We'd been sat directly in front of Mrs Arrowsmith! She said how pleased she was to see us and invited us over to the Rectory to have coffee. After coffee, the Reverend Arrowsmith said, 'Would you like to see the garden? I'll take a gun in case there's a pigeon.' And, sure enough, there was a pigeon and Bang. I was disgusted, seeing that we'd just been in church and Sunday was a day when you didn't *do* they sort of things. On a Sunday at Endsleigh we didn't shoot or fish. It's only the 12th Duke's Trustees and the Syndicate have brought that on.

This Reverend Arrowsmith was a personal friend of the Duke. He used to stay with Keeper Buckingham at Carthamartha for a fortnight, three weeks, a month, spring or summer and autumn, but never at the same time as the Duke. His granddaughter, Caroline, turned up out of the blue this afternoon [August 1]. I hadn't seen her since she came and stayed at Carthamartha in the 12th Duke's time when she was about six. She, Prebendary Arrowsmith, his wife and myself were going fishing, and she'd a wire-haired terrier with her and a trout rod with three flies dangling. I said, 'For goodness sake watch the dog!' and, right on the same, the dog jumped at a fly and it got caught inside his upper lip and he went berserk. The little girl was screaming, the Reverend Arrowsmith was panic-stricken. I said, 'It's no good getting like this. We must find a pair of pliers.' So Mrs Arrowsmith went to the car, found a pair of pliers and I got hold of the dog by his scruff, caught hold of the fly with the pliers and twitched it out. The little girl turning up again brings my story right to 1984! Queer, really, as I began talking to you about Prebendary Arrowsmith this morning. I said to her, 'If you talk about the devil, you're sure to see his horns.'

Sometimes the Reverend Arrowsmith would motor down along from Carthamartha, cross himself over from the Cornwall side in the keeper's boat, and pick up a push-bike he kept in an old shed at Inny Foot among the rhododendrons. One morning in mid-July I stopped at Dunterue Stage to catch a fish for a farmer. It was about 7 a.m. and I'd already caught one fish at Woodtown. I caught another fish immediately, so I thought, 'I'd like a third.' I was getting a bit greedy. This is human nature. But I wasn't greedy for myself, I was thinking, 'I don't want to take a fish to X and Y without taking one to Z.' Suddenly I heard the rattle of an old boneshaker coming upstream through Dunterue Wood, and the Reverend Arrowsmith arrives and the very first words he said to me were, 'Oh!' he said. 'So I've caught the poacher!' I said, 'What do you mean "the poacher"?!' He said, '*I* was going to fish here!' This was one of his favourite pools and it was in easy cycling distance. I said, 'Well, bad luck!' I mean, he'd got fourteen miles of river to fish and he'd got to come on to the pool that I was fishing on behalf of the farmers. I think he expected me to give one of the fish I'd caught to *him* but I left, saying, 'I must get on now. By the time I've push-biked home and had breakfast there'll be a hundred and one things to do, including the distribution of these fish to tenant farmers.'

I met the Reverend Arrowsmith on several occasions after this and accompanied him fishing. But, after about five weeks, I had a letter from His Grace saying the Reverend Arrowsmith had complained to him that I was fishing at the crack of dawn at Dunterue Stage. I'd been reported by a man I'd helped! Me who's in charge of the river! But His Grace said, 'It's like this, Adams. All you have is one boss, and I happen to be your boss, so you just carry on in the normal way and take no notice of anyone but me. If people treat you rough, I must remind you to treat *them* rough. Do your best but don't be trodden on. If people stand on *my* toes, boy, I give it to them, I cut them in half!'

His Grace stayed at Endsleigh House for the first time in 1949 because a suite was at last ready, though other redecorations were still going on and there was a lot of banging. His arrival was far more simple than that of his father before the war. His wife never came because they were adrift, so just him and his secretaries and his valet/butler, James Foley, would arrive by train at Exeter where a chauffeur met them in an old runabout, a converted London taxi. The chauffeurs' residences at Harragrove were now turned into workmen's cottages and a housekeeper and a cook were awaiting everyone, including the chauffeur, at the house with about four daily staff. That year, Miss Margery Russell, a sister of Russell Pasha, and Lord Hugh, the Duke's younger son, were staying there as well. Along with the secretaries — Miss Houseman and Miss Dix — there was a young, pretty under-secretary called Miss Williams.

Though His Grace was approachable and easy to get on with, you had to be on the ball. One year he noticed that the fencing around the box tree at Bush Pool had been broken so he said to me, 'I'd like for you to ring the agent and tell him to have that fence repaired by the estate carpenter.' The next day we came up to Bush Pool and the fence wasn't repaired. He said, 'Have you been in contact with the agent?' I said, 'Yes.' He said, 'Well, please ring him again.'

Another thing was time: everything had to be on time. I'd to meet him every morning bar Sunday he was in residence at nine o'clock out in the colonnade where the tackle was kept and, if the clock over the entrance to the stables yard had started to strike nine and I wasn't there, he'd been and gone. So, if possible, I was always waiting for him at nine when he came out into the colonnade which is outside, in front of the passage joining the main house to what was still called 'the nursery end' but is now sometimes called 'the cottage end'. In front of the colonnade there's a flower garden and a pool with a little fountain. The garden was more beautiful in they days. Each little flower-bed was surrounded by a box bush kept trim to a height of about one foot six, and it was full of wallflowers and tulips in May time, and phlox and nemesia later in the year. Any rate, he'd say, 'Good-morning, Adams!' and I'd say, 'Good-morning, Your Grace!' and then he'd give me my day's duties. In the morning he might be with Herbie Symons down at Gunnislake and I'd be with the secretaries on my stretch, or the other way around. I'd set off with whoever it was at approximately half past nine, driven by his chauffeur or the under-keeper, Charles Broad. His Grace would always come home for lunch and then he'd write literature or go for walks on his own till half past four, five o'clock when we'd usually go off fishing until dinner. His favourite rod was an old twelve foot six Farlow — I'd have to make it up on the river bank. His favourite fly was the Silver Grey. We crossed in a boat with Miss Russell one evening to fish Parson's Pool — it's our only left-handed pool; it was fished from the Devon bank till His Grace thought it would fish better from the other side; he had one or two trees cut down to enable this, though you'd still to fish over your left shoulder to avoid the bushes. He asked me to put on a No.8 Silver Grey and he was into a fish immediately. It was around ten pound. I've told you there was a stake with a net and a priest at every pool, so I netted it, killed it and that was that. We came back across the stream, got in the car and went up to Inny Croy where he said, 'Let's put on a bigger Silver Grey. What about a 2/0?' And when I went to put on this bigger Silver Grey I noticed it wasn't a Silver Grey that I'd put on in the first place, it was a Mar Lodge! So I started to put on a No.2/0 Mar Lodge. His Grace was watching me and he said, 'I though we were going to put on a Silver Grey. You're putting on a Mar Lodge.' I said, 'Yes, Your Grace. We've caught a fish, and the fly you caught the fish on was a Mar Lodge. My mistake,' I said, 'but I was always taught by Mr McNicol never to change the jockey in the middle of the course.' He said, 'Well, carry on,' and I remember taking Miss Russell out in the boat and her losing a fish which was a disaster when I needed a triumph.

We got back here and His Grace called me into his study, now the Quiet Room. He said, 'I want you to go through all my fly cases and, if there's any Mar Lodges there, would you let me have them in the morning.' So I took the cases home with me and I remember he'd got a hundred and eight Silver Doctors and even more Silver Greys, and the Mar Lodges I wrapped in a piece of newspaper and gave to him personally the next morning when I met him at nine o'clock. He said, 'Thank you very much.' Now I was very curious about all this so later I asked Miss Dix what he did with them. She said, 'He've destroyed them. He've thrown them in the fire.' It took me years and years to get to the end of the story. In the early Sixties someone told me that Mar Lodge, after which the fly was named, was a lodge on one of the rivers in Scotland and its owners were once at loggerheads with the Bedford family and His

Grace was still not going to fish with anything connected with them. But he never murmured a word to me about this feud and time after time after that I put on for him the old Silver Greys he liked best. *I* liked Jock Scotts, Silver Doctors and, above all, Dusty Millers best until the introduction of the brass tube.

Keeper Hall lived at Carthamartha (Buckingham had retired and was living at Endsleigh Lodge) and Charles Broad, the under-keeper, lived opposite in what used to be the rabbit trapper's house on the Devon side. We always thought Broad had preferential treatment. He had been a cowman on the Woburn Estate and His Grace brought him down to Endsleigh special. It was 'Good-morning, Charles' — you know, very personal. Broad came once with Keeper Hall at the wife's invitation to have coffee. We didn't know then that Keeper Hall was full of jokes. He said, 'Coming down river this morning, I saw a tremendous salmon lying on one of the big rocks just inside Dunterue Gate.' Dunterue Gate is only about a mile from Fishery Cottage so I left him and Broad with the wife and cycled to this rock where I found it wasn't a salmon at all but a damn great smelly pig washed down in the flood!

The keepers were roaming around keeping down the vermin, but His Grace was all for Nature and things were being conserved more. Otters weren't to be trapped or shot so if the odd one was killed and disposed of for three quid we didn't talk about it. Shortly after we got married the wife and myself were out walking — we don't go for walks any more — and we saw something bubbling in the water. This was an otter pushing a salmon down river. He pushed it past us as far as Black Rock where he pushed it up on the shingle on the Cornish side. I threw a stone and he was gone. Then I told the wife to stay put while I ran like a train back to Fishery Cottage for my waders. I found the fish hadn't been dead very long — it was edible though a piece was nipped out from the back of the head. I've never ever, before or since, seen an otter pushing a salmon down the stream. You'd have a hell of a job to see an otter *at all* now, and you can't kill them because they're protected. They're wonderful animals but I've always regarded them as vermin.

You could shoot some foxes but no badgers. Late in the evening on the drive, I'd see as many as seven badgers in the hedgerow looking for their evening meal. One evening after His Grace had been out trout fishing, he asked me to put a couple of trout down into a badger track to see if they'd take them. Well, I thought this was a little bit mad because you wouldn't be able to tell *what* had taken them — a badger, a fox or a rat. Any rate, the next morning, the trout were gone. We done the same thing two or three times and, each time, the trout were gone. Then we staked the trout down on a piece of *string* and they were pulled away and the old Duke would inspect the string. Then he had the brainy idea of tying a salted kipper down and that *wasn't* pulled away, it wasn't even touched, not even by a cat, which didn't prove anything really. Seeing that he was so full of Nature, I suppose he was trying to discover something new but I couldn't understand the idea. It was part of the funny ways he had like trying to catch and examine every spider he saw, and nibbling like a donkey at a raw carrot wrapped in a piece of paper while he was fishing. He had green lizards on the stone-walling at the edge of the herbaceous border on the terrace and he would ask me, 'Have you seen any of the green lizards?' Well, *I* didn't run around looking for green lizards.

He imported into here from Woburn quite a few golden pheasants. He said to me once, 'Have you seen many of the golden pheasants?' I said, 'No. I'm not really interested in golden pheasants.' There was a fir tree — we have it still — up beyond the Yew Walk before you come to the Grotto or Shell House. It has two dead bare branches — the shorter one was much longer in they days but some of it have broken off — and the agent wanted to cut the whole tree down because it looked untidy. But His Grace wouldn't allow this because it was a resting place for the buzzards. As many as fourteen would be lined up on the two branches, and he could look out and see them from the dining-room window in the morning.

His Grace was up at dawn one year when he was staying at Cartha-martha, and he sighted through his binoculars a wonderful red deer, a stag. So he had about ten acres of scrub- and woodland by Inny Mere enclosed with a fence of good stout wire, eight, ten feet high. Hinds from Woburn were put inside and, outside, walk-ups were built with faggots of wood so that, when the hinds came on heat, the stag would jump in and couldn't get out. In fact, the first time he got in — in '49 — the hinds weren't on heat so he had to be released. Then in 1950 he goes in, he's in there, and all of a sudden he goes missing and there's a great hue and cry. Me and Keeper Hall and Under-keeper Broad had to search and search. Hall or Broad probably got the credit but I was the person who walked in on him, lying dead in the enclosure in the bracken. He'd been there several days — you could tell because he was well blown up. I think he died of a broken neck, trying to get out. He'd a record head of eleven points on the left antler and nine on the right. The head was cut off and handed to the Duke, but I believe it's now owned by people called Price in London. He's known as the Endsleigh Stag. I won't make an elaborate description — my tongue would slip away and I'd say something false, a little bit rash — but there's nothing more beautiful than a deer. August, about three year ago, I was down river between the lights with Sir Ernest Woodroofe, one of our directors, at Southcombe Wood Gate. I said, 'My God, look! There's a stag up there in Leigh Ham!' He must have heard me because he trotted away, and over the hedge. You wouldn't think that with a damn great head they could go over a hedge so graceful. There's never been very many stags here. That's why the Duke considered the Endsleigh Stag so important. The hinds in the enclosure were returned to Woburn.

There's a publican in Sparkwell, a Mr Dryden, who's going to write a book about deer. He knows that it was Horace Adams, the water bailiff, who was the lucky one to stumble across the body of the Endsleigh Stag. Five or six year ago, Nick Pitts, a pal of Mr Dryden's, was fishing here with a gentleman called Captain Locke when they saw a salmon floating down, more or less on its back. They assumed it had got off the hook of a riparian owner and they unsuccessfully tried to foul-hook it. Then, for a lark, Nick Pitts had his dog bring it out and they barbecued it that same evening after entering it in the register as a twelve pound salmon caught by Nick Pitts on a 36 inch Black Dog. I was quite upset. There were complaints. The entry had to be crossed out.

In the May of 1950, the year I found the Endsleigh Stag, I was fishing one evening with His Grace and in conversation, right out of the blue, he said to me, he said, 'You know, Adams,' he said, 'I'm seriously thinking of allowing people to stay at Endsleigh as paying guests when I'm not here. This isn't for the money,' he said, 'but because, really, this day and

99

age, to have fourteen miles just for me and my personal guests and so few others is a waste of water. What do *you* think of the idea?' I said right out, 'What *type* of person?' You see, I'd only ever had in the house one type of person — what I call the bettermost person, people such as Mr Cansdale, Sir Thomas Russell, a Colonel Craig-Scott, the secretaries, Lord Hugh, Miss Margery Russell and Mrs Burkin and their sister, *they* sort of people. His reply to that was, 'The sporty type. A person that will take an interest in the river, and respect the locality and other people's property and my tenant farmers. I want people that, if they go fishing, whether they walk or take their motorcar, won't strew the rides with litter or light picnic fires. I want people that will remember to secure the gates.' And before he left, he appointed Mr Porter, the man at present managing the house for short stays, to be permanent manager and appoint a few staff to look after about eight fishers and their wives or hangers-on.

Endsleigh was soon to be fairly humming because later he got in touch with Ranny (Randolph) Luke, another pet of his, the estate carpenter who lived at Coombe Lodge, and told him to build an aviary for some budgies which he'd bring down next year. They decided to build it on the tennis court which was just down under the bank below the *Acers* in front of the house here, though you can't picture it now because it's all brambled over. Ranny was helped by his son, Maurice. The job took three to four months. It was an exceptionally big aviary with a roosting enclosure and a place for the birds to fly around by day. The base was damn nigh the size of the tennis court which they cemented in. Any rate, in '51, His Grace passed it as OK and, when he left, thirty, forty birds duly arrived, and in '52 and '53 he put in a tremendous lot of time at the aviary instead of being down the river with me fishing. Ranny made him an oak rustic seat with rhododendron branches for the arms and legs and he'd be on that or in the aviary feeding or watching the birds or teaching them the homing instinct. I'd have to *look* for His Grace sometimes. A secretary would say, 'You'll find him at the aviary,' and I've gone down and he've chatted to me about the grey green and the cinnamon grey green and the slate cobalt and the Australian pied budgerigar, and about their food and about how they were breeding, though I didn't know one from the other. He said to me one day, fishing, he said, 'Are you interested in the budgerigars?' I said, 'Well, I think they look charming.' He said, 'They're good for the eye but bad for the pocket.' Eventually it got that birds would fly out as far as Edgcumbe Pond, and the old sparrowhawk got so many that Ranny had to make a trap and put it near the aviary. It was a square frame in two sections. In the bottom section there were one or two bright canaries, and the sparrowhawk would fly in to try to get at them, and he'd touch a little tiller and the roof of the top section would close over him. One fortnight there was thirteen sparrowhawks caught in that cage. Sometimes a canary would die of fright.

The gardener that lived at Dairy Dell Cottage, not far from the aviary, was Charlie Alford so he was to be in charge of the budgies when His Grace wasn't around. In '51 he was sent to Woburn at the Duke's expense to get an insight from watching the birds up there. I was detailed to keep an eye on the aviary. Unfortunately, while at Woburn, Charlie was taken very seriously ill and it was two or three months before Claude Masters was appointed in his place. During that time five albinos that hadn't the homing instinct found their way out. I'd to get in touch with His Grace through the agent. Poor old Adams! The damage had to happen when he was in charge, feeding and watching the birds, cleaning the nesting boxes, scrubbing this and scrubbing that, removing the funnel in the escape hole in the morning, replacing it a few hours before sunset. A hundred and twenty birds, and a hell of a lot of droppings, a hell of a lot of mess, all to be dealt with in addition to my other duties.

Eventually there were about three hundred and fifty budgies here, so many that an extra aviary had to be built. A room, even, at the back of the house was made into a Budgerigar Hospital which contained an electrically heated cage for birds suffering from a chill. Birds which didn't look very well were caught with a little net and brought to this room. You'd watch that the damned things not in the heated cage didn't fly out. His Grace gave me a grey lopsided one with a damaged wing. This meant I'd to dip my hand in my pocket and buy a budgerigar cage. We kept this here budgerigar at Fishery Cottage for four or five years. As I say, it was a bit lopsided but it was company for the wife.

In 1951, His Grace stayed from the 14th of May until the 23rd of June and, during that stay, he and his party caught more fish than they'd ever

101

caught at Endsleigh before — forty-two fish on my stretch and twenty-three on Herbie Symons' at Gunnislake. And most of those fish were given away — to the tenant farmers, to the minister, to Miss Gale, the postwoman, to men he saw trimming the bank... He only kept two. You see what a hell of a kind gentleman we'd got in the 12th Duke of Bedford?! He wasn't even interested in making money out of the paying guests. Mind you, he *was* a millionaire.

The house opened for paying guests (who had to fade away, of course, before the Duke's arrival in May) on the second Sunday in April with four rods allowed on each of the two sections of water. First to come were Mr Brian Reeves, an eye, throat and nose specialist from Salisbury, Mr Geoffrey Taylor, a tummy surgeon from Gloucestershire, a Dr Bourne from London, and Mr Walter Blundell who had a furniture business in Luton, Bedfordshire. Mr Walter arrived with his brother, Herbert, in a chauffeur-driven Rolls. Here are the Blundells arriving in state in a Rolls while the Duke uses an old London taxi! I'd offered to take in a chauffeur or two at Fishery Cottage so, after introducing the Blundells to the manager, Mr Porter, I proceeded with the chauffeur, a shy man in his sixties called Tokely, who parked the car by my front steps. We sat down at the dining-room table for afternoon tea. The wife was as shy as Tokely because she'd never had anyone staying with us, not outside the family. She said, 'What sort of car have you?' He said, 'A Rolls. It's parked at the bottom of the steps.' She looked out the window and said, '*I* can't see a car.' He said, 'I parked it at the bottom of the steps.' She said, 'Well, it's not there now!' *He* looked out the window then. He said, 'My God! So it isn't!' It had rolled back about two hundred yards into a clump of laurels. Luckily the laurels had been trimmed over a number of years so they were pretty stable — any rate there was two trees behind them. But if the car had missed the laurels or the trees, he'd have tumbled two hundred and fifty to three hundred feet straight down over the cliff. So that was poor old Tokely's introduction to Endsleigh. He never enjoyed his tea after that. He was a bundle of nerves and he kept coughing.

After tea, the wife and myself walked around part of the estate with him. There wasn't leaves on the trees yet, but the rhododendrons were just breaking and he was intrigued by Swiss Cottage where we introduced him to Mr and Mrs Percy. We wandered down over the hundred and eighty-nine steps and along the path leading to the river, quite a long trail. Then I showed him the hatchery which was temporarily out of action — later, in '53, it was loaned to the River Board who purchased it in 1959. Back at Fishery Cottage Tokely had a bath and then a real Devonshire cooked meal. We weren't paid very much to put him up, so what we got only paid for his grub.

I remember Mr Walter Blundell was the first of the paying guests to catch a salmon — fifteen and a half pound, so that was a good start. And the medical men caught quite a sizeable fish, too. They said, 'Come on now, Adams! Let's celebrate with a wee dram!' So I'm breaking out for the first time. Till then no drink was partaken on the river. Inwardly I didn't want these odd people here, but I've got them and they're offering me a drink, so I partake. And I don't know whether the hard stuff was getting the upper hand, but they started acting the goat. Dr Bourne had gaffed this fish and, as they'd no bass, he hung it on a door handle of the others' car and, with me in the front, raced them up through the fields in his to the house. Although the fish was secure and undamaged, you've never seen such a mess as the blood made. I thought, 'Well, if this is the kind of thing I'm in for, it's going to be chaotic. Good fun, but chaotic.'

In October, we broke our London holiday to stay with Tokely at Flitwick near Luton. He drove us for meals to Mr Walter Blundell's home in Luton and to Mr Herbert's home in Market Harborough. We were made very welcome but, from the next year on, we phased off a bit, we wouldn't let anyone know when we were going to London as our holidays were becoming rather too organized; we also thought we might be imposing on people which was the *last* thing we wanted to do. One day, Tokely drove us into Luton, and we took the bus over to Woburn to see His Grace and James Foley. Next day was Election Day. The wife was wearing a red mac and the conductor said to her, 'If I were you, madam, I'd dispose of that mac. It's the wrong colour for these parts.' We had coffee in the Abbey with His Grace and Miss Dix, and then he took me around the park while Miss Dix escorted the wife. He showed me scores of different kinds of birds in the aviaries, and bison and different types of deer in the park — even in they days the place was like a zoo. He said to me in conversation, 'I understand there's been a grey squirrel shot at Endsleigh. I didn't think there was *any* grey squirrels down in Devon.' I said, 'Well, there has been because it was me that shot one.' He said, 'What did you do with it?' Foolishly, without thinking, I said, 'I threw it in the river.' He said, 'That wasn't a very clever thing to do!' I said, 'No, it wasn't. But it was a grey squirrel definitely.' He said, 'Do you see any brown squirrels now?' I said, 'There are still a few about but as the grey squirrel is increasing so the brown squirrel is disappearing. They're starving them out.' Now it's only grey, what we used to call tree rats. The funny part of it was his father introduced them into Devon years previous.

One evening in '52, His Grace and myself walked down to Black Rock after he'd had dinner. We caught a fish almost immediately. His Grace was in what I call 'good form' because everything was ticking over so well at Endsleigh — the fishing, the guest-house and, above all, the budgies. He asked if I enjoyed my work, if the wife liked it at Fishery Cottage, even though we'd no electricity ... things like that, which he'd never asked me before. I was met by Miss Dix, now the Senior Secretary, when I arrived next morning. She said, 'Oh, Mr Adams,' she said, 'His Grace would like you immediately in his study.' I went in. He said, 'When we were enjoying ourself last night, there was someone up at Edgcumbe Pond poaching.' Poaching! And the Duke in residence!! He told me that one of the Miss Russells had been out walking and as she approached Edgcumbe Pond — she didn't show herself — she saw a man there fishing, and the description she gave of the back of this man and the texture of his jacket was of me! He laughed. He said, 'It's a good thing you were with *me* last evening!' I said, 'I can't understand it. Do you know, I'm sure in the whole locality there's only one person that's got a jacket like me and that happens to be Tom Bray.' I was quite upset now. I said, 'I can't think it's him! He would never do this!' Tom Bray was my best pal in they days. He was the man who cleared all the rubbish at Harragrove Gardens with the horse and cart. We would often dress alike if we went out for the evening, if we were going on the beer. His Grace said, 'I want you to try to find out who this poacher is.'

That evening in the village I went and seen my mate at the Edgcumbe Arms. I said, 'By the way, you never went down Edgcumbe Pond last night, did you?' He said, 'What would I be doing at Edgcumbe Pond?' I said, 'Well, it's been reported that there was someone trout poaching, and the bad part of it is it was my description back view and

104

my jacket, and who else have got a jacket like me?!' He said, 'I wouldn't go down there poaching, and you know better!' I said, 'Yes, but I've got to analyse everything.' It was the jacket that was worrying me. It was quite a show-off jacket, speckly tweed with a lot of green, red and white.

Next morning I said to His Grace, 'I've challenged my pal because I had to make sure. It wasn't him.' He said, 'All right. This will be a job for you when I've gone back to Woburn. Report what you find out to me personally.' And he went back, leaving behind his Woburn mouthpiece, a Mrs Osborne Samuel, who'd been staying with him at Endsleigh. In fact, she came down about twice a year to keep an eye on things. She was an old battleaxe, a domineering sort of woman with a bit of a limp. I didn't like her — nobody did — although me and Ranny Luke got on best with her because we knew our jobs and weren't afraid of her and were too well in with His Grace. She'd a habit of watching people to see if they were leaving work at ten to five. On one occasion she invited me into the office for a cup of tea. This was a sprat to catch a mackerel. She was at the window making remarks about the time the gardeners, painters, carpenters went past. I said, 'They've got travelling time. Probably they're running *late*! Nothing to do with me, madam. *I* can't do nothing about it. I'm not being involved in this. I'm enjoying my cup of tea and biscuit, and then I must be on my way.' Then she said, 'About this poacher. What are you going to do about it?' I said, 'Track him down and report to His Grace personally when I've done so. It's as simple as that.' She'd a friend in the house who was very, very intimate with the manager. When she disappeared back to Woburn without him, I thought, 'I'll watch his movements.'

One evening — end of July/August — I came down here from Fishery Cottage on my push-bike and I got down to Dairy Dell Pond where I met a gardener. He said, 'What's on?' I said, 'I'm looking to see if there's anybody fishing without permission.' He said, 'Two have been here. I think they've gone up the valley to Edgcumbe Pond.' I twigged who they were. I said, 'Thank you very much. I won't hang about,' and I left my bike, picked up a stick and walked very cautiously up the incline to Edgcumbe Pond. I looked out the gateway down to the pond, and there they were — Mrs Osborne Samuel's friend, who wasn't fishing, and the manager of the house, who was — and with my identical jacket on him! I pounced. I said, 'Good-evening, gentlemen!' They jumped around. I said, 'You're not allowed to fish here!' The manager said, 'Who are *you* to tell me I'm not allowed to fish here?!' I said, 'Now look. You've got no right whatsoever to fish the ponds unless His Grace have given you permission. May I be allowed to tell you that you were actually seen fishing this pond when the Duke was in residence!' Of course, he coloured up. 'Because', I said, 'His Grace approached me on it. I was fishing with him one evening down at Black Rock and the next morning he approached me about a poacher at this pond. I've said nothing till now, just kept my eyes open, but I was informed by His Grace that I was to try to get the poacher. Now I'll have to report you.' 'Oh,' he said, 'you wouldn't do *that*!' He said, 'I'll see Mr Finnie.' A Mr Finnie was now the agent. I said, 'It's nothing to do with Mr Finnie. I've been told to report to His Grace personally and I must say to him that I saw you fishing in an identical jacket to mine. Then it's up to *you* to sort it out.'

The next afternoon I was down the river with some guests when Mr Finnie approached me. He called me to one side. He said, 'Now, Adams,' he said. 'About the manager fishing Edgcumbe Pond.' He said, 'We'll forget all about it.' I said, 'I *can't* forget all about it! How can *I* forget about it?!' I said. 'Between you, me and the gatepost, he was seen fishing Edgcumbe Pond on —,' I stated the date when I was fishing with His Grace at Black Rock. 'And His Grace laughed the next morning when he was telling me the story because I had the identical *jacket*! Now was it *me* fishing the pond or was it the manager fishing the pond?! Well, it was the manager, and His Grace told me that *I* was to inform him.' He said, 'You leave it to me.' I said, 'But I *can't* leave it to you! I've *got* to tell him! I wasn't told to come to tell you. I've got to write and tell him. I must for my own sake. Otherwise the man has me — *and* you — in the palm of his hand. It's as simple as that.'

I wrote to His Grace, and the manager had instant dismissal. There wasn't no backchat. Mr Finnie didn't come into the picture, Mr Finnie wasn't informed. There was a letter came through the post to say that the manager's services would be no longer required. And up the road he went. Now, that's pretty sad because I feel responsible. But I was only doing my duty in a proper way. Say he'd made an apology and I hadn't reported it. The Duke would have thought to himself, 'Well, what's the use of keeping Adams down there?! He's supposed to be looking after my fishing rights, and the manager and probably *his* friends, and probably

Adams and *his* friends, is running around fishing!' So out he went, and his wife with him. I was a loner then, and Mr Bradbury, the present manager, will tell you I'm a loner now. I'm friendly in a way, but I'm not so friendly as that. I talk to everybody and I would do them a good turn but I was taught as a boy 'Never trust your left hand with your right hand. You never know who's who.'

So a Mrs Henderson was appointed manageress in time for the '53 season. She struck me as a bettermost person. She was well bred, well educated and she knew her job, knew how to cater for the guests and for His Grace, a bit of a loner like myself, who arrived in May with his secretaries, his chauffeur and his valet, James Foley. James was an Irish boy, a hell of a nice fellow, quite a little toff, well turned out. He'd often come up and have a meal with us at Fishery Cottage, or a cup of tea with the wife if I was out. He was a great Roman Catholic. There's a big ceremony on the Castle Green at Launceston every June for about two thousand pilgrims — something to do with the skull of a martyr called Cuthbert Mayne. Probably it's someone else's skill, but it doesn't matter. James was very interested, so we went over there with him one Sunday on the bus from Milton Abbot. Of course, he understood all the jabber and when to kneel and stand. The wife and myself was a little bit embarrassed.

One year, when Mrs Burkin was in the Duke's party, she asked me to shoot some rabbits for her two dogs. So, late in the evening, I took the Cogswell and Harrison and went just up river from the bathing pool where there was always hundreds of rabbits. James and the wife came with me. The wife was in the cutting between the bathing pool and the river and James and myself had gone a little further on when James said, 'Come on! Let me have a shot!' I gave him the gun and a rabbit runned across us and downstream. James, who couldn't have hit a haystack let alone a rabbit, swung the gun around and, Bang, he nearly shot the wife. That was the beginning *and* the end of shooting for James. It frightened the hell out of him.

James was usually an inoffensive person, wouldn't say boo to a goose. But, one night, cor, he was bloody mad with me. Miss Dix and a glamour little secretary called Miss Synott persuaded His Grace to let me go with them because they wanted to hear the nightjars at Carthamartha. We took the staff car, the Austin saloon. Miss Dix drove. She was very much the spinster still. I always remember being with her when Mrs Burkin was fishing Parson's Pool. Mrs Burkin, an old lady, played a fish for about twenty minutes and it got off. Miss Dix could have cried for her. She said, 'What a shame!' and Mrs Burkin said, 'Better to have loved and lost than never to have loved at all!' Well, I felt sorry for Miss Dix because I didn't think she'd ever been loved... As I say, Miss Dix was driving and she drove Miss Synott and myself to Inny Ford and I crossed them over in the boat to the Cornwall side. They wanted me to walk up with them through the woods to Carthamartha House. I said, 'No. I'll have a sleep in the boat.' About an hour later, at about midnight, the girls returned. I said, 'Have you heard anything?' No. I said, 'Well *that* was labour in vain!' Suddenly Miss Dix said in her high-pitched voice, 'Listen! There's one! We've been all the way up to Carthamartha and there's a nightjar over there on the Devon side!' So I rowed them quietly back and we sat in the car listening to the nightjar while, with the moon glistening through the trees, I told them creepy tales. There I was at one o'clock at night in the middle of the woods with two girls, and a wife at home longing for me to return and not knowing where I was!

Do you know, we didn't get back to Endsleigh House till two o'clock in the morning?! His Grace had expected us back at about half past eleven and had gone to bed, instructing James Foley to wait up for us. James immediately went for *me*. He said, 'Where on earth have *you* been?! His Grace has been fussing!' I said, 'Hey! Hang on, mate! Don't talk to *me* like this!' I said, 'You want to get on to Miss Dix — she was driving, *she's* the culprit! His Grace gave her and Miss Synott permission to go out to hear the nightjars and he asked me to go *with* them! *I* didn't want to hear the bloody nightjars! I've been out from ten o'clock till two, and now I've got to push-bike the two miles home!' Of course, next morning we buried the hatchet — in they days you'd got to — and, when I met His Grace at nine o'clock, he said to me, '*You* had a very late night, Adams! It was quite foolish of Miss Dix and Miss Synott keeping you out.'

Any rate, in May '53, mid-afternoon, there was a knock on the front door of Fishery Cottage. The wife assumed it was James Foley. She said, 'Come around to the back door! I'm cleaning the hall.' Knock again.

She said, 'Come *around* — to the back door!' Knock again. She shouted, 'If you can't come around, you must stay *out* there!' Knock again. She was fed up, she opened the door. And there was His Grace! She's a little tiny tot and he was six foot one, two, and probably he'd heard her. She felt such a fool she could have went in a mousehole. He touched his hat to her and said, 'Good-afternoon, Mrs Adams. I hope I'm not intruding but I'd like to see the inside of your house.' So she showed him round, downstairs and upstairs, and — I've told you she was very, very house-proud — the lino was highly polished and everywhere he went he left his imprint, the marks of his studded shoes. Before he left, he said, 'Thank you very much, Mrs Adams. I think it would be nice if you had electricity.'

We were over the moon. We lived in the best worker's cottage on the estate rent free and we were going to have electricity. My take-home pay was still £2 a week. This seems very little but in 1953 — I'll read to you from the wife's Housekeeping Account — half a pound of butter was a bob, half a pound of margarine was eightpence. A pound and a half of sugar was tenpence halfpenny. Cheese, half a pound, was one and tuppence. Six pounds of self-raising flour was three and a penny. A large packet of Persil was a bob. Half a pound of tea was two and tuppence, a two pound jar of plum jam two and eightpence. A pound of lemon curd, one and eight. One ounce of tobacco, one shilling and fourpence halfpenny. A packet of Shredded Wheat, a shilling. Two tins of sweet milk, three bob. One tin of stewed steak, three bob. One toilet roll, sixpence. A bar of salt, one shilling. Custard powder, one and seven-pence halfpenny. Elevenpence for a loaf of bread... That all comes to about two pound for the week, same as my wages, most of which I've always handed to the wife. Why would *I* want money? When we pull up to a petrol station now, I say, 'What shall we have? Ten quid's worth?' and out comes the ten quid from her purse. She buys me my clothes, the old-fashioned way. At the bank, we've a joint account and she's her own account. She cashes my wages from the Syndicate for necessities, then banks what's left over, with my pension, in either account. To me it doesn't matter which. Health before wealth... It says here a dozen Oxos in '53 was a bob. Mind you, I don't know what a dozen Oxos is now. Do

109

you? Two razor-blades, sevenpence. A round box of Cheddar cheese, one and fourpence. Quarter of ham, two bob…

You see? We could get by, and I was working for a thoughtful and unselfish man, a perfect gentleman, make no mistake about it. I'll give you another example of how unselfish he was — I've already told you how he gave most of the fish he caught away. One morning — this was back in '51 — I set off fishing with Lord Hugh and Miss Rooke, a young ladyfriend he'd got with him, to fish Leigh Wood Croys. Lord Hugh was the second son, the present Duke's brother. Again, a wonderful gentleman. It's a pity he never became the Duke. He would probably have got rid of Woburn and kept *this* place because he'd fished from the cradle. Unlike his father who didn't smoke and was a teetotaller, Lord Hugh liked a pipe of tobacco and a drink. He married a Cornish girl who met later with a very severe accident riding a horse — she's been paralysed for years… Any rate, I went down with him and Miss Rooke in the staff car to Leigh Wood Croys and he got a fish. Then we went on to Underhill and Miss Rooke got a fish and Lord Hugh got another fish. Then he said, 'Let's see if we can catch a fish upstream,' and we got one in Bush and another in Inny Croy. We got back here about eight-twenty, eight-thirty because one of the staff had to go and fetch other staff from the village in the car to get them here for nine o'clock. So we'd been doing a little bit of running around, but in they days the gates were all posted open so you could drive right through.

I was putting the rods away in the colonnade when His Grace spotted me from the terrace. He shouted, 'Oh, Adams! Just a moment!' Then, as he came towards me, he said, 'Has Lord Hugh had any luck?' I said, 'Yes, Your Grace. We've killed five and lost two.' He put his hand to his ear and I knew there was something wrong, he wanted a recording. I said, 'Lord Hugh have had four. Miss Rooke have had one.' He said, 'Disgraceful!' and Lord Hugh wasn't allowed to fish again that day and he sent me straight home. Now there was the type of person he was. He'd got all this fishing, but he wasn't greedy, he thought it was disgraceful catching four fish before breakfast. And what a sportsman! I once failed to net a fish for him at Bush Pool, partly through his own fault. I was standing at the top of the steps, lost for words, which was unusual, and he tapped me on the shoulder and said, 'Bad luck, Adams, but', he said, 'the fish lives to fight another day.' *Then* he turns round to me and he

110

says — we'd already got a ten and a twelve pound fish — I think, after all that, you'd better take the smaller of the two fish home to Mrs Adams.' I said, 'Well, thank you very much, Your Grace, but', I said, 'Mrs Adams is away at her parents' and I wouldn't know what to do with it,' — in they days there was no deep freezers. He said, 'Oh, that doesn't matter! Take it!' I said, 'I'd rather not. I'd rather for you to give it to a farmer.' I was telling His Grace what to do, which was quite rude. Later that day, Lord Hugh said to me, 'It'll serve you right. Because you've refused, he'll never offer you another fish again!' And he never. Around that period when he caught forty-odd fish and never kept more than two for himself, he'd say to me, 'Now who could we give this fish to?' I had it in the back of my mind to say, 'Well, *I* don't mind having a fish *now*,' but I mustn't stoop that low, you see. Any rate, he knew that I could always help myself if I wanted to. When you *can* help yourself, though, you never do. It's when you're not allowed into the orchard that you whip in and whip an apple, isn't it? But he was very good in other ways. You'd have a portion of venison sent down from Woburn, or a brace of pheasants — not that I'm very fond of pheasant…

So His Grace offered me electricity, not fish! And, in June 1953, before he decided to leave, he said to me, 'What's the fishing like in the autumn? I think, this year, I may come down again.' You see, he'd never been down to Endsleigh fishing in the autumn before. (The season varies. Now it closes on September 30th: in '53 it was October 14th.) I said, 'Some of the fish are a little bit coloured if you haven't the right type of water and they've been in the pools a long time, but you can still pick up a fresh one.' He said, 'We'll be in touch.' I think he wanted to see for himself what the autumn fishing was now that he'd paying guests. He was also hoping to spot a stag in Dunterue Wood which was said to have even more points than the Endsleigh Stag. But, of course, his *prime* object was the budgerigars. The budgerigars now were really built up, they were flying everywhere. I must admit it was a wonderful sight out on the terrace or down in Endsleigh Ham. First thing in the morning, the sun shining on them, there they were swooping in batches and flying up and down, all colours of the rainbow. Very, very attractive. They added to the natural beauty of the place. I say 'natural' because His Grace didn't have everybody trimming everywhere like it had been under his father. We had brambles where there never used to be brambles. He was

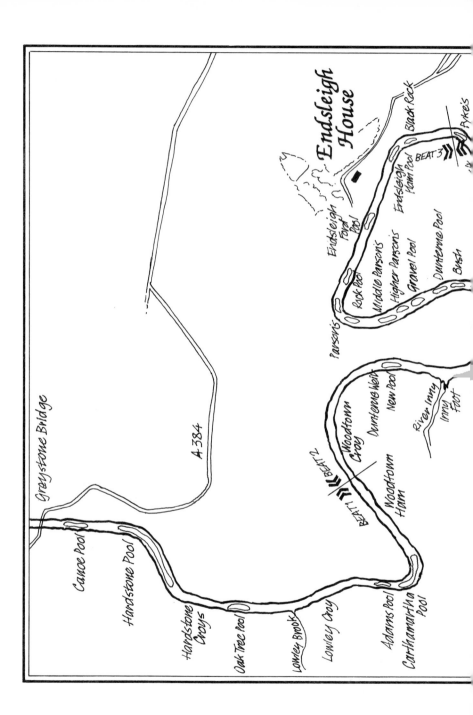

Greystone Bridge

Canoe Pool

Hardstone Pool

Hardstone Croys

Oak Tree Pool

Lowley Brook

Lowley Croy

Adams Pool

Carthamartha Pool

A-384

BEAT 1

BEAT 2

Woodtown Ham

Woodtown Croy

Dunterne Weir

New Pool

River Inny

Inny Foot

Parsons

Rock Pool

Middle Parsons

Higher Parsons

Gravel Pool

Dunterne Pool

Brash

Endsleigh Foot Pool

Endsleigh House

Endsleigh Ham Pool

Black Rock

BEAT 3

Pykes

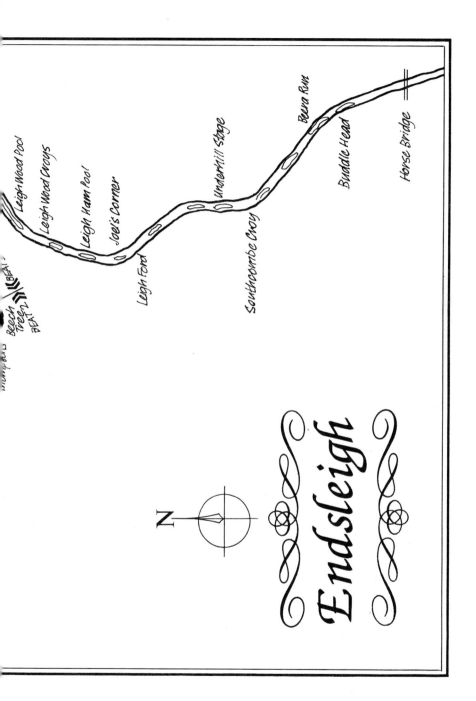

Endsleigh

N

Leigh Wood Pool
Leigh Wood Groys
Leigh Ham Pool
Joe's Corner
Leigh Ford
Underhill Stage
Southcombe Groy
Beeva Run
Buddle Head
Horse Bridge

BEECH TREE
BEAT 2
BEAT 3

a great naturalist so he liked to see a little bit of nature in the rough state, little bits overgrown, nature coming back. But the place was still very beautiful. There were flowers everywhere. At Fishery Bend leading up to my cottage from the drive, there was a large bed of eight or nine different coloured azaleas, and at night in the spring and early summer the perfume was so overpowering you had to keep your bedroom window shut. I remember once Mrs Burkin passing a remark as we motored up through the flowers of Leigh Wood. She said, 'Well, Adams, if heaven is like this, I'm ready to go now.' And that's the describing of Endsleigh as it was in they days in a nutshell.

During the season I was up at half past six. After making tea and having a cup myself, I'd take one up to the wife and my father — I still take the wife her cup of tea — then push-bike down the rides through the woods to Leigh Wood croys, three-quarters of a mile away, where I'd read the gauge-board (the Syndicate had it moved to Endsleigh Ham) and write the height of the river in my notebook. Then I'd walk along the bank to Endsleigh Ham, up Ham Hill and home. I loved that morning walk, out with nature, alone, watching the movements of the fish, seeing where they lay, for the benefit of His Grace or the guests. I might, as I've told you, do some fishing myself, or I might shoot a rabbit for the pot, or a cormorant. The sun might be casting its first shadows across the river, or glinting and playing on parts of the water. A flight of mallard might fly upstream. You might see a shepherd checking his sheep, a farmer bringing out his milking cows. You'd hear the thrush and the blackbird. In the spring of the year you'd hear the cuckoo; you'd stop and listen, keeping yourself under cover, and all of a sudden he'd break from the bushes, going ooh ooh, ooh ooh, ooh ooh. This was April and, in April, the early rhododendrons are just bursting into flower. From the fairyland days of winter everything's coming alive again…

For breakfast I didn't eat a lot — I've never been very much for porridge or toast. I'd have, say, a fried egg, some fried spuds and a bit of bacon — our own cured bacon — and saffron cake and tea. After breakfast, I'd glance at the *Daily Mail* or the *Western Morning News* — first the 'hatched, matched and dispatched', then the sport and then the scandal. If His Grace wasn't in residence I might then push-bike to a pond to see if the gratings was clear — the trout were no longer being fed. Fishing with someone until lunch-time. Home for lunch (we called it 'dinner') — say, beef or pork or lamb and boiled potatoes and cabbage followed by apple dumpling or rice or suet pudding. Then perhaps I'd trim some steps or visit other ponds before fishing from five till seven. We'd supper at half past seven — say, a cold salad, then tinned pears or peaches with lashings of cream. Then I might potter in the garden, feed the pig if my father forgot, check for eggs, shut up the poultry. Father went to bed at nine. I'd be reading the *Fishing Gazette* while the wife was sewing or knitting and listening to the radio. I'd go to bed first about half past ten, eleven, after a cup of tea and a piece of bread and butter. Just when you'd blown out the candle and was dozing off, you'd hear an owl outside — woo-wooo. In the middle of the night my father might come into the bedroom. He'd say, 'There's somebody down in the woods screaming!' But what he heard was the screaming of the foxes. Or he'd say he'd seen a light. Well, of course he'd seen a light! — a car light or a light flickering from a farmhouse or a cottage as far away as the Cornish hills. He came running in, time after time.

Though our daughter hadn't been born yet and my father was probably a bit of a bore and a lot to cope with for a young wife, there was more laughter at home than there is now. I wanted to tell, and Nes wanted to hear, the interesting or amusing things that happened during the day — His Grace teaching me how to hand-tail; how Miss Dix was lost up a tree for an hour, struggling to release her tail fly and droppers caught in the branches! ... Then there was the story of how I was down at Leigh Wood with His Grace, Miss Dix and Miss Synott or it may have been Miss Gordon. We had a Farlow rod, twelve foot six, a very light, whippy rod, an old rod — a lot of the Duke's tackle was very old. A fish head and tailed two or three times but they just couldn't catch it, so His Grace said to me, '*You* have a go!' So I had a go and the fish took me. His Grace said, 'See how quick you can land him!' Now this will take a bit of believing, but it's perfectly true. There was a boat tied up at the bottom of some wooden steps. I ran upstream, jumped into the boat, still playing this fish, went out in the boat, and one of the girls threw the net to me and, within four minutes, I netted the fish which was fresh as a rose, covered with sea lice, and sixteen pounds. His Grace said to me afterwards, 'You didn't spare the rod!' I said, 'You told me not to, and see what happened!' It was one of the differences between us. I was always saying to people, 'You don't play it hard enough!' He didn't like landing fish quickly. He liked to have a little bit of fun with them, keep them on for a time.

115

Six

His Grace arrived on Monday, October the 5th, 1953, with James Foley, his valet, Scott, his chauffeur, Miss Dix and Miss Gordon, his secretaries, and some other lady who was tubby and a little deaf but whose name I can't remember. I went fishing with him in the afternoon to Bush Pool, Gravel and Dunterue, but we didn't catch a fish. On the Tuesday he didn't do anything fishingwise — perhaps he was concentrating more on the budgies. I know I was occupied getting in one or two boats before the winter floods. In they days I'd always umpteen men to help me. Wednesday the 7th I met him nine o'clock as usual, and he said he'd like to fish Woodtown Croys. Scott motored us up in the house car, the Austin. There was quite a drop of water in the river. I rowed him out and he caught quite a decent little fish — seven, eight pound, very clean. He was thrilled.

There happened to be a tremendous lot of cormorants at that period so, on the Thursday morning, when His Grace asked me to take Miss Dix and Miss Gordon and the other lady fishing, I said, 'Can I take my gun with me?' He said, 'Yes. See if you can get a couple of cormorants.' We went to Bush Pool. Miss Dix was driving. I was sat in the back with Miss Gordon. The other lady was sat in the front. They were all a bit perturbed that I'd got a gun in the car. I spotted a heron and I said, 'Slow up! I'll have a shot out the window.' I was acting the goat, showing off. When the gun went off Miss Dix got a fright and the car jumped. Any rate, we caught nothing and I killed no birds before coming back to lunch. In the afternoon, Miss Dix said, 'His Grace is busy writing, but would you come with Miss Gordon and me to Leigh Wood Croys?' So I put them fishing down at Leigh Wood and I walked back with my gun and shot two cormorants which both fell in the water and drifted downstream. I rushed to Miss Dix and I said, 'I've shot two cormorants! Here they come! Quick! Give me your rod!' and I hooked one and reeled in. His Grace was in the entrance hall when we arrived back at the house. He said to Miss Dix, 'Any luck?' She said, 'No. But Adams has shot two cormorants.' 'Oh, good, good!' he said. 'Did you manage to bring them back?' 'I got *one*,' I said. He said, 'Would you please cut it open and find out what's inside?'

I cut the cormorant open in the stables yard, in what's the Rod Room now but was called the Ballroom for a while as a gimmick to attract guests. A floor was laid over the cobbles where there used to be five stalls. Probably it was Mrs Osborne Samuel's idea. She was always on about how she'd like a golf course. Well, the ball would have been in the river half the time. You can't have everything... Any rate, I took out what was in the stomach, put it on a piece of paper, took it over to the house. James said, 'His Grace wants you to come with it into the study.' So I took it in to him on this piece of paper and he probed it with a pencil and we identified four or five small salmon parr. He said, 'We must curtail these cormorants.' I said, 'I'm always trying to do that but they're coming and coming and coming.' One winter I shot forty-two. I was paid a bob a beak as perks. He said, 'Well, keep trying. Thank you very much, Adams. Good-night.' I said, 'Good-night.' It was about half past five, six o'clock, the last time I saw him alive.

The morning of Friday the 9th I arrived here as usual just before 9.00 a.m. I was about to go into the house to walk through to the colonnade when I was met by James who told me that His Grace had gone out for an early morning walk with his gun (not unusual) and hadn't come back for breakfast (most unusual as he was so punctual). At nine-thirty James came to me in the yard outside. He said, 'You haven't seen His Grace? I'm beginning to get worried. Something must have happened.' So we walked out on the terrace and you could see that somebody else had walked towards the Shell House because there were footmarks in the grass still wet with dew. As soon as you left the grass just by the Shell House you lost the track, but we decided to walk along the path there as far as Rixall Drive behind the hatchery. Then we stopped and returned to the house. The secretaries said His Grace still hadn't turned up. I said, 'I'm wondering if he wandered up to Edgcumbe Pond to shoot a cormorant.' James said, 'Good idea. Let's look.'

We didn't find His Grace at Edgcumbe Pond so then the hue and cry went out properly. Miss Dix informed Mr Finnie who came to

Endsleigh immediately and then informed Woburn and the police at Tavistock and mobilized foresters and anybody on hand to search the grounds. Fearing the worst, I walked parts of the river from Bush Pool to Underhill. We searched until dusk. Still no trace.

Saturday morning at daybreak the search was resumed. The place now was like hell let loose with the house turned into Search Headquarters for the police and Royal Marine frogmen from Bickleigh and troops from Plaster Down, and Mrs Henderson, the manageress, making sandwiches for everybody. There was even a plane flying overhead. Most of the estate workmen set out again to search hundreds of acres of undergrowth in the heavily wooded areas surrounding the house. I was detailed with five others to search the river from Greystone Bridge to Horsebridge by boat — three boats in all, two men in each boat; a very difficult and exhausting exercise because of the rapids. Before lunch, when we were still well above Inny Croy, I was brought back to the house in a police car and questioned why I'd shot two cormorants and about the last things the Duke had said to me. I was beginning to wonder if the police thought I was involved in his disappearance. I suggested he might have slipped into the river off the staging at Underhill Pool after shooting at a cormorant and trying to retrieve it. In they days Underhill was one of our deep pools, fifteen feet, if not more, in places. There's an old story that in years gone by it was the deepest pool on the whole of the River Tamar and that if you took a wagon rope and put a stone on the end it would go down twenty, twenty-five feet. Now it's shingled up and probably only nine feet or ten. Any rate, I was taken down there by a Police Inspector with Lord Hugh and Mrs Osborne Samuel and two marines. When he saw the staging the Inspector said to me, 'I don't understand how you think the Duke could have slipped off *that*!' One of the marines started to walk along it and, bang, he was on his back in a jiff — a trained man who could hold his balance! I said, 'There you are, sir, and don't forget the Duke is about sixty-four!' But the marines found nothing and I spent the rest of the day roaming the bank with different people, pinpointing pools.

On Sunday the 11th the search reached as far as Gunnislake on Herbie Symons' stretch. Then at about three forty-five, four o'clock, the message was sent out that the body had been found by two estate workmen — William Jordan and Ernie Masters. They found it about

118

seven yards down the bank under the path leading to the main Swiss Cottage steps. If James and myself had only went another three or four hundred yards beyond Rixall Drive on the Friday morning we might have found the body then. It was brought back to the house and rested downstairs in what is now No.12, the double bedroom with the french windows at the cottage end. I was so upset Mr Finnie asked me not to help to carry it in and sent me home. His Grace had gone down the bank through the rhododendron bushes and his gun came across him and shot him in the head. After a year or two I decided to stop carrying a gun myself. Lord Hugh told me that his father taught him as a boy always to slide down awkward places on his bottom — it was a family joke. Now, whether His Grace slid or crept down the bank I don't know, but he was probably after the sparrowhawk, the enemy of his budgies, in the ivy-covered trees growing there.

Pressmen were all over the place. They even took photos of where His Grace was found; the *Daily Express* got it wrong at first and showed Edgcumbe Pond. Some of the papers mentioned he'd been anti-war and thought there should be no poverty in the Land of Plenty. In the *Plymouth Times* the Duke of Westminster described him as 'the bravest man in England'. He was taken to a crematorium in Plymouth. I helped to carry him out and to put him in the hearse. The 13th Duke, the new Duke, arrived from his farm in South Africa too late for the inquest and the cremation. I went with Nesta to the Memorial Service at Milton Abbot. We wrote afterwards to Miss Dix saying friends and workers at Endsleigh would like a stone of remembrance set up where His Grace fell. She wrote back asking how much they would care to contribute and suggested inscribing a verse from his favourite hymn 'Dear Lord and Father of Mankind'. I talked to half a dozen people. They said they couldn't afford to contribute anything and asked why Miss Dix hadn't sent any money herself to set the ball rolling. But, a few years later, the Bedford Trustees had the carriage stepping-off stone outside the entrance moved as a marker to where His Grace went off the path, and a fir tree was planted where the body was found.

So there you are. That was the end of my Duke. I was down in the dumps I don't mind telling you. A lot of people were distressed, but I was distressed *terrible*. I tossed and turned in my bed. This isn't being big-headed but, of the work people at Endsleigh, I was the one that was most intimate with him, outside the carpenter, Luke, who soon had to dismantle the aviaries as the budgies was sold (the concrete bases were broken up and dumped where the river banks were eroding in Dunterue Wood). His Grace was very good to me, very human. As regards the locality, the Grandfather Duke dying was bad enough. To lose the next one so shortly after the war when things were starting to straighten out was a tragedy. He was our bread and butter. I was thinking, 'What's going to happen to Endsleigh? What's going to happen to *me?!*' He'd talked about installing electricity at Fishery Cottage but never mind about electricity, electricity's no good to you if you haven't got a job. You think everything will go for a burton under a new boss. But — it's easier for me to say it now I'm seventy-one and more mature — life must go on. And, under the Trustees who took over, it *did* go on. In fact 1954 produced more fish than ever before: the guests at Endsleigh caught two hundred and seventy-five.

The new Duke caught his first fish with me in July. There was a photo in the *Tavistock Times* of him and his family arriving at Plymouth from South Africa. With him was Her Grace, Lydia, the young Marquess, Robin, who was about fourteen, and Rudolph, the second son, both sons of His Grace's previous marriage, his first marriage. There was also Their Graces' little son Francis and Her Grace's two youngsters by her previous marriage, Gavin and Lorna Lyle. Underneath the photo it said, 'They're now at Endsleigh', and they stayed here for ten days or so before going on to Woburn. Staying with them was Her Grace's sister, Lady Cadogan. She was called Primrose which I thought was a beautiful name. And she was a beautiful person, a hell of a good-looker. There was one or two guests around, but His Grace didn't object to that: the house didn't have to be cleared like it was for his father. His Grace wasn't at all snobbish. I don't think he knew even the first thing about what being a Duke involved. He certainly didn't know anything about fishing. He didn't *come* here to fish. It was only through my persuasion that he decided to have a go.

July the 20th I was instructed to meet him in what was classed as the Quiet Room — the Writing Room they call it now, though it has the library in it. My first impression was what a nice gentleman and how relaxed he was. He was about five foot ten, with glasses, and he was dressed very casual in a pair of slacks and a blazer, and he was very, very easy to speak to. He immediately introduced me to the Duchess. She was charming. And pretty, too. Well, everybody knows that — all the Yarde-Buller girls were pretty. Being very shy, I felt a little bit out of place. We talked about things in general. He wanted to know if we were fishing the ponds. Rudolph, I think, wanted to fish Edgcumbe. I said to His Grace, 'Have *you* ever caught a fish?' He said, 'No. I was never *allowed* to fish in my younger days.' I said, 'Would you like to fish with *me*?' He said, 'I wouldn't mind.' So I said, 'Well, what about this evening?' and I took him into the passageway where the fishing tackle was and gave him a few details about the rods and the flies, showed him a Silver Doctor and a Jock Scott and what have you. He said, 'All right. We'll have a trip up the river this evening. See you five o'clock.' It was arranged that Symons would come up from Gunnislake to meet him then, too.

His Grace and I stopped at Gravel Pool and Symons went on with Lady Cadogan to Bush. I was a little bit perturbed about that. Symons is an exceptionally good fisherman and I understood that Lady Cadogan was quite good also. I didn't want either of them to catch a fish and us not, and His Grace had never caught a fish in his life. I put the rod together, his father's old fishing rod, the little Farlow, showed him how to put the reel on, thread the line up through the rings, tie on the gut, put on the fly, a Silver Doctor. Then I escorted him out more or less into the middle of the river and asked him to watch me make one or two casts. I said, 'It's easily done. Now, come on. All you do is take the rod and cast your fly out into the water like I did.' He made quite a hash of it so I just stood behind him, put my arm over his shoulder, caught hold of the rod and lifted it so the fly would come back and went, 'One, two, three, out!' so he could get the rhythm. Then I said, 'Come on. You try again,' you know, quite casual, and, believe you me, it was like providence, like a miracle: bang, a fish!

Then it was pandemonium because he immediately dropped his rod, pointed it at the fish. I said, 'Get your rod up! Let all the line go, don't hold the line at all! Change your rod over to your left hand! Get your right hand on to the handle of the reel! Stick the butt of the rod into your tummy and start reeling!' He did this, and then the fish started splashing. I said, 'Now let the reel go and, if the fish wants to swim away, let him!' We went on like this for five or six minutes, and I was praying hard that the fish didn't get off. Any rate, we were lucky. I'd already been to the bank and picked the net up, and the fish came around within reach and, bang, he was in the net. I said, 'Now come on into the bank because the fly is still in the fish's mouth in the net. The best thing is we'll walk up the steps and I'll take the fly out on the bank.' Which I did. Then I took my priest out of my pocket, gave the fish a couple of cracks across the head. Then I said to His Grace, 'Well done, sir!' and shook hands with him. He said, 'Wonderful! That's my first fish and it's enormous!' I said, 'Well, it's not enormous!' and I weighed it and it was seven pound. Then I took him straight back into the river and I showed him one or two tricks of the trade like, when you cast, how you should wait a little bit longer at the top when the line is upright so it can straighten itself up at the back, and how you should then come forward so the line flies out in front of you and the fly lands gently onto the water. But, being a newcomer, he was splashing about, couldn't keep his balance. After about ten, twelve minutes he said, 'Well, Mr Adams,' he said, 'I've had a wonderful hour with you so', he said, 'let's call it a day. Lady Cadogan will be here in a minute or two because we're going back to dinner, and time we've had a bath...' And, all out of the blue, Her Ladyship and Symons arrived. I was longing to find out if they'd caught a fish. They hadn't and, inwardly, I was pleased that the Duke had pipped them.

Back at the house Symons and myself were invited in for drinks in the small lounge. There was no bar here in they days — there wasn't one installed till the late Fifties — so you either had to bring your own drink with you or the management got it in specially. I remember His Grace saying to me, 'You'd betterway have a whisky. I'll give you a double.' I was sat on the arm of a chair. It was all very, very casual. And, right at this point, he asked me, 'Would you like to take Robin and Gavin out fishing tomorrow? The difficulty is', he said, 'I shall need Scott and the car from eleven o'clock onwards.' I said, 'Right. As soon as the boys have had breakfast, if Scott can take us up river and drop us, we can manage from there.'

So next morning Scott ran us up to Dunterue Stage. He'd got three parts of an hour before he had to meet His Grace so I asked him to hang around. Then I got the boys to toss a coin as to who was going to fish first because I didn't want no preferential treatment. Gavin Lyle won and I took him onto the staging and showed him what to do, went through the same process as I did with His Grace. He soon got the rhythm. Youngsters pick it up immediately. Almost within seconds he was into a fish! And, being a youngster, he wanted to drag it right in. I had to explain to him, 'Now, come on! Change hands, get the butt of the rod into your tummy and keep the rod upright so much as you can, let the fish bend the rod!' The fish ran downstream. I said, 'Now reel in a bit. Keep reeling. Keep reeling. Keep reeling. The fish is coming. Keep reeling.' And then the fish stopped and started to splash. I said, 'Right. Let him go. If he wants to go, let him run. Let him run.' The fish stopped again. I said, 'Now reel! Reel so fast as you can!' I'm excited and Gavin's excited, and I'm watching at the same time that he doesn't fall in. I shouted to the Marquess who was with Scott, 'Bring the net down!' After about ten minutes the fish was coming near the staging. I said, 'Keep your rod up! Keep reeling! Keep a tight line! Don't let the line go slack!' and he brought the fish around and, bang, he was in the net. I said, 'Well done, my boy!' and we upped the steps and I released the fly and gave the fish a crack across the head. I said, 'We'll weigh him right away!' And he was eleven pound. Wonderful! I put him in a bass, threw him in the boot and I said to Scott, 'Now you'll be able to take him back and dump him on the slab.' I said, 'Run us down to Inny Croy on your way.' He turned round the car. I said, 'Come on, boys! Jump in!' and I jumped in, too, and held one hand out the window with the rod, and on we go.

At Inny Croy I said to Scott, 'How long have you got?' He said, 'Oh, five and twenty minutes. We're still all right.' I put on a bigger fly as the water was a wee bit deeper here, and I showed Robin the procedure. Robin was taller than Gavin and a little bit more clumsy. We're stood on the bank now, fishing above the croy, the slack water above the croy, and it's harder because the flow of water doesn't stretch your line out so it can be all in a hell of a bunch if you're not casting very well. I was standing behind him and I'd caught hold the rod with my arm over his shoulder and, as we went to pick the fly off the water, I saw a fish swing around! I said, 'My God! A fish came to you!' I said, 'Try to cast out there!' and he made quite a good cast, seeing that he'd never cast before until today. I said, 'Let the fly swing around. Let the water take it around.

123

Strip in a little bit, pull your line back with your left hand.' Bang! A fish was on! Unbelievable! Unbelievable! Here's a family who had never fished! I said, 'Now, come on! Play him! You watched Gavin so you should know the technique. I'll scramble down the bank for when you bring him in.' He wasn't very long getting him there and I slapped him in the net. If I'd been with a professional fisherman I'd have been a little bit cautious and probably we'd have lost the fish. So that's No.2 fish, and ten and a half pound!

I said to Scott, 'You've got ten minutes longer?' then to Gavin, 'Well, come on! You do exactly the same as Robin have done.' Before, he'd been on the staging. On a sloping bank you've got to dig your heels in a wee bit, you're keeping your balance. He started fishing. I said, 'Cast a little bit farther!' He cast a little bit farther and, bang, there was another. It was as simple as that! He played it a bit hard. Probably he wasn't playing of it right but I wasn't bothered. I'm not teaching of him. Now all I'm after is the fish. So I netted this fish and we're up on the bank, the fish is killed, the fish is weighed and he's *another* ten and a half pound! Scott said, 'I must go.' I said, 'Take these fish too. His Grace will be over the moon. He'll think to himself, "What's all this fishing talk? Bloody easy!" ' And it *is* easy. If the fish will co-operate, any fool can catch a fish. You have all this literature that's written about fishing. Well, of course it's written! It's written to be sold!

I sat down with the boys and I showed them the colours of some flies and the different tyings, but they'd really had enough — you know, they were excited. Then they asked *me* to fish, they said, 'We'll watch *you*!' So I started to show off, you see, trying to fish properly, two or three hundred yards down at Beech Tree. But there was no fish going to come to *me*! They thought if they hang on to *my* fly they'm *bound* to be dead! Then Lady Cadogan appeared on the scene and, after we'd had packed lunches, I left her fishing Beech Tree and went back with the boys to Inny Croy where I'd the devil to make them fish, they just didn't want to fish any more. I said, 'You'd betterway watch me again,' and, while they were half watching me, I came up with the tip of the rod pretty smart. They said, 'What was that?!' I said, 'If you'd been watching carefully, you'd have seen what was that! That was a fish came around and touched me!' It wasn't true: I was just trying to keep them interested. I said, 'One of you'd betterway have a go,' so one of them had a go and mimicked me. I said, 'Now, come on! We've hardly known one another for five minutes and you're being cheeky!' Youngsters, you see. Then they threw stones in the water saying, 'There's a fish!' I said, 'You've to cut that out!' They got a little bit out of control. I've noticed with youngsters that, if they catch a fish fairly quickly, they can be spoiled — they either take to it and start asking you questions, finding out about the lies and whatnot, or they know all the answers. At about half past four, when I was getting worn out, we heard a car. This was Scott with His Grace. They'd brought a tea out for us — fresh, beautifully made beef sandwiches and strawberries and cream. So we tucked that back. Lady Cadogan joined us. She hadn't caught a fish, I hadn't caught a fish, but there were these two boys who'd caught three! I took a photo of them holding them with my old box camera, my Kodak Brownie No.2.

After tea, I said to His Grace, 'Would you like to wander up and have a look at the river?' He said, 'Yes, I'd be delighted,' so all of us except Lady Cadogan, we jumped in the car and wandered up the river. We were up to Lowley Croy, beyond Carthamartha, when I got His Grace fishing. And, by God, he was into a fish again! But this is what happens in fishing: it's all or nothing. And this fish was also ten and a half pound! Yet there was a gentleman called Saunderson staying at the house, an exceptionally good fisher, and he didn't catch a fish that day. Nor the next, July the 22nd, when, woe betide me, Lorna, Gavin's sister, got a nine pound fish at Inny Croy. When I netted it from the boat for her she grabbed me round the shoulder, said, 'Thank you very much!' and give me two or three good kisses.

So here we are. I've only known this Duke and his family for three or four days, I've only just got over the tragedy of his father, and I'm in another world which is even more relaxed than the one before. I say 'relaxed', but I was still nervous at the back of my mind about what was going to happen to the estate. Although I say this myself, and it's easy to praise yourself, I was and am really dedicated to Endsleigh, and I didn't know what the future held. Was the river going to be split into little portions? Was someone else going to take it over? Would I be wanted though no one knew it better than I did? The wife, at last, was expecting a baby. My take-home pay was only about £3 per week and we'd need every penny... I was inwardly worried, there's no mistake. As it happened, my position remained secure under the Bedford Trustees till

1962. His Grace had a lot of sorting out to do at Woburn and, let's face it, he didn't take up fishing, so I lost touch with him for a long, long time, but the guest-house filled up more and more with fishermen each season and, by 1962 when the Syndicate took over, my take-home pay per week as ghillie, water bailiff, waterkeeper, riverkeeper, what have you, had risen to £7.18s.10d.

Any rate, going back to the Sunday before His Grace left Endsleigh in July, 1954, he asked me to meet him before he went to church. 'Mr Adams,' he said, 'would it be possible for you to catch me a couple of fish?' I said, 'It's a tall order, but I'll try. You and the children may have been successful, but you can't just ask a person to go down the river thinking he'll come back with a couple of fish.' Mr Saunderson was at the side door at the end of the passage. I can see him now, off to Constantine Bay near Padstow for the day because he never trusted his gardener to cut the lawn. I said, 'His Grace wants me to catch him two fish!' He said, 'You haven't a hope!'

Symons had a car, but I'd still only got a push-bike so I push-biked to our one left-handed pool, Parson's, holding my rod and with my gear in my shoulder bag and my bass strapped on the carrier. I crossed over in the boat and, by God, Adams was into a fish! I played him pretty hard and got him, and he was nine pound! So I was home and dry; I wasn't bothered any more; I didn't have to go back empty-handed. They say if there's a fish in Parson's there's a fish in every pool in the river, so I jumped on my push-bike and away I went upstream to Bush. I waded into Bush, fished for a minute or two and I saw a fish come to me. My tummy turned over. I still get the feeling now. So I cast again. Bang, he was on, and I eventually beached him, nine, ten pound. I was very, very proud of myself. The tall order was achieved.

His Grace was back from church. I went into the house. I said to Miss Cook, the new manageress, 'Would you ask His Grace if I could speak to him in the hall?' His Grace came into the hall. I showed him the fish. He said, 'Well done! Right. In we come!' and in I went with him to the lounge for a drink — a whisky again, though I'd have preferred a Double Diamond — then home to lunch and feet up. So that's what fishing's all about. You can go on for week after week, week after week, and not get a fish. You can hook a fish and lose him, although people never believe you when you tell them this have happened. Or you can get two of three in a day. The most I've had is five.

While I'd been at Parson's, Keeper Hall came along. Probably he was out hoping to meet the new Duke and create a good impression. He said, 'Fancy fishing on a Sunday!' You see, he hadn't yet got used to the idea: in 1954 Sunday fishing was allowed on the Endsleigh water for the first time. The late Duke was always, always against Sunday fishing, even for himself. He often spoke to me about it. I'd point out that there was fishing on the Tavy, the Taw and the Torridge, and he'd reply that Sunday was a day of rest. After his death it was decided to try to make the place pay for itself. Things was becoming commercial. The river-keeper was going to have no rest at all.

I said to you that I lost touch with the 13th Duke for a long, long time after 1954. In fact I didn't see him again until 1960 when he was working up to his marriage to the Frenchwoman, Nicole Milinaire. I was sat on the bank, watching a Captain Turner fish the lower part of Inny Junction. A car passed up and parked at the junction. Next thing I heard was someone coming through the bushes who then tapped me on the shoulder and said, 'Mr Adams?' This was His Grace! Of course I jumped to attention. I said, 'My God! Fancy seeing you!' He said, 'Would you mind coming out to the drive for a moment. There's a lady I'd like to introduce you to. My fiancée.' I said I was pleased to meet her which I wasn't because, after all, the Duchess was a marvellous person, lovely, and I got on well with her the short time she was here and there was always good write-ups about her in the papers — you're always watching the papers, getting to know. Any rate, we were introduced and, on the same, Captain Turner decided to come out of the river and up to where His Grace, the lady and I were talking. I immediately said, 'This is one of the guests of the house. Captain Turner, this is His Grace, the Duke of Bedford.' Then I wasn't sure what the lady was called so His Grace introduced her. He'd caught a fish earlier, this Captain Turner, seven or eight pound, and he said to His Grace, 'I'd like to take a photo of you. Do you object?' His Grace said No and the lady said to him, 'Well, why don't you hold Captain Turner's rod and the fish in the photo?' Captain Turner sent me a copy. It's in one of my albums. That's what I call fantasy — His Grace with someone else's rod and a fish he didn't catch.

It was rumoured that the marriage was going to take place on Sunday, September the 4th, and, to mislead the Press, the staff here were asked

127

by Woburn to give the impression the couple were coming to spend their honeymoon at Endsleigh, you know, to tie the journalists down. Bert Moore and myself went to the Edgcumbe Arms about half past twelve, quarter to one that day to return the empties. The pub was full of journalists and one of the local lads shouted, 'This man, Adams, he knows *all* about Endsleigh.' And there was a very crippled lady. She said, 'So you *must* know, Mr Adams, where His Grace is going to spend his honeymoon!' I said, 'Why should *I* know? He isn't marrying me or any connection of mine!' A young boy representing the *Daily Mail* called me a big-head for that, and one word led to another. I said, 'I can't understand youngsters like you being on the *Daily Mail*, a paper my father has taken all his life. I've a copy at home dated 1906.' He said, 'Utter nonsense!' and he bet me and my mate a double whisky each I wouldn't find it. So I'd to whip off home and get it and he paid up like a man.

I never did find out where His Grace spent his honeymoon. I lost interest in him a bit because, let's face it, he lost interest in Endsleigh. All that seemed to interest him now was Woburn and making money. Probably he couldn't help himself. Times was bound to be hard for him because I think the death duties when his father died worked out at about five million. It's a hell of a lot of money, isn't it?

My daughter, Jill, was born on the 27th of January, 1955. The pregnancy came as a great surprise to me and the wife as we'd been married for twelve years and she was thirty-four. We'd wanted a child all the time, and the doctor didn't think there was anything wrong with either one of us. A lady fisher had suggested we get in touch with the adoption people but I wasn't keen. I mean, I know the poor devils have got to have a home but if you're going to have a child you don't want somebody else's. We were really looking forward to our baby. The only trouble was getting the wife from Fishery Cottage to Freedomsfield Maternity Home in Plymouth. At Fishery Cottage we were isolated, out in the wilds, and January there was snow. Nes went to Freedomsfield three times by ambulance — for inspections twice, and once because of a false alarm. She stayed there for a couple of days after the false alarm and then a Mr Concannon performed a Caesarian. After three or four days she came back to the Maternity Home in Tavistock for ten, twelve days.

I remember walking down to the house here at about six on January the 27th. I rung the hospital and Mr Concannon told me there were complications but I wasn't to worry, I should ring him back half past nine to ten o'clock. I walked back up to Fishery Cottage with my heart in my mouth. At about quarter to ten I push-biked down and was put through to the sister that helped deliver the baby. She said, 'Mr Adams? ... I'm delighted to say you've got a beautiful baby daughter of eight and a half pound.' I said, 'My God, I could kiss you!' And, come to, my daughter was christened Jill and that sister's name was Jill Ashley, a marvellous coincidence. We'd have called a boy Tony. You can't put into words how you feel when you're told you've become a father. I was over the moon. I couldn't sleep: I tossed and turned. And my father was some pleased to be a grandfather at last. Unfortunately he fell ill soon after and was too much of a handful for the wife now she'd Jill, so he had to go into an Old People's Home in Tavistock. Eleven years later, July 1966, he died at St Mary's, a Home for the bedridden in Launceston. He was ninety-six. He wouldn't come to see us once he'd left Fishery Cottage. He said he'd find a visit too much of an upheaval.

The day after Jill's birth, I left my bike in the Coxes' garden at No.2 Milton Green and went down by bus to Plymouth. I bought the wife some flowers. The baby was brought into the room as soon as I arrived. Oh, I was like a dog with two tails! It was in a robe and the nurse put it into my hands and I looked at it and smiled and the wife smiled. But I was scared stiff to hold it; I soon handed it back again. It's like a piece of china, isn't it? Once it falls, you've had your chips.

We had her christened in St Torney's at North Hill where the wife was christened and we were married. Jack Adams, no relation, and his wife were Godfather and Godmother — Jack Adams was put in charge of the hatchery when the 12th Duke handed it over to the River Authority in the early Fifties. I taught him.

The christening was the second Sunday of April, the 14th April, 1955, in the afternoon. In the morning, a gent caught his first fish with me at Inny Croy. I took him out in a boat, gave him thorough instructions, and he just flopped his fly in the river and, bang, into a fish! Towards the end of his stay I gave him a fish I'd caught, and I thought he took it in to people called Poole at Tavistock to put on ice as was the practice in they days if they weren't going to leave for a little while.

When it came to the day of his departure he gave me half a crown but I picked up on the grapevine that he'd sold the fish I gave him for £11.10s. So instead of him giving me a tip, I tipped him pretty heavily. Yet this was a man who'd got everything in life — a good business, his own aeroplane... When you come about tips, you just don't know. The person that you expect a 'drink' from doesn't give you one and another person will. I was given a note by a gent this year and I'd never given him much attention, just shown him around. Yet someone else you'd done something special for mightn't say thank you. Of course you've got to be careful. Tips might be a bribe and there must be no preferential treatment. If someone arrives and says, 'Here you are, Adams. Have a drink,' and offers me a ten or twenty pound note, I'm probably being a fool to myself but I've a habit of saying, 'That's against my grain.' At the *end* of the week if they'm inclined to tip me, it's a different matter.

When Jill was coming up to four, Mr Finnie gave us a choice of three cottages in the village where there'd be company for the wife and friends for Jill to play with. Also we still hadn't electric light at Fishery Cottage, and the two miles to school would be too far away for Jill when she started going there. So we moved to 18 The Parade, Milton Abbot, on the 18th of December, 1958. We'd a kitchen, living-room, dining-room, two bedrooms, bathroom and front and back gardens (twenty-five yards by twenty-four and thirty yards by eleven) and an allotment measuring forty-two yards by fourteen, all rent free. We'd to pay for the electricity, of course; also for using the phone. The Syndicate installed the phone for us in '62. We were glad to be able to ring up my brother in Ireland and so on, but a phone meant I was always on call, it was hard to get an evening off. I'm a devil for not answering the phone, so I don't feel so guilty when I'm out. You see, it could be the wife's mother ill, something serious. But, during the season, poachers ring to see if I'm at home.

Jill wasn't a bit nervous about going to school. She went when she was five. The wife had always read to her and she could skittle off a lot of words. She didn't even want to come home to lunch. I can see her mother dressing of her up with a little shoulder bag with two or three sandwiches

130

in. We didn't go to London for our holidays from that time on, and I've never been there since. I don't miss it, you've got to adapt. Paignton, where we always went after, usually with the Lukes next door, has a good shopping centre and you can watch from your bed all the oil tankers going up the Channel. It's got a wonderful beach of its own and it's in easy reach of other beaches. Jill lied in the water, but she really only started to learn to swim last summer in the big baths in Launceston.

She went to Tavistock Comprehensive when she was eleven. She came on quite well there and joined the school choir, but her weak subject to begin with was Mathematics. To earn some pocket money she helped Saturday morning in the Market Café, Tavistock, where the wife, who knew the owners, worked all day Mondays to Fridays. One evening in 1967, she came home and said, 'Can I go on a school trip to Belgium and Holland?' Well, her mother started fussing and fluttering because she's only twelve years old. But I was all for it from the word go. I said, 'We never had a chance like this.' So, in the end, we left her to it. We paid the fare of about £40 and Jill took the pound or two she'd saved as spending money. I let her take my camera, a Halina, the best camera I had. When she came back after a week or so, we met her in Tavistock in the square. She come rushing up to us, keen to talk about everything, and then she suddenly became a bit stand-offish. She said, 'Dad,' she said, 'I let the camera fall in the sand in Belgium and I can't get the sand out.' I said, 'Never mind about that, maid. You'm home!'

Come 1969, she's fourteen, and there's a Mediterranean cruise come up on the map, and a ship called the *Nevasa*. Her mother was quite concerned again. I said, 'Other kids go. Let *her* go. She'll enjoy it. She wants to go. She's got her own mind.' She'd saved up the money and was willing to pay but, though we hadn't got it, we dipped pretty low — you know, we looked under the old carpet and there it was. I can see her mother now waving her off with tears in her eyes because Jill's going to be away fourteen, sixteen days. She never slept again for nights: she was fussing and fussing and fussing. She had a letter from Jill. She was lying in bed and I was sat on the side of the bed while she read it to me. Jill said how everybody had been sick but she hadn't and how there were a lot of steps and ladders from her sleeping quarters to the upper deck where they had to do their drills every day in case of emergency. She said, 'God help us if the real thing happens, but don't worry, Mother, I'll

131

survive!' That upset her mother even more. They went to Portugal, Gibraltar and on to Italy where they had a day at Florence. She brought us home a decanter with a leather cork. The kid was as pleased as Punch with it and, of course, we were. She told us how the Italian shop assistants said they liked English children — to sell them rubbish, I suppose. I was very big-headed at Endsleigh about Jill's holiday. All the guests wanted to know how she was enjoying it because I would say, 'My daughter's gone off on a Mediterranean cruise.' On this one holiday she was doing more than what we *ever* did. Some kids from the village were too nervous to go with her. Jill has never been nervous. Jill is pretty out and about.

She left school in '72. She'd been picking up on Mathematics and thought she might like to become a schoolteacher. Then she came home one night — she was hardly seventeen — and she said, 'I don't know. I don't think I'll bother.' Just like that, though she'd four or five O Levels. She wanted to earn money as soon as possible. So at the end of term, she went in to the Labour Exchange at Tavistock who soon put her in touch with a chartered accountant called Mathias in Drake Street. Jill went to the old boy's office accompanied by her mother, and I think he was taken up more by her mother coming than he was by Jill. He was quite intrigued by this. He said, 'You know, my dear,' he said, 'the trouble with mothers and fathers today is the children's out on the street and they couldn't care a damn. But', he said, 'I'll have to get a reference from the Head of your school. I'll get in touch with you one way or the other within four or five weeks. Are you pleased with that?' Jill thanked him and, within three days, the phone rang and this was the old boy saying, 'I've had a good report. Will you come in for another interview?' So she went in, again with her mother, and she got the job and she's been with the same firm ever since. She sometimes wonders if she's wasted her life because top bankers staying at Endsleigh used to say to me that they'd get her a job in their banks and, when I told her, she'd answer, 'What do I want to go in a bank for?! No, I'll stand on my own feet. If I go in a bank and I don't come up to expectations they'll shun you and they'll shun me.' But I think she's done very well for herself with Mathias — the old boy is retired now; a Mr Frost and a Mr Stone is the two bosses. She's highly respected and she'd got an office of her own. She's been taken by Mr Stone to Bristol on a big job which have taken a week. They stayed in a first-class hotel — you know, with a telephone beside the bed and a

132

tea-maker and a coloured television. Outside of work, she's the Secretary of the Milton Abbot Players — in 1980 she was President. Recently she played the glamorous teacher in *The Happiest Days of Your Life*. She's quite an organizer; she's done more for the community than I have. She's looked up to. For ten years she helped to run the village Youth Club. Also, for a time, she was a Methodist Sunday School teacher. Before then, in 1968 when she was thirteen, she was crowned Methodist Queen of Milton Abbot by Mrs McNicol, the widow of my former boss. She had a little crown put on to her and a blue sash.

The biggest fish that have even been caught when I was actually working on the river was twenty-six pound. Sir Kenneth Peppiatt, the Bank of England's Chief Cashier, the 'pound note man', caught it in 1968 and I wasn't present. But I *was* present when his brother, Sir Leslie, a lawyer, caught almost as big a one in 1955, the year Jill was born. It was April time, April the 14th. I had Sir Leslie in a boat at Inny Croy. (Actually he wasn't knighted till 1959, the year he was made President of the Law Society.) It was getting late in the evening. He hooked a fish. There were three pairs of steps attached to the pool. I dropped down to the bottom pair where the water swings around forming some depth, and Sir Leslie brought the fish quite near the boat for me to net. We were both stood up in the boat which was tied to the bank. I said, 'My God, this is big!' so he said, 'You go up into the stern and I'll step back into the bow,' and, as he stepped back over the seat, he fell into the bottom of the boat. At first I laughed, though it was no laughing matter. Then I said, 'My God, the fish is gone!' because, you see, when he flopped down, his rod dropped forward and everything went slack. Any rate, I got him up from the bottom of the boat — he was still clasping the rod — and everything was under control again, the fish was there and, when I netted it, it was twenty-five pound. Marvellous. The biggest fish *I*'ve ever caught was twenty pound. I've caught three of those.

Another event of '55 was the appearance of the Endsleigh Ghost, the Man in Grey. A lady guest here in August — I think she was called Mrs Oliver — claimed she saw a strange man on three occasions: once coming along the passage from the main house towards the Cottage End, once coming down the stairs at the Cottage End, and once coming out of her bedroom, No.12, at the Cottage End. Two estate carpenters, Mr Luke Senior, the late Duke's carpenter, and his son, Maurice, who is still alive and does all the carpentry work for the Syndicate, it took them three whole days searching the house to find this ghost. Out over the colonnade there's a manhole goes up into the loft, so they put a ladder up and found a lot of bully beef tins, baked bean tins, spaghetti tins. The schoolboys here during the war had probably pinched them and stored them there; no importance was attached to them. But the ghost story went on and on. I took it as a huge joke, but the wife was quite frightened. When I was home of a Friday evening, she would go up at eight o'clock to get the groceries at Mrs Dawe's shop in the village — it didn't close till eight. In winter it was pitch black and Mrs Dawe would say, 'Now, Nesta, you're not afraid to go down through the woods to Fishery Cottage, are you? You're not afraid of the ghost?' You see, the ghost was tall and slight and dressed in grey, and everybody was trying to say it was the late Duke come back.

Early one afternoon in the middle of December I came in with my push-bike at the Horsebridge end and I was walking up river with my gun across the handlebars when I saw a strange man coming down towards me through the fields. He wasn't a farmer and it was unusual to see *anyone* by the river at that time of year so I immediately thought, 'I wonder if this is the Endsleigh Ghost.' Even *I* was getting a bit ghosty now! I stood still and, when he got near to me, although he wasn't actually dressed in grey (he'd a blue overcoat and an old tweed cap on), he looked grey in the face. I said, 'Good-afternoon!' and he said, 'Good-afternoon!' There was wee bits of hay on his coat, he looked as though he'd been sleeping rough, but I then said, 'Are you staying in one of the farms, sir?' He didn't know what to do with his hands and I was getting a little bit fussed because he was a hell of a big bloke, a bigger bloke than me. He didn't answer. I said, 'Have you got permission to come down here?' He said, 'I'm doing no harm! What's this gun for?' I said, 'To shoot a cormorant.' He said, '*Gluttonish! Devour!*' I don't mind telling you I was a little bit on edge. I put the push-bike up against a tree and my gun under my arm. He said, 'What part of the country do *you* come from?' I said, 'I was born here.' He said, 'Well, you don't sound like a Devonian to me!' He looked so big in his tummy that I thought he had something inside his coat like a turnip or even a pheasant. I said, 'You haven't got a pheasant there?' He opened his coat with a hand bigger than both of mine, a 'shovel', and he said, 'No pheasants! No rabbits! Myxomatosis!' Then he said, 'War! How do you expect nations to agree when next door neighbours can't agree?! I've just passed a row of houses where one woman threw a bucket of water at another!' I knew where *that* was — it was a well known ritual at Leigh Cross Cottages. Then he stepped right over to me: he was cheek to cheek. I broke my gun, let him see I'd a couple of cartridges. I thought, 'It's man for man. Better to be a live coward than a dead hero!' He walked on.

That same evening a cousin of the wife's came over from Callington to see us with her husband. I started telling the story and the husband said, 'Oh, I know who that is! That man's what they call Bushy Beard.' He said, 'It's always been rumoured on the Cornish side that he was very friendly with the 12th Duke. He's mentally retarded.' He didn't say 'mentally retarded' but them's the words you've got to use today. 'He's supposed to be in Bodmin Asylum for dropping insulting literature in people's letterboxes. He's very, very odd. I can't understand why he's out.'

Well, a few days later a couple of policemen came from Milton Abbot to see me in the hatchery where I was putting some men from the River Authority wise, helping them because they were new to things. One of the policemen was from the Police Station in Milton Abbot which used to be opposite the church gates. This twenty years it's been a private house. There's no village policemen anywhere in the district. They all work from Tavistock. That's why there's so much crime. People see a Panda car go through the village and then, if they want to commit a crime, it's just too easy. In the old days, when the policeman was *in* the village, he was intimate with everybody, he knew everybody's business... Any rate, the police had heard I'd seen this man and they asked me for a bit of a description. They told me he'd escaped from Bodmin Asylum, though now they'd say 'released himself' and it's called Bodmin Mental Institution. Then the local policeman asked, 'Was he offensive at all? Did he threaten to hit you or anything?' I said, 'No, but at one time he was getting a bit close to me and I was a *wee* bit scared. I broke my gun to let him see there was a couple of cartridges there.' He said, 'What would you have done if he'd attacked you?' I said, 'I'd have shot the bugger and you'd have been looking for me instead of him!'

135

The police searched around and, come to, he'd gone back to Callington. They found him in January, working for a farmer who'd taken him in and he was re-certified. The Endsleigh Ghost was never seen again so it could have been him. Everybody assumed it must be, so that killed the ghost stone dead.

Seven

When someone says they know all the answers, well, you can take that with a pinch of salt. For instance, people will tell you if there's a mist on the river fish will never take. Rubbish! One thing that *is* true is fish won't take if they're going hell for leather up the river when there's a slight rise after a dry spell. And if the distant hills are on the palm of your hand that probably means rain within twelve hours. And if all of a sudden the river starts to rumble, that means he's crying for more water and, I'd bet my last penny on it, there'll be rain within twenty-four hours.

You'm learning something new every minute. Two gents arrived today [August 2] with cane rods. This reminded me that, in what I call 'the Trustee Period' after His Grace was killed and before the Syndicate was formed, I saw a Mr Towgood — who taught me how to roll-cast — rubbing the brass furrow of his cane rod in the creases at the sides of his nostrils to make the joins easier to put together. He said, 'There's more grease there than anywhere else on your body.' Until then, being an Air Force boy, a Brylcreem Boy, I'd always rubbed the furrows in my hair. Those old cane rods were well built. Bad enough if a car door slams on one of those — the rod may crack or it may not. But if a door slams on one of the new fibreglass or carbon fibre rods, the rod will definitely break. At the moment I've a glass fibre rod. Ideally I'd treat myself to a thirteen foot carbon fibre rod with a decent reel — the Prefect reel made by Hardy's, that's the best reel there ever *have* been. And I'd have a No.10 line, sinking tip, instead of my present No.9. As regards flies, I'd stick to the brass tubes introduced to Endsleigh by Colonel Macintyre in the late Fifties.

So guests taught *me* and I'd something to teach most of *them*. People down from Scotland expected the fish to take the fly on its swing with the current when they cast. I'd to say, 'Strip in immediately! Draw the fly towards you! Keep it moving!' Scotch rivers are gin clear. People

137

found it hard to accept that in most of the West Country the rivers are coloured, coming down through clay, so the techniques here must be different. After heavy rain in the old days, the river became pea soup and you were finished for about seventy-two hours. For the last fifteen, twenty years, through land drainage, there's a faster flow. Even after a tremendous storm you usually can be fishing within thirty hours.

Another thing some people could never understand was the need, again because of the coloured water, to have a biggish fly with a bit of yellow or yellow and black bucktail in. I now always recommend a Yellow Torrish or a brass tube (I don't go much on the Esmund Drury). The Yellow Torrish should have a single hook and the brass tube a treble — there's more fish caught at Endsleigh on the tube treble than on any other fly. 'Go out', I say, 'carrying flies of three or four different sizes so that, if you're fishing with a medium-sized fly and a fish comes to you, you can immediately drop down and, if he comes to that, you can drop down again.' I don't personally fish below a No.8. If you go down to a very weeny fly you've to have a very fine cast and you've got a chance of it breaking, especially in low water when there's rocks showing. And, outside of that, a weeny fly hasn't got the hooking power. I'm inclined for a sizeable fly that'll hook in the scissors or the jaw and stick there. The scissors is the side of the fish's mouth. In the old days, there's no mistake about it, you always hooked a fish in the scissors. This day and age — some scientists reckon it's due to pollution — the majority of fish don't turn on a fly, so they're hooked on the lower or the top jaw. By the way, there's no need to 'strike' a salmon. You strike for trout because trout's feeding: as soon as you feel something, a sharp wrist movement, up with your rod, you've struck! But — here I agree with the Scotch ghillies and I hate to say it! — you should give a salmon room. As soon as you feel him, you lift the point of your rod gently, and gradually, not too quickly, you tighten by stripping or reeling in, and he strikes hisself.

In the Trustee Period, and before, I used to write away for Scale Readings. If someone argued the toss about whether, say, a grilse wasn't or was a kelt and shouldn't or should be buried, the only way to settle the matter seemed to be to whip some scales off and send them away to be read by Mr Macfarlane of the Scottish Home Department in Edinburgh or Commander Charlie Brittan, a dental surgeon in Tavistock who invented the Seabrit fly. You'd take the scales off by the dorsal fin,

138

put them in a bit of greaseproof paper, enclose them with any relevant facts such as weight and length in an envelope, and back would come the most fascinating information.

For instance, I sent some scales to Mr Macfarlane in April, 1954, and he told me the fish migrated as a two-years-old smolt in 1952 and then spent a year and a half in the sea before returning as a grilse in the late summer or autumn of 1953; the severe marginal erosion of the scales and the fact that the fish was full of milt indicated that it ripened to spawn in the recent winter as, in most rivers, a few unspawned fish, both male and female, may be found in the spring of each year. In a letter, also dated April, 1954, he told me that a sea trout ($6\frac{1}{2}$ lb.; 25 in.) migrated as a two-years-old smolt in 1948 and then spent a little over a year in the sea before returning to fresh water for the first time in the summer of 1949; it spawned in each of the five winters 1949–1953, with an interval of a few months in the sea between spawning visits.

A letter from Commander Brittan, dated May, 1953, about a fish caught in April ($20\frac{1}{2}$ lb.; 38 in.), said the fish spent two years in the river as a smolt, went to sea for two years, returned to spawn, went to sea for a further year, returned to spawn a second time and had just completed its fourth year in the sea! A letter dated the 4th of June, 1954, about a fish ($13\frac{1}{2}$ lb.; 37 in.), said the length according to the Arthur Hutton Scale of length for weight should have corresponded to a fish of 19.1 lb., and the amount of scale erosion didn't comply with a 1954 peel run fish; the scale reading indicated a two year river life followed by a three year sea life and that the fish was a kelt!!

I only wrote away to verify and, this isn't being big-headed, nine times out of ten I was right. You only learn through catching fish and I'd been on the river enough, seen enough fish pulled out. I didn't send away at all in the Sixties and I've only sent away once since then — to the South West Water Authority in the Seventies. They've altered the names all the way up. The Conservatory Board, the Cornwall River Board, the Cornwall River Authority, the South West Water Authority (all Cornwall, all Devon and part of Somerset)... In the old days the Water Authority and the River Authority was different things. Now it's amalgamated. I've to ring up the South West Water Authority, River Section. They'm *always* altering names. Like 'ghillie'. Ghillie became water bailiff, water bailiff became riverkeeper. River Board boys aren't classed as water bailiffs any more: they're *wardens*. It's something for the secretaries and the clerks to do on their blasted typewriters. The Syndicate now officially call me their 'Fishery Manager'!

It was in the Trustee Period that some of the guests started calling me Horace. I remember Colonel Macintyre saying to me, 'It seems a bit stiff me calling you Adams. What's your Christian name?' and I said, 'I've got a horrible Christian name: Horace.' A lot of people called me Horace from then on. Everything was becoming more and more familiar. What a difference from the Grandfather Duke's days! At Milton Green my father referred to Sam Branch, an estate worker and a pal, as 'the late Mr Branch' when he died!

But, funnily enough, our first American visitor always called me Adams. I arrived back from the river one evening, about ten, ten fifteen, and the Manageress, Mrs Young — Miss Cooke married the chef, Mr Young, in 1954 — she said, 'There's an American would like to see you.' I said, 'Where *is* the American?' She said, 'He's gone to bed.' I said, 'Well, how can he *see* me?!' She said, 'I'll go and tell him you're here.' When I met him in the entrance hall, he was tucking his shirt in. He said, 'So you're Adams! I'm very pleased to meet you!' He said, 'I'd like to go fishing tomorrow morning, early.' I said, 'What do you call early?' He said, 'Five, six, seven…' I said, 'What are you going to fish for?' He said, 'Trout or salmon. I don't mind what I fish for.' I said, 'I'll meet you seven o'clock tomorrow morning and we'll fish for salmon.'

I met him at seven o'clock and he introduced me to his chauffeur. 'This is my man, John,' he said. 'John have got the pole.' We proceeded down Ham Hill to the river and, as we were going down Ham Hill, he shouted, 'Stop, John! Stop!' We stopped. I thought he wanted to go back to the house, but he jumped out and got on his knees and started photographing a cobweb.

Any rate, we ended up fishing at Joel's Corner, Leigh Wood way, and he was immediately into the rock there. He shouted, 'I've got him! I've got him!' He was jumping about and putting pressure on, and the rod was bent. I said, 'You're in the rock!' He said, 'No! It's a mammoth great fish!' Eventually I persuaded him it was the rock and I put my waders on, went out and released the fly. Then we started off on the croy, and he's into a rock again. We came back to breakfast. He went with John, the chauffeur, somewhere else till lunch-time when he told everyone that he'd lost two or three fish. I'm sure he hadn't. I'm sure it was all rocks. I said, 'The sort of fish you catch is what we call rock salmon!'

Americans are always welcome at Endsleigh. Though they exaggerate, they're good fun, good value for money, true sportsmen. We'd three arrive here in the Seventies — they'd been up north on a business trip. They'd only got short eight foot six, nine foot rods. I said, 'My God! Is this all you've got?! You shouldn't use small rods on big water!' They said, 'Ah, but we travel the world over, you see, and we've got to pack it small!' — they'd to pack these small three or four piece things in metal cases for transport. Any rate, I started them off at Bush Pool, which is Beat 3. There's forty-two pools all told and the pools is divided up pretty evenly, about ten, twelve pools in a beat. There isn't a fairer allocation of beats than at Endsleigh.

I wandered up river — you can't, just because they're Americans, stay with them all the time. When I returned about two hours later, one of them had caught a seven or eight pound salmon. He said, 'This is the first fish we've caught in England so we must eat it. When you go back to the house, take it with you and tell the Manageress we want it for our supper.' Then they said, 'You'd better have a drink.' So they poured me a whisky and I thought, 'Well, we're friendly enough now for me to ask *them* a question,' — not that Americans aren't friendly all the time: from the moment you first meet them, they're very, very free; they're all over you; they're probably a little bit *too* gushing. I said, 'Why are you dressed so loud?' One had on a red, almost a crimson anorak! The other was in *yellow* of all things! And the other was in bright green, real bright green! They didn't understand what I meant by 'loud', so I said, 'such gay colours', and one of them said, 'Well, Adam, boy,' he said, 'why we're dressed so *loud* as you call it is, out in America, everyone has guns and, when they go out shooting, they shoot at anything and, if you weren't dressed *loud*, you'd hear a gun go off and then probably you'd be dead for ever!' That was the very words he said to me.

This was on a Saturday morning and they were going away on the Monday morning, and the conversation turned to where one of them could buy a good gun. I said, 'There's a firm down at Plymouth called

Jeffery's that sells fishing tackle, and they're also gunsmiths.' So he instructed their chauffeur, John — all Americans I've met call their chauffeurs 'John' — to go to Plymouth in the afternoon to see some guns. John came back at five o'clock. 'Did you find a gun, John?' 'The dearest they'd got was six hundred and eighty quid!' 'Aw, that's no bloody good! You'd blow your head off with that!' — he was prepared to pay a thousand. So I said, 'Oh, you want an *expensive* gun! There happens to be a gentleman here tied up with a firm in Dulverton in Somerset, people called Lance Nicholson. I'll introduce you to him.' So I made the introduction when everyone was back for dinner, and they got on like a house on fire.

The Sunday morning, I was watching this American fish when he said, 'Oh, by the way, Adam, boy,' he said, 'I'm going to Dulverton later today. The gentleman you introduced me to is opening his shop for me to have a look at his guns to size them up. Would you like to come too?' I said, 'Thank you very much for the invitation but I mustn't be involved.' I didn't see the American again, but apparently he made a deal. The other gent said to me, 'We did very well on that. I'd like to give you something.' So I had an anorak out of his firm. Not a loud one — mellow green.

I've never met an American snob so far. Snobs is people what I call 'jumped up'. One moment they've got nothing and then, the next, they've got the world at their feet yet they can't afford it; they've got the lolly, but they haven't got the sense. They're few and far between at Endsleigh — I have them for a week's fishing and then it's always very difficult, but they don't often come back the second time. A lot of my mates used to say to me, especially in the old days, 'You're working for snobs.' I said, 'Can you explain the word "snob"?' They'd say, 'The gentry.' I said, 'Yes, but the real gentry are more down to earth than the working man.' If people are born into money, they're wonderful sort of people. But take a schoolmaster, for instance. When he's gone to the top of the ladder, he thinks he's God Almighty. In the Trustees' days we had a barrister here called McCarthy. He was a snob and he didn't fit in. You could never tell him anything yet he always wanted you at his heels. One day he came back from the Lower Stretch and I overheard him say to another guest, 'That bloody Symons!' he said. 'I've had no help from him again today. He makes out he's not well but I happen to know he's been trying to sell his car!' I butted in. I said, 'Now look, sir! That's not right saying that!' I said. 'Herbie Symons is a hell of a good bloke. I don't like this backchat. Let's be fair. He *is* unwell and he *has* been trying to sell his car, but he's been doing it from his living-room.' I was talking about this later to Sir Leslie Peppiatt, a real gentleman, and I said, 'If Mr McCarthy's like that about Symons behind his back, he's probably the same about me! I don't like it! Mr McCarthy, hell to him!' I was so upset I went home to Fishery Cottage. Dear old Sir Leslie, he followed me up. He said to the wife, 'It doesn't feel a bit like Endsleigh when Adams is like this.' Then he talked to me quietly, he said, 'Take no notice of him. He's only here for a short period of time.'

So this is the sort of thing that I've learned you've got to let wash off your shoulders, and, due to Sir Leslie, when Mr McCarthy made his next complaint, I was feeling better and decided to help him. The Trustees were allowing netting again and, when Mr McCarthy went down to fish the Lower Cottage Run on the tidal water, there was a damn great boat there with four blokes in it, netting through. So he came back here and he was on to *me* about it. Mind you, he was right on this occasion, because the men shouldn't have been netting when paying guests wanted to fish. I said, 'Well, it's none of *my* business. It's not *my* estate. The estate is being run by the Bedford Trustees. You must get hold of the agent.' It happened that the sub-agent, Mr Walkinden, was here and I had a word with him. I said, 'If you get a chance,' I said, 'would you meet Mr McCarthy a bit later in the day? I'm taking him down river fishing because he's fed up with everybody and I want to try to put things right.' So Mr Walkinden came down river and I introduced him to Mr McCarthy. But he foolishly asked, 'Have you had any luck, sir?' '*Luck!*' he said. 'How the hell do you expect me to have any luck when there's a bloody net now down below Gunnislake Weir pulling all the fish out?!' And he just carried on fishing, really snubbed Mr Walkinden. I felt *terrible* because Mr Walkinden was young and probably didn't know the ropes. So there. That's what I call a snob, a nick-nack, a fly-by-night. It all means the same.

Round the same time, there was an old boy called Sparrow who came here, something to do with Lucas, the motorcar accessories. He thought he was the Duke! He came here with a Rolls. Now, in the Grandfather Duke's days, you could drive a Rolls *anywhere* on the estate as there was scores of men to keep the drives and banks trimmed, but, even then, Ford cars were used for fishing. In the mid-Fifties when staff were retiring and drifting away and I'd only some woodmen to help me, a Rolls on the river bank was out of place. A wonderful old boy called Mr Goslett, who had a Sunbeam Talbot, said to me, 'I *told* him', he said, 'that he shouldn't go up and down the river in a Rolls-Royce because he'll get it scratched and he answered, "I've nothing else to go up and down the river *in*!"!' One year he arrived in the Rolls, his wife arrived in a Daimler, his son arrived in an MG sports and his chauffeur brought an old Morris Traveller, a rougher car for the river; so he'd realized. But I didn't realize he was a snob — I just thought he was odd — till one day I went fishing with him at Woodtown and, as I'd nobody to help me at all by now, the steps there was getting a little bit dilapidated, a little bit shaky. I said to him, 'You must go carefully down over these steps. If a step should break, you're doing of it at your own risk.' Any rate, that was all right. Then, as he walked into the river, I pointed out a shelf of rock and a little duct of water rushing through where you've got to strike. Well, he stepped into this duct and knocked his leg pretty nasty. Later, back at Endsleigh, I heard him saying to some guests, 'Adams didn't point it out to me. I don't think he likes me. Probably he was hoping I'd *break* my leg!' I thought it was terrible he should speak like that! So he turned out to be another snob. High and Mighty. You can tell them anything and they don't take notice of you.

When Lord and Lady Trenchard came here first, in '54, I was a little bit fussed. He's the youngest son of Lord Trenchard who was head of the police and head of the Air Force, and being a wee bit deaf, he's very, very loud. His father was called Boom so they say the son turned after him. He'd a black labrador called Porgy and, if he shouted, 'Porgy!' you could hear him in the village almost… But he turned out to be so nice. As did Her Ladyship. Almost as soon as I met her, she asked, 'Have you got a family?' I said, 'It won't be long now probably. But, seeing you've asked *me* that question, may I ask you the same?' She said, 'Yes. I've got two boys.' Then she said, 'You look astounded!' I said, 'I'm sure I do! I never thought you were *old* enough to have two boys!' One was Johnnie, then a baby, and the other, Hugh, was two. Late in life they had another

144

boy called Henry who caught his first fish at Endsleigh, but not with me. Hugh caught his first fish with me at South Coombe Pool when he was twelve, and Johnnie caught his first fish with me at Leigh Wood Waterfall in Boat House Pool when he was ten — Johnnie's was the only fish that was caught here that day.

Another charming couple was Lord and Lady Hollenden . He was coming up to eighty-nine, ninety, and Her Ladyship rung me up one morning and said, 'Lord Hollenden would love to have a birthday picnic on the river bank at Carthamartha, and he wants you to join us.' We had quail and all the best drink. Picnics on the bank could be quite lavish. The Hollendens brought their own, but you could order a picnic basket from the house. The present Managers, Mr and Mrs Bradbury — they've been here nine or ten years — introduced a system by which the guests every evening tick in a Picnic Book what they'll want the following day.

Since we've lived at The Parade in Milton, the wife has packed me a lunch, so I've always got a couple of flasks of tea and some chicken thigh or ham sandwiches with me. Six or seven years ago, Sir Edward and Lady Caffyn, members of the Syndicate, invited me to join them for lunch. They opened up the packs in their basket and found almost no lunch there, just a wee bit of cheese, some biscuits and a couple of pieces of bread and butter! I said, 'Would you like some of my chicken?' Lady Caffyn said, 'No, thank you. A little bit of cheese and a biscuit is good enough for me. But my husband... If you've got chicken enough...' So I pulled off a hunk of chicken and Sir Edward joined me with mine. This is on the Friday. On the Monday evening I was leaving the house here just before seven o'clock when a friend of Lady Caffyn came into the yardway and said, 'Oh, Adams,' he said, 'Lady Caffyn wants to see you up at Gravel Pool.' So I drove up to Gravel in the Land Rover — the Syndicate gave me a motorbike first, then a Land Rover — under the Trustees I'd never anything but a push-bike — and Sir Edward was sat in his car and Lady Caffyn was fishing. 'Oh,' she shouted, 'give Horace that little parcel that's in the back! Thank you very much for last Friday!' So I took the package. I didn't open it there and then: I opened it further down the river. It was three beautiful lamb cutlets in lieu of my little bit of chicken. So I'd gained. I'd got three lunches now for the price of one...

Where was I? Oh, yes. Guests under the Trustees — some of the nicer ones. There was a dear old gentleman called Canon Coupe. In fact, he was one of the first gentlemen to fish here when His Grace, the 12th Duke, began to open Endsleigh as a guest-house. But, round about '57, Canon Coupe invited a bishop and his wife to come here to fish with him, and, one Sunday morning, he introduced me to them in the hall after the three of them had been to church. The bishop said, 'I didn't see you this morning, Adams.' I said, 'Where might that have been, sir?' He said, 'In church.' I said, 'Well, it's like this, sir,' I said, 'I haven't got any time to go to church because I've to come down here and get the rods ready for the clergy to go fishing.' So Mrs Coupe, the canon's wife, said, 'If you'd known Adams like we know Adams, you wouldn't have said that to him. But you've got your answer now. Although he've only known you for two seconds, you've got the true Adams.'

Well, during the week, I had the opportunity of going along with the bishop and no one else, and we were at Carthamartha Pool and he asked me to join him for lunch. So I sat down and he had his picnic lunch and I had mine. He said, 'Well, my boy,' he said, 'are you a Church of England?' I said, 'No, not really. I was brought up in the Wesleyan which is now Methodist but,' I said, 'I shouldn't say this probably but, I've got to be truthful about it, I only go just occasionally, either to a Harvest Festival or to an Easter Service, something like that. I'm not a communicant. But, while we're on about churches,' I said, 'the young people is drifting away from the Church, and I'm not sure if it isn't partly your fault, you the Church of England.' When people come fishing, they let their hair down and they ask you a question and therefore you try to answer it to the best of your ability. I mean, you don't make up a fairy tale and say Yes when you mean No. He said, 'How right you are! And especially in the country! I think a lot of it's to do with the motorcar because the family can get to the beach today, whereas in the past you relied on a coach trip.' I said, 'Yes, but there's another side of the question because', I said, 'don't you think it's a lot to do with your clergy? In my schooldays, you could never avoid the parson. It didn't matter where you were. If you walked into the shop, there was the parson buying some groceries or some cigarettes. If you went to the school, there he was, a governor of the school and always in and out because he was so devoted to the children's religion. But today', I said, 'you've a hell of a job to find the parson because he keeps himself to himself. It's true he turns up at a

146

wedding and a funeral, and he probably turns up at church on Sundays, but', I said, 'I know he doesn't associate enough with the young people. Seeing that I don't go to church, I'm the wrong one to criticize, but', I said, 'I can give you an illustration. Every summer in Milton Abbot youngsters go to the Cherry Fair. It's only a hundred yards away from the vicarage, but the vicar never turns up. He should be *amongst* those youngsters. Probably he'd be given cherries, he wouldn't have to buy them. If the clergy don't associate with the youngsters, they're never going to get them into church.' And then I went on and gave a description of Tavistock Football Team. I said, 'There was a young curate in Tavistock was an exceptionally good footballer so he joined the team and helped entertain people on a Saturday afternoon. Probably it's not religion, but', I said, 'the team had quite a good following and youngsters patronized his church because he was one of *them*.' The bishop thought that was a good point.

Next we went right away from the Church and on to fishing. He told me that he'd started quite young, unlike me, and used to go down the streams and creep up behind the trout and tickle them underneath with his hands and flop them out on the bank. He said, 'Later, when I was at college, studying to go into the Ministry, I used to take some of the other students down to the streams surrounding the college and show them how to tickle trout.' We went on in conversation about trout and about fishing in general, and then he said, 'You know, Mrs Coupe has told me that you're pretty clever at putting a name to a face though you meet so many people in a year.' He said, 'How do you do that? Sometimes one of my flock says, "Hallo, Bishop!" and I haven't a *clue* who they are, though they may be one of my leading church wives.' I said, 'I associate them with some story or distinguishing feature in my mind. For instance, I'd look at you and say to myself, "The poaching bishop!"!' I wonder if he thought about that afterwards, because he *was* a poacher: what he did as a child and at college was illegal.

Right. Endsleigh is being run as a guest-house with all these paying guests coming (six people now instead of four fishing each of the two stretches), some of them knowing more about fish than I do as they've fished from the cradle and in various rivers. I'm bragging that my heaviest fish was

147

twenty pounds and they cut me off by saying they've caught one twenty-six, twenty-nine and, one gent, thirty-five, so I'm only a small fisherman. And it's not just guests coming into the house: agents and solicitors are being sent down from Woburn, wondering whether to dispose of the whole estate. Then prospective buyers start roaming in, and I've to meet them, show them the best pools.

One Saturday afternoon I was off on the bus to watch football in Tavistock — the wife was coming too with a collapsible pram to push Jill round the town during the match. There was a knock on the door of Fishery Cottage just as we were starting lunch and a gentleman said, 'Oh,' he said, 'I've come to look at the place and I wondered if you could take me down around and show me the river.' I said, 'Well, I was going out for the afternoon but I'll cancel it.' Your entertainment was being pushed aside to escort these people, and probably you were cutting your own throat because, if they bought the place, you'd be the last person they'd want. By many of the pools there were bunches of beautiful azaleas, lovely. A gentleman came one day and he bought a tremendous lot of these azaleas. He had two cattle lorries sent down from Surrey, and they were dug up and taken back to his estate, spoiling Endsleigh. Some of the guests had only seen them for a short period, some had never seen them, so they didn't miss them the next year, but I missed them.

The asking price for the fourteen thousand acres of woodland and agricultural land (including the village) plus the guest-house and the fourteen miles of fishing was three hundred-odd thousand.

There was an old boy called Richards. Apparently he had a chain of butcher's shops. One minute he didn't know anything about fishing yet when you tried to explain he knew it all. I was pleased that in due course nothing happened with *him*. A gentleman called Mr Williams, he wanted a tree taken down here, a tree taken down there to make room for extra rods. I said, 'No. You don't know anything about it. You'd be commercialized right away and kill Endsleigh within a couple of years. You'd spoil the beauty of the place, it would be like fishing on a canal. You must have the beauty or the people won't come back a second time. Any rate, you're choosing parts of the river where the fish push though and wouldn't lie.' Mr Finnie and a forester took Sir Charles Clore, the big financier, around the woods and I escorted him along the river. He seemed quite nice but some guests spotted him and said to me, 'That's the last man you want to buy Endsleigh. He'll split it up.'

But, from '59 on, Endsleigh *was* split up. Lord Bradford, one of the best foresters in the country, bought most of the woods. He was a marvellous man. He allowed no shooting, but he took on most of the Duke's foresters. Seven, eight years ago, I was fishing at Carthamartha with the Harris twins when I got up on my hinder legs and stopped his Land Rover, thinking it was poachers. He said, 'That shook you, but I've come up here purpose so I can introduce Her Ladyship to you because', he said, 'with your running around keeping an eye if there's anyone here that shouldn't be here you're helping me so much as you're helping yourself.' When he passed on in '81 and his son took over, everyone said, 'He'll never be the man his father was.' Well, of course he *couldn't* be, because you can't expect a man walking out from a restaurant and the antique business to go into woods and have the same character.

A Mr William Tuckett of Ludbrook, Buckland Monachorum on the Tavy bought Leigh Wood and all the farmlands from Leigh Wood Gate downstream to Horsebridge — in other words the lower two miles of the Upper Stretch, what we now call Beat 4, Tuckett Trust — and became an original member of the Endsleigh Fishing Club, the Syndicate which was formed in 1962. He was very, very dictatorial, but you knew where you stood: if you put your cards on the table, his would be there too. I remember Bert Moore and myself — the only two the Syndicate kept on — had been sawing logs and we were taking a couple of bags home at five o'clock when Mr Tuckett came along. All he said was, 'I see you're going to keep the home fires burning!' Another person might have said, 'You can't take any of those!' In the 12th Duke's days I always had ten tons of logs supplied to me, cut, delivered and stacked, and I've taken them as of right ever since. Mr Tuckett was a very generous man — he helped the Church considerably — though once, when he had a party here for his daughter, and Bert and myself had helped with parking the cars and whatnot, he put his hand in his wallet and gave Bert a fiver and then turned to me and said, 'You've got enough, Adams, haven't you?' I think it was supposed to be a joke. Mr Tuckett Junior, who lives at Leigh Barton in the centre of all this land, is now the local director of the Syndicate, and the land he owns here and on the Tavy is part of the Tuckett Trust. Some of his money's tied up in Hughes and Wilbraham, an estate agency in Tavistock. The father didn't shoot, but the Trust have a shoot here this side of Christmas.

Next on the scene came a Mr Walton, a gent with spinning mills in the Nottingham area. I showed my stretch of river and Herbie Symons showed him his. Whichever stretch went first, Endsleigh House was supposed to have went with it, but that idea fell through and, in '59, he bought the fishing rights and farmland from Horsebridge down to Impham Meadows below Gunnislake. He kept things as they were before, barring Endsleigh was only allowed to have two rods fishing down there — he stopped them after three or four years — along with two rods for himself and two for his personal guests. Herbie Symons was *his* river manager now. He was sad, but glad to be employed. Mr Walton had said to me, 'May I ask your advice? Which stretch of the river would *you* buy if you were in my position?' I said, 'I'd rather have my stretch. The fish have to come through the tidal stretch first, but this is prettier — down there was knocked to pieces in the mining days and you can still see the stacks. In the long run, over a period of seasons, especially in the freshwater, you'll pick up so many fish on this stretch as you will down there. Of course early in the spring you'll get more fish on the tidal stretch, and when the river's very low you'll always get more fish down there because the devils can't run up.'

So the estate was getting smaller. What was left was the fishing on my seven miles from Greystone Bridge to Horsebridge, the house, the grounds around the house, and hundreds of little outlying bits including Milton Abbot Village and No.18 The Parade, where I moved to in '58. Up here kept ticking over till 1961 for the Bedford Trustees. To fish cost eight to fifteen guineas per week according to the season, four guineas extra for Sundays. Now it's £11 to £15, Sundays included. To stay in the house with breakfast, lunch, tea, dinner, baths and services was two guineas per day or fifteen guineas per week. Now it's about £38 per day.

To begin with, the Trustees only allowed one free fish per day but after about three years the rule had to be abolished. I remember a gentleman catching a sixteen pound fish early in the morning and immediately taking down his rod. He said, 'I shan't catch a better fish all day. Why should *I* catch a fish for the house? I'm off to tour Devon and Cornwall!' If a husband and wife was fishing and the husband caught two, Symons and myself used to put one down for the wife. You were having temptation thrown at you all the time. There was a bit of an uproar once when the agent accepted money from a person who could afford to pay for all the fish he kept.

A popular innovation was allowing guests to bring their dogs. The 12th Duke never allowed a dog, didn't have one himself, and they're 'out' with me still — they're not really supposed to be used for catching poachers because by law they'd be called an offensive weapon. There's more dogs in this country now than there are human beings. They're everywhere, fouling the beaches, fouling the streets. Although Torquay's supposed to be the Riviera of the west, every other yard you step is a lot of dogs' mess. I've told you of the full-time man who, when His Grace was in residence, sanded the stagings and washed the boats. Well, now you'd need one to clean up all the dogs' dropping. The yard's full of it.

In '61 it was on the grapevine that a group of fourteen gentlemen — a lot of them had fished the Endsleigh and lower waters as day-fishermen or guests — were combining together to buy the house and the fishing rights on my stretch. Their eventual names were Lord Roborough, Mr George Coryton, Lord Boyd, Sir John Carew-Pole, Sir George Hayter-Hames, Mr Claude du Cros, Mr William Tuckett, Lord Trenchard, Sir Leslie Peppiatt, Mr W. H. Wykeham-Musgrave, Mr Egbert Barnes, Captain R. M. Thompson, Dr L. H. B. Macleod and Mr Arthur Best. Their Chairman was going to be Sir George Hayter-Hames and they were going to form a syndicate called the Endsleigh Fishing Club.

I'd known Sir George over a period of years. He was a local celebrity and Chairman of the Devon County Council. He was running around the river in his little Morris Traveller with a pencil and paper, drawing up a list of members to prevent Endsleigh getting into the hands of the wrong type. He'd have this list on the bonnet of his car and he'd say to me, 'What do you think of this person?' and I'd say, 'Well, I'm not too sure about him. Probably he's got a lot of money but money isn't everything,' and he wouldn't go any further with him. I'll give you an idea of the sort of man Sir George was. One day he arrived here about nine o'clock in the morning to fish Inny Croy. He said, 'You know, Adams,' he said, 'I won't be able to fish very long because I've to go to

151

a funeral this afternoon.' He fished right up to the last minute, had a quick snack and then he said, 'You can fish for me whilst I change,' and he whipped into the wood as a fisherman and came out as a town gentleman with white shirt, black tie and pinstripe trousers. On another occasion he *forgot* to change. He'd been out on his farm in Chagford and he went to a big ceremonial parade in Exeter and marched down the street with yorkers on and bits of string tied around his legs.

Lord Roborough was the Lord-Lieutenant of Devon, and you couldn't have a nicer gentleman to be a Lord-Lieutenant of *any* county. In height he was on the short side like you. He and his wife were always very, very kind to people. He stayed here in the beginning of the Syndicate days and the fishing was out of order, so he said to me, 'Would you like to come over and fish with us on our stretch of the Tavy?' I thought that was very considerate. I went over with him for the day. We didn't catch a fish but we shared lunch, that sort of thing. It was Her Ladyship who earlier suggested the wife and me adopt a baby.

Lord Boyd, Lennox Boyd, one time Colonial Secretary, was another very considerate person. He'd a wonderful estate called Ince Castle, near Saltash on the estuary of the Lynher. As a member of the Coalition Cabinet he received a medallion personally inscribed by Winston Churchill himself. That's what Churchill thought of him. That's the type of gentleman I've been mixing with all my life. He never done no fishing before he came here as a member of the Syndicate. He had to have all new tackle and I showed him how to start off. He was about six foot tall and, the first time I took him out in a boat, the boat struck a rock and, by God, he was overboard, rod and all. Straight in the river! Why I thought he was a sailor I don't know, but I said to him, 'I thought as a sailor you'd have more balance!' He said, 'I'm no sailor. It doesn't look like it, any rate!' He'd to strip off and hang all his clothes out — he'd got a change of slacks in the car.

Going back to the days of the 12th Duke, if he hadn't died he was going to have cattle grids put everywhere to save opening and shutting gates. Early in the Syndicate Lord Boyd said to me, 'I'll donate six grids as well as the labour.' I said, 'You don't want to bother about the labour because Bert Moore and myself will put them in.' He approached Sir George, but the Syndicate wouldn't have it. They probably didn't want an individual giving anything; they thought he would take over probably, which was stupid. So they bought six grids in Tavistock instead through the Syndicate funds. If they'd only allowed Lord Boyd to give his section there could have been cattle grids all the way. *But*, I must say this, it don't matter how deep you put them or how wide you put them, the modern bullock, the Friesian, he walks across them. Terrible. Especially with the three foot old-fashioned ones up the river, they walk along the edge. Even if there's stones and a gate by the side, once one comes they all come. They'll even jump it...

Lord Boyd was a wonderful gentleman, he always treated me well. I telephoned him once and I said to him, 'I'm awfully sorry I've rung you. Probably you were at dinner. I never know when to ring.' He said, 'Horace, my friend,' he said, 'you ring me any time you want. It doesn't matter if it's first thing in the morning or last thing at night. If I was entertaining the Queen, I would leave the dining-table to speak to you.' And he meant it with all sincerity, he didn't say it in a sarcastic manner like *I* would to you. His wife was Patsy, one of the Guinness family, the daughter of Lord Iveagh. Twelve o'clock was always Guinness time whether anyone had caught a fish or not. If a friend was a little way up the river, he always sounded his car hooter so we could all come and have a Guinness or a Harp lager.

He always used to say, 'Why don't you come down to Ince? You can bring a friend or bring your mother-in-law or bring your wife and daughter. You've got he freedom of the place.' In '64, when Jill was nine year old, the wife and myself went down with Jill. We didn't make any appointment, just come into the grounds, and we ran up against him. I introduced him to the wife and Jill and the first thing he said to Jill was, 'If you want a swim, dear, you can go down and have a bathe in the bathing pool which has a shallow and a deep end.' It also had changing rooms by the side and a little freezer with drinks. Jill said, 'I haven't swimmed very much. You know, at the beach I've paddled with a bathing costume on but', she said, 'I haven't got any bathing costume with me.' 'Oh,' he said, 'it doesn't matter about that. Her Ladyship's not all that big. Put Her Ladyship's on.' Of course she'd get in one part of Her Ladyship's costume and out the other. 'If that doesn't suit you,' he said, 'jump in in the nude and if I come around do whistling.' Jill was too shy to swim in the nude, but we went down there on many occasions after that, and Jill took her bathing costume with her. I've got photos of her by the pool. He was so good to us. But we didn't eat with him. It comes back to me being a loner again. I don't like to impose.

Sir John Carew-Pole, who'd been invited here once by Sir George to get the swing of it, was the Lord-Lieutenant of Cornwall. He was very military, always immaculate and dressed to kill. If you seen him on a station platform to meet any of the Royalty, he was always smarter than them. I took him on that first occasion to Inny Croy. I said to him, 'Have you fished very much, sir?' He said, 'No. I've only caught one salmon in my life and I lassoed that.' Apparently he was spinning and the spinner had gone into its back and the line got wrapped right around. This is the story he told me and it's quite feasible.

Mr Wykeham-Musgrave was a tiny man, very, very wiry, with a very red face and gingery hair. He was a real country man with quite an estate near Cirencester. Although he owned a motorcar, he always push-biked around his estate to see his cattle and his men. He was really interested in Endsleigh, he fell in love with it enormously. I always said and I let people hear that he should have been Chairman of the Syndicate when Sir George died because, although he could be dictatorial, he had the place at heart; he wanted this and that done, he was trying to keep Endsleigh nice and he saw it slipping away from him. What he said was right and nobody likes being told what to do. One day we were fishing up at Carthamartha and in the Tavistock Woodlands (Lord Bradford's estate) on the far side they were felling trees and one tree fell in the river. Mr Wykeham-Musgrave shouted across, 'What are you going to do about *that*?!' Whatever the woodsmen replied was a little bit cheeky so he said, 'Right! I'll give you twenty-four hours to get that tree out!' It was retrieved with the help of a tractor within forty-eight. Eventually he became so aggrieved about things he pulled out of the Syndicate. The last time he came here during his Syndicate reign he didn't even stay at Endsleigh House, he stayed at the Arundel Arms. Sir George told me to give him the same attention as I'd give anyone else.

Mr Egbert Barnes had a wonderful garden in Wiltshire and he was Chairman of the St Austell Brewery. Whenever he sent me a present he addressed it to 'The Master Caster of Endsleigh'.

Dr Macleod, a doctor in the Sidmouth area, played his fish too hard and therefore he lost more than his share. Him and his wife were always inviting me to join them for tea and they used to love China tea. Well,

154

personally I'd never tasted China tea before I had a drink with them, and China tea is not my cup of tea. In the morning Mrs Macleod would say to me, 'We're going to Tavistock this afternoon. What sort of biscuits would you like for us to bring for tea?' A homely old couple. Typical old country doctor. Any rate, I remember they gave me a present of half a pound of China tea and, of course, I took it home and I put it in the cupboard and Jill, who was a small girl now of seven or eight, she invited her pals in and, you know what kids are, they love to make their own tea. They got hold of the packet of China tea, put it all in the teapot and stunk the place out.

Mr Coryton was a very tall, red-faced, big-nosed gentleman and a very, very good mixer. His daughter always used to say to me, 'Father gets on well with you because you can natter away and bring him out.' He was full of complaints and he never stayed in the house although he was a member. There was wisteria growing on the whole of the front side of the roof of the colonnade and it really looked beautiful, but Mr Coryton said, 'You can't have a pretty roof and a dry roof.' He kept on about this till the wisteria was all cut off. When the slates were taken off the roof to re-slate it there was found underneath another roof of very small slates and that's the roof which is there now.

Mr Claude du Cros, Sir Philip's son, was the opposite of Mr Coryton. He was always smiling, never grim. I've seen him sit on the bank between the trees and rollcast his fly across the stream and not even stand up to play the fish when he hooked it. Once, the net slipped out of his hand — it was his father's and it have never been found — and he just stuck his fingers in the gills of the fish and lifted it up alive to me. One afternoon he caught three fish at Lowley Run while Sir Philip was snagged in front of him on the inner tube of a tyre, thinking he was playing a fish.

Mr Arthur Best was an exceptionally good fisherman. The poor old boy have gone on now, but his widow have become a member instead. Before his death she used to come here with her mother, Mrs Thacker, and act as his ghillie. One day, about 1969, he was fishing Gravel Pool. Mrs Best was down on the shingle watching him, Mrs Thacker was in the car and I was leaning up against the car nattering to her when Mr Best had a bout of coughing and all of a sudden spit his false teeth out. They were gone. It's as simple as that. I had to get a net, the trout net because you had to have something fine or the false teeth would flow through, but we never found them. Talking of teeth, one of my relations was a coroner's officer in London and they didn't know what a person had died of and when they post-mortemed him they found he'd swallowed his bottom denture. So, before I go to bed, I always take mine out and put them in a basin.

Captain Thompson died shortly before March, '62 when the Syndicate started fishing. I'd once boated him down from Inny croy to the bottom of Lower Inny Run and, on the way, he'd hooked a fish and lost it. Some days after, we were up there again and he decided to scramble over the bank and fish from where a tree stump had washed in and the river had shingled up, and he flicked his fly out and got a fish. So I asked Mrs Thompson, because *she* became a member instead, if I could name this part of the river Thompson's Pool. The pool below that, I named Beech Tree Pool because of the old beech tree stump that used to be there — the River Authority's cut it down since. It was also known as 'Ghillies' Paradise' because you could get a stick after people was gone and wriggle out the flies caught in the old ivy. So what used to be Inny Croy and Lower Inny Run was now Inny Croy, Lower Inny Run, Thompson's and Beech Tree.

Everything was signed and sealed in 1961 and the Syndicate started in March '62 after this quote appeared in the *Daily Mail*:

Some of Britain's anglers have done a curious thing — formed a club to fish a river which did not yield a fish last year. The new Endsleigh Fishing Club bought rights on the River Tamar in Devon. But the Chairman, Sir George Hayter-Hames, who used to fish it last year when the Duke of Bedford owned the rights, told me, 'I don't know what is going to happen this year. Last year we didn't catch a single fish [they caught forty-four]. Among the distinguished list of members are Viscount Boyd, Viscount Trenchard and Lord Roborough, Lord-Lieutenant of Devon. The fact is that the Tamar, once one of the best known salmon rivers in England, has been having a lean period. 'The last good year was 1957,' he said. 'We have good hatcheries [these and Fishery Cottage had been bought by the Water Authority] and there is no pollution. I don't know what the trouble is at all.' If the season which begins in less than a fortnight does turn out to be bad no one will be more disappointed than Lady Trenchard. 'One of the best rods,' Sir George assured me.

Things improved as I'll be telling you, but I want to put in here a wee grumble. When the sale of Milton Abbot and all the remaining bits and pieces of the Tavistock Estate came up in 1962, my new house at 18 The Parade was included. It was described in the particulars and plans as a house 'in a block with Nos.19 and 20, each containing living-room, sitting-room, scullery, WC, fuel storage, larder, and three bedrooms, bathroom over, mains, electric light and drainage and piped water, let to Mr H. Adams from the 29.1.62 on a weekly tenancy at £65 per annum. Rateable Value £22.' (Mr Finnie banged on the rent for the purpose of the sale. I never actually paid it.) Well, the starting price was £500 and the Syndicate got the house — they also bought some others — for £750. So I could have bought it — £750 would have been easy to get from the bank. Lord Ampthill, one of the Bedford Trustees, said to me, 'I can't understand why you didn't go to the sale.' I said, 'Because me and some other sitting tenants like Mr Percy were put off by Mr Finnie, your local agent! He said we wouldn't have a chance of buying as we lived in blocks and we'd have to buy the whole block. I'm one of a block of three and Mr Percy's one of a block of six!'

In fact, the houses were sold individually so several workers or ex-workers for the Bedfords could have bought their own properties. We were only told that after the sale. It's like shutting the gate after the horse have bolted. Perhaps I shouldn't have told you this. A man is like a fish: once he opens his mouth he's in trouble. And when I say the bank would have willingly lent me money, I could be wrong. My take-home pay from the Syndicate was only £9.11s.11d. at the start and ten years later it was only £13.5s.4d. But don't forget they charged me no rent and rates, and wealth is wonderful but health is even more wonderful. I've had health but no wealth, and now I don't want the wealth because I shan't have the health to spend the wealth.

Eight

The Syndicate employed me from January the 1st, 1962, to take charge of the river, and I'd Bert Moore (he didn't retire until about '74) to help me trim the banks and get ready generally for the beginning of the season. The Trustees had made Endsleigh tick and I was a little bit frustrated. I was still unbalanced by the sale, I didn't know what the future held and I was starting life all over again. If it's just your wife you can pick your cases up, but with an extra mouth to feed you'm scared stiff. Let's face it, everybody's human. I knew most of the Syndicate already but it's different altogether people here fishing under someone else's roof than when they become bosses: they might change overnight. In fact, they've turned out to be a really first-class bunch. On the practical side, they immediately fixed me up with a telephone, and, as I think I've said already, I was given a motorbike in '63 and then a Land Rover in '68.

Sir George Hayter-Hames, the Chairman, was a type of person who put you at ease socially. When I first met him in 1960 I was sat in the back of his car and he said to me, 'How long have you been married then, Horace?' He called me Horace right away. I said, 'Eighteen years and I've got a daughter five and a half.' 'By God,' he said, 'you've wasted a lot of time!' I said, 'Have you got a family?' and he looked to his wife who he married late in life and was much younger than him and he said, 'Good gracious, yes! We've got three daughters, haven't we, Ann?!'

Early February, Sir George rang me up. It was a Sunday and I wasn't feeling very well as I'd just had a bilious attack, and he asked me to come down to Dairy Dell Cottage. You've to cross a stream to approach Dairy Dell Cottage, the stream that runs into the pond, and right up to this period there was only a narrow wooden footbridge over so, when staff moved out, they'd to carry the furniture across because no transportation, not even a horse and cart, could get there unless they came up

158

through a field. Sir George thought it would be a good idea if Moore and myself built a concrete bridge to take cars — the cottage was eventually let to holiday-makers, though it's just been sold to the Landmark Trust. (Swiss Cottage was sold to them long ago by the Tuckett Trust after standing in ruins for years.) I said, 'What do Moore and myself know about building a bridge?!' He said, 'You've just got to shutter it off and put a base on and lay in some ironwork and pour in concrete. I'll leave it to you. You order the concrete and try to do your best.' So Bert and myself laid old pieces of staging, three, four inches thick, across and built up the sides and put in bits of wire netting and bedrails. We'd got the bedrails because another of our jobs for Sir George was to chuck out unwanted furniture. The amount we burned, thinking it was rubbish! — dressing-tables, chests of drawers, chairs, things that'd be valuable today. Then it was only in the way, wasn't it? If only you could look to the future. Now you go to a sale and the sort of stuff that we smashed up and put on the bonfire is making pounds and pounds. One didn't *value* things then, you see. At home we threw out letters from His Grace about his sick budgerigars, yet the wife's kept all our love letters from when we were courting which *is* rubbish...

Any rate, we sweated buckets building this bridge, and the concrete arrived in one of those revolving concrete lorries and we had it pumped in while we added this and that. The result was very amateurish and makeshift but we stuck a stone in the side engraved '1962 AM' which people probably thought meant 'before lunch' and not 'Adams and Moore'. Sir George came down to have a look and he said, 'That's a damn good job you've done, boys! I wonder if you could now patch up the walls of Dairy Dell Cottage.'

So I'm not a riverkeeper for the moment, I'm Jack of all trades with a trowel in one hand, a paintbrush in the other and a damn sweeping brush somewhere else. But all our decorating was labour in vain. Electrical people came in and drilled holes in the ceiling. Bert and me came in one morning and heard gushing water. First we thought it was from the back of us, from the stream going into the pond. But what had happened was the toilet went to overflow and the overflow pipe out into the garden got blocked by a spider's web and the water was running down through all the electricians' holes. It was one hell of a mess. Water was running down the walls. One ceiling had collapsed. They had to have proper tradesmen in — and all because of a spider.

Well, what with this sort of thing and the poor season the previous year and no fish caught in March, Sir George was panic-stricken and wondering if the Syndicate had spent their money wisely. He said to me, 'You know,' he said, 'I'm not sure if our club have really done the right thing.' I said, 'In the Dukes' days the river wasn't overfished. But salmon fishing's a gamble anyway. *Life*'s a gamble.' I remember going home to the wife and saying, 'Sir George is beginning to have second thoughts. With this crowd is my job secure? Under the Grandfather Duke and my Duke I knew my bread was buttered provided I kept my nose clean.'

Luckily, April was pretty good. The first fish was seven and a half pound and it was caught by Mr Critchley, not a member, right down below Endsleigh House at Black Rock. The second fish was a nine to ten pounder. That was caught by Dr Egbert Barnes at Underhill, my second favourite pool (my favourite is Leigh Wood Croys). The river was quite coloured so he used a 5/0 Yellow Torrish. The third fish was also caught at Underhill — twelve pound, by Mr William Tuckett.

Catching the fourth fish — on the 2nd of May — was a hell of an experience. We'd a dear old boy here from Somerset called Dr Bain. He was over eighty and no longer practising and he'd just met with an accident — his car had been turned over and he was badly bruised. I'd met him once before, and he was game, you see: he came back here fishing, really bruised. I told him that if I could get him down the bank and down the steps at Woodtown Croy I'd take him out in the boat there. He said, 'Good boy! But', he said, 'I'm so stiff, mind, I can't move hardly. I'm not sure if I can cast a fly.' So I rode up to Woodtown Croy in his Humber Snipe with him and his wife, also very old, and his housekeeper, about forty. Some people call them a companion but I call them housekeeper. She did all the chores for him, looked after him as though it was her father. He was stubborn, but at the same time he was a marvellous gentleman, and he knew a lot about flies — he told me that in his younger days a Silver Wilkinson was called a Lilac Rose. His wife was very frail and a tiny little person so the housekeeper helped him down the steps below the croy. I got him in the boat after a struggle — he was so taut and sore because of his bruises that he couldn't twist and turn. But you can sit down in the boat and fish with ease providing you can cast. The boatman is doing the fishing in as much as he's making the fly swing around.

He started off and he said, 'You know, I don't know if I'm going to be able to carry on.' I said, 'Well, yes, but it was a struggle to get you in the boat so you must make the effort!' He was casting all right. Mind you, he was an old-timer, he'd fished from childhood. It's like driving a car or riding a push-bike — whatever you've done in life, as soon as you do it again it comes naturally, and within ten minutes, at exactly eleven o'clock, he was into a heavy fish. There was pandemonium. He knew how to play the fish, although you could see this was hurting him, and he wasn't going to give up now, so I'd to keep swinging the boat around to follow it. There was quite a stream coming through the croy so the boat took a little bit of handling. The old boy was sat just like he was in a vice and I was playing the fish with the boat. I shouldn't have *had* him in a boat but I did it to get him *out* of hisself. Well, we played this fish and played it and played it, and it was now coming on quarter to twelve so we'd been playing it for three quarters of an hour. Then all of a sudden the fish went across the stream behind a rock. Now I'm stuck, so I said to Dr Bain, 'Drop your rod and think nothing more of the fish. I'll have to try to get us across the stream somehow.'

So I got the boat over, and one of two boys that was working in Lord Bradford's Tavistock Woodlands crept down the bank and held it, and I took the rod from Dr Bain and stood up in the boat and played the fish myself because we were wrapped around this rock. And I got the fish free. You mustn't panic. You must forget how difficult it is to do. You must forget that if anything goes wrong it's always your fault although you're working like a bloody Trojan. I suppose the two women on the other bank didn't know if the old boy was ever coming out of the river again. Any rate, the fish was downstream and I'd got it under control so I said to the boy that was holding the boat, 'I must get the boat across again. There's too many bushes hanging over and too many snags on the Cornwall side. We'll never land the fish here.' I said to Dr Bain, 'Take the rod and keep in contact, keep a taut line!'

We got back into the slack water. The fish was sat in the stream: being a big fish, he'd gone to the bottom of the river and he was staying there. The old boy can't stand up because if he stands up he's going to be in the river and then he's sunk because I can't swim and if I'm saying it's pandemonium now, well that *would* be pandemonium. I said, 'Hand me the rod! It's a flat-bottomed boat so it will sit on the pool in this slack

161

water,' and eventually I moved the fish by 'pumping' it, that's getting it on so short a line as you can and keeping raising the rod so that you'm putting a bit of pressure on. As soon as the fish moved, I said, 'There! Take the rod!' He said, 'Yes, but I'm exhausted!' It was now a quarter past twelve so we'd been playing the fish for an hour and a quarter. It could even be foul-hooked although I didn't think so because it was doing a *little* bit of what it was told. Then I spotted it was a much bigger fish than I thought at first. I guessed it at fifteen pound before. I said, 'It's in the twenty pound mark. We've got to keep at it, we've got to have patience. I'll try to get the boat back to the bank and I'll get your housekeeper to hold the chain.' Which I did. But then the damn fish started to go round and around the pool and jumped. He said, 'My God! It's a bloody whale!'

So the fish now is over into the stream again. I said to the lady, 'Give me the chain!' and she threw the chain back into the boat and we went out again. Stupid of me, perhaps, although he was really enjoying of it. But was it all going to be too much for him? You hear of people playing a fish and dropping dead, and I didn't want that to happen. These things were flashing through my mind.

At a quarter past one I said, 'Come on! Put a bit of pressure on!' and I rowed back to the bank. The housekeeper held the chain again and I said to the gent, 'Hang on because I'm going to stand in the boat with the net… Now reel!' The fish was coming on to the surface and it swam near the boat and it was in the net first time. It was in the bottom of the boat behind Dr Bain and he couldn't turn around to see what it was like when I took it out of the net and cracked it across the head. I said, 'By God, this is quite a weight, sir! Sit tight while I carry it up the bank!' He said, 'Don't leave me!' But, when the housekeeper had tied the boat to the stake, we took everything out except the old boy. I weighed the fish. I said, 'It's nineteen and a half pound!' and I went down to Dr Bain and shook hands with him. He said, 'I'm dead, boy! Bloody dead I am! I can't move!'

The housekeeper came down with his wading stick to help me get him out of the boat. She held the boat to try to keep it from rocking — I didn't want the old boy to fall overboard after the event. But to get him off the seat, well I wanted a crane almost because he was a big gentleman and he'd been sat there for two and a half hours. To get his leg over I'd to turn the boat around. Then I got out onto the bank again and, with the housekeeper holding the boat and me holding the boat, I said, 'Put your hand on my shoulder!' and, instead, he caught hold of my shirt and I wasn't sure if I was going to fall into the river. Though his wading stick was a third leg, he'd no sprawl, he could hardly move even yet. Any rate, we got him out of the boat on the ledge between the river and the bank, just on the bottom of the steps, and I said to the housekeeper, 'You get hold of one arm and I'll get hold of the other,' and we got him, quite exhausted, up to the car, and after we got him up, Mrs Bain, the dear old lady, she gave him a kiss and so did the housekeeper, and I shook hands with him again. He was all shaky but he didn't want to sit in the car, he said, 'Let me lean up against it.' Then Mrs Bain said, 'Out with the bottle!' and we all clinked glasses and had a stiff whisky.

We were over two mile away from the house and they were supposed to be back for lunch at one. I said to Dr Bain, 'Well, come on then! We've got to get you in the car. I'll put the fish in the bass and in the boot. It's gone half past one and I shall get grumbles that end.' He said, 'Bugger my lunch!' I said, 'Yes, but that isn't the thing. The ladies want theirs.' The housekeeper had to drive. When we got back it was almost two o'clock. Well, we got out of the car and I went in with the fish so proud as Punch. This was the fourth fish that had been caught in the Syndicate days and it was nineteen and a half pound! But I was met with contempt. Mrs Young, the Manageress, said, 'Where have you been?! Dr and Mrs Bain and the companion haven't been in to lunch yet!' I said, 'They've just gone in.' She said, 'See what time it is! It's nearly two o'clock and my staff is still here!' I said, 'Yes, but now wait a minute, madam. Don't you speak to me like that! I've been out on the river working bloody hard all morning and we've had a bit of fun and I'm not letting you spoil it, Manageress or no Manageress! Let's face it, the Syndicate's only a couple of months old yet, so we don't want to start this way. Otherwise the Manageress and the riverkeeper is going to be crossed swords right through!' She flinked away. It really put paid to me again. I thought, 'Is it going to be worth it?' But next morning everything was honey. If a person fall out with me today, I'm not crossed swords with them tomorrow. You've got to go out and forget all about it. I brought the fish into the fish larder and put it on to the slab — no deep freezers till the late Sixties, don't forget. And that's the end of the story,

163

barring I had instructions that the Bains would like to send the fish away to have it smoked, so I had to pack it ready to be sent to Totnes by bus.

That season, the first season of the Syndicate, there was just sixty-five fish caught on the Endsleigh water — the average is now running at 250 — so it was a bad season on the whole. Although two rods were still allowed on the Gunnislake water where Herbie Symons was, fish caught there counted as Mr Walton's. At the end of the season, Sir George reminded me what he was talking about at the beginning — 'Was it a mistake?' — and he was now making me frustrated again. I reminded *him* that there was only forty-four caught the year previous so we were twenty-one fish up. 'And', I said, 'you can't always go by numbers because you've got to have the right conditions.'

The next year, which was successful — we had 230 fish — Dr Bain was back. The big fish he'd caught with me did him more good than medicine: it brought him to life again. But he'd have been drowned if he'd fallen out of the boat — in places the water was ten feet. Your bible, the Rules and Regulations, say that if a person fall in you must let them get out theirself. It's bad enough to have one drowned; you don't want to drown two. And if they'm playing a fish it's your job to get the fish, never mind about the person. I've had many a person with high blood pressure and angina and whatnot say, 'Quick, Adams, take the rod! I'm going to die!' and I've said, 'No! Hang on to it yourself! Playing a fish is a glorious death!' ... Any rate, Dr Bain came here again in '63 and he was much improving and, on Mrs Bain's birthday, Mr Critchley said to her at the dining-room table, 'What's the old boy going to give you for a present? Another diamond ring?' She said, 'I don't want no more diamond rings! What I want is the doctor to catch another fish!' And, sure enough, from Dunterue Stage that morning, he caught an eight pound fish while the housekeeper held the tail of his jacket. When I arrived on my motorbike, a little AJS, Mrs Bain was rocking of the fish in her arms as if it was a baby.

Dr and Mrs Bain never came to Endsleigh from then on. They were getting so old. You see, this is another part of your job. You become acquainted with people, and you become very intimate with them although you're in a different walk of life, and then you pick up a paper or you hear over the grapevine that they've left this world for ever. It's happening all the time and it unbalances me. You lose a friend and you shed a tear. The brother of Sir Leslie, dear old Sir Kenneth Peppiatt, he died last year at ninety. I shed a tear for *him*. I liked him because he was a jovial sort of person. He was very, very fond of cricket and, though he hated Jeff Boycott, my favourite cricketer, he gave me a copy of his book. Sir Kenneth's son, Mr Brian, and his daughter-in-law, have four children — Quinton, Giles and two daughters. Sir Kenneth and his wife, Lady Pamela, were here with all the family last year at Easter time when there was the usual Easter Egg Hunt. At lunch-time, Lady Pamela and Mrs Brian Peppiatt hid away about twenty eggs in the bracken. I'm a child with the grandchildren and we've got to find the eggs. Each Easter egg we find, up to four, we're allowed to keep.

Of course Lord Boyd's death, also last year, upset me *terrible*. The Duke and Duchess of Cornwall came to Tavistock on the 9th of March. Charles was presenting a Royal Charter at the Town Hall to the new borough of West Devon, and Diana was visiting an under-five playgroup. My daughter, Jill, got time off from the office to see Diana, this new bride, this girl that's become so popular, and the wife wanted to see her too, so I just took the day off though there were guests in the house and it was a thing I shouldn't do. I stood on the churchyard wall and the wife was on the edge of the pavement, hoping to shake hands with the Duchess. The Duchess shook hands with the person next to the wife and the wife held out *her* hand and, as she held out her hand, so the Duchess waltzed around, went to the other side of the road and shook hands with half a dozen there and then came back further down. It was a long shot, but I got a picture of her going into the Bedford Hotel to have a tidy up and go to the loo. The loo had been really dished up, but I'm not sure if she used it.

There's a midday edition of the *Evening Herald* which is no more 'evening' than I am — well, I'm now in the evening of my life so I suppose I *am* evening. Any rate, at one, quarter past one, I spotted somebody reading the *Evening Herald* which showed a photo of Diana with a lot of children. So I dashed to get a copy as I thought it would involve today in Tavistock, though I couldn't at the same time understand how the photo was so quick. It turned out the photo was taken at Bovey Tracey earlier in the day. But, with it, there was a picture of Lord Boyd and the

165

words 'Killed last night'. The news had been broadcast on the wireless and I hadn't picked it up. Thank God I *hadn't*, because probably I wouldn't have went to Tavistock, it would have knocked me over.

So there I was enjoying myself, taking photos of Diana, really enjoying of it, when I should have been sad because one of the most important members of the Syndicate had been killed by a car in London as he was crossing a road with Lord Moyne to look at an antique shop. I was choked, I don't mind admitting it: I was really choked and the rest of my day was spoiled. And Jill was upset because Lord Boyd had been so very, very good to her. The wife said, 'What are we going to do now?' and our first reaction was we went straight into a card shop and bought a memorial card so we could send it to Lady Boyd...

More about 1963.

Firstly, there was a Mr and Mrs Carr appointed as Manager and Manageress in place of Mr and Mrs Young. Secondly, early in January, it turned very, very cold. The old saying is, 'As the days lengthen, so the cold strengthen' and, sure enough, the cold *was* strengthening and by the 13th of January the river was in parts froze solid. Now, never in my life had I seen the river frozen, not even when I was a kid. On January the 14th, Bert Moore and myself walked across at Hardstone on the ice, and the width of the river there was round a hundred feet. We did it again on the 23rd. On the 26th, a Saturday, the day before her eighth birthday, we walked Jill across Carthamartha. Carthamartha in they days was fourteen, fifteen feet deep so it was pretty dangerous. I left Bert and Jill out in the middle of the river and I took a photograph of them which I eventually showed to the wife. She probably regretted ever meeting me. She thought I was insane to run such a risk with our eight-year-old daughter after we'd waited for her for thirteen years.

We decided, the Monday, to go up with mattocks and try to break some of the ice on Hardstone near the bank. The ice was seven to nine inches thick — unbelievable but perfectly true. We broke this ice and I brought home a piece and I put it outside of our front door and it stayed there solid, it didn't really go to water, until well into March. The ice on the river started to break up in places on that same Monday. From Parson's Pool to Hardstone, which is three and a half to four miles, it was one of the most wonderful sights you could ever see, with ice breaking away and washing downstream and congregating and building up like little mountains. A lot of trees — oak, beech, sycamore — were either killed or damaged very badly; melting snow was putting pressure on the ice and great lumps of ten, twelve feet thick floated down making a noise worse than thunder, cracking and crashing, and striking the trees and barking them. In places, the ice even cut the banks. In the Grandfather Duke's days, if the banks were slipping and they hadn't got the labour or the time to build them up with stone, they would plant little willow bushes. All people, this day and age, think about is having more people fishing so they'm trimming the banks, trimming the banks and they're just slipping away for ever. By 'trimming' I mean cutting the bracken and the brambles. Wesley Lee was down river trimming with the mechanical trimmer on Friday [August 3, 1984] and it cut a viper in portions of about two, three inches; he said every bit was wriggling. Immediately after, he went through a wasps' nest…

1963 was also the first of thirteen consecutive years when Sir Philip du Cros invited me to stay with him for three or four days in March at his home near Parkham in North Devon. The Taw and the Torridge, especially the Torridge, were classed in they days as earlier rivers than the Tamar, so we did the Torridge together — and on occasions we went over to the Taw with some of his acquaintances by invitation. The house would open up here on the last Thursday of March and I'd be up there round about the 12th on a busman's holiday. I used to love it because he had a beautiful garden with a couple of gardeners and I'd get up early in the morning and walk around the lawns and out through the woods and then come back for a hell of a breakfast with all his family. The wife didn't come — she's not interested in fishing, the farther she can get away from it the better. And Jill's the same. If I start talking about fishing, she slams the door in my face. She says, 'It's fish, fish, fish!' The dear old gent died after I went to stay with him in '76 and that was the end of that.

In May — also '63 — the present Mr Tuckett's sister had a birthday party at Endsleigh. A large marquee was put up on the lawn. There was a hundred and eight cars, and Bert and myself packed them all in around the house and on the drive. Mr Tuckett Senior was stood at the entrance hall and he'd given us instructions that no cars was allowed to go down

Ham Hill to the river. When he saw a car go down there with a young gentleman driving, he said, 'Where's he gone?!' I said, 'Down in the Ham to turn.' He said, 'Didn't you try to stop him?!' I said, 'Yes, but he took no notice of me.' He said, 'Right! I'll have him when he comes up,' and, when he comes up, he said he wasn't needed to the party, he could go home, and he sent him up the road. Mr Tuckett was that strict.

Four days before his son, Philip, the present Mr Tuckett's, twenty-first birthday party in October '65 at Tavistock Town Hall, Bert and myself were bringing the boats all down to Endsleigh Ham where we could pull them out dead easy to store them for the winter. It was a fair-sized river and I was bringing the Inny Croy boat down from Inny Croy and, as I came through Parson's Pool, I hit a rock and the boat turned over. My waders was full of water and the skin broke just behind my big toe. This was on the Friday and I went to the party on the Tuesday with a new pair of shoes on and that didn't help. On the following Friday I was in hospital for sixteen days and they thought at one period I'd have to have my left foot off. Poison. I picked the poison up through the dirty water that had been in my boot.

Later this year there's going to be three hundred people coming here for Mrs Philip Tuckett's birthday. Derek Bradbury, the Manager, is letting all the cars park in Endsleigh Ham. The only way to stop a traffic jam is to let the cars down in batches. He and Wesley have a walkie-talkie now, so there'll be one at the house with a walkie-talkie and Wesley will be down in the Ham with a walkie-talkie. I've warned Wesley about the mud if they'm parked in the field and it's a wet evening. And, as Wesley's said, 'What about them stepping in the cow dabs?' You see, this is where it all breaks down. I call it a bloody good giggle. No organization.

Derek wants *me* to have a walkie-talkie, but the phone is bad enough. Say I was up at Greystone Bridge, they'd call me back to Endsleigh — I'd be up and down like a bloody yo-yo. At night, I suppose, it would be a protection against poachers, but during the day it'd become a gimmick; if anybody wanted Adams they'd get on to the walkie-talkie, probably to ask me to come and have a cup of coffee.

From 1963 on, the Syndicate have held a dinner after the Annual General Meeting on the last Saturday of the season. In '64, because they

Horace with Lady Trenchard and her son, Henry, aged thirteen, holding his first salmon, 11 lb. (hers was $17\frac{1}{2}$ lb.), 6.4.78

Major Dore, aged eighty-nine, fishing from Joel's Corner croy, assisted by his wife

Horace rowing the Harris twins, 1978

Horace preparing to trim the river bank, 1978

The only catch of the morning. l. to r. Mr Peter Medd, Mrs Heather Bell, Mr Peter Bell, Mrs Julia Medd (with grilse), Mrs Sybella Medd, Lady Pamela Peppiatt, Sir Kenneth Peppiatt and Dr William Medd, 1979

Wedding reception at Endsleigh, 26.9.81. Jill and her husband, Mr Rodney
Hill, stand in front of her father's portrait

Horace at Weir Pool, 28.6.86

Horace at Leigh Wood Croy, 2.7.86

said I was such a good old yapper, they invited me to make a speech, and I've made one every year since. To begin with, these dinners were on a very small scale in the dining-room. Now so many people attend they've got to lock the outside door and eat in the hall with a top table and two long legs which can sit up to about forty-two. The wives is allowed and, if the wifie don't come, they can invite a friend. They have a good old tuck-in with plenty of drink.

I'm asked to join them at table after dinner when the coffee's being brought. At first I was invited to the dinner, but they'm like the 12th Duke: when you refuse they don't ask you again — I don't want to go anyhow. You're outside, all tensed up, waiting for the cue. It's like going on stage. When you walk in, you can hardly identify anyone for a pall of smoke, and they'm all talking across one another. There's a seat for me beside a lady and they ask me what I want and I'll have a double whisky. I've had two or three doubles beforehand because, it's all very fine, it's like leading Daniel into the lion's den, isn't it? And *they*'m all half cut, they've been drinking all evening. Then odd people that's nominated make speeches and then the Chairman makes a speech and then, after praising me or running me down, he says, 'And now I ask you all to stand and toast Horace Adams!' 'Horace Adams!' — the glasses clink, and I reply to the Chairman, wind up, while people take the mickey. The lady I'm beside usually pinches my bottom or tries to take my notes. It's fun, you see. But there's a serious side to it, and I enlarge on the number of fish that's been caught or I say, 'Well, it's been one of those years. My opposite number downstream have knocked me for a six,' and I tell them about the lack of water and whatnot and whatnot. Then we all adjourn to the lounges and I'm toasted again and kissed by the ladies and I get a bit sozzled. When I arrive on Sunday morning, I'm asked, 'How's your head?'

The gentlemen's dressed in dinner jacket and the ladies in their nice evening dresses. Adams is in his best sports trousers and a velvet jacket. Once upon a time I used to wear my suit but I can't get into it any more and I can't afford to buy another: I'm not in this world for all that long so a new suit would probably be money down the drain. Jill now types out my speeches and makes them a bit posh — you know, she'd change, 'The old Atlantic salmon is taking a hell of a pounding,' to 'The Atlantic salmon is taking a terrible pounding.' Despite the interruptions and distractions, I always try to be short, sharp and to the point, and I've very often got a torch with me because the lighting system's so bad. All good speechmakers, even Maggie, even the Queen when she's making her Christmas Broadcast, they have it there in front of them; if it isn't on a piece of paper there's a tele-prompter going down: even *they* can't do the whole thing otherwise.

For my first speech I was sat between Mr Tuckett Senior, Mr William Tuckett, who was acting as the Chairman for the evening, and Lady Boyd. I was like a little boy: I was scared stiff; I didn't know *what* to say. They poured me out a drink — probably it was a beer then. Mr Tuckett got up and said, 'You know, Adams, who's amongst us this evening, is like my gamekeeper. He's not a five o'clock man...' Sir Kenneth Peppiatt called out, 'No, four o'clock probably!' Now, Mr Tuckett was very serious about things, very domineering, very thorough, and you knew where you were with him, he put his cards on the table and you could play him. If he put the Queen down and you had the King you could beat him, but if you hadn't for the King you'd betterway keep your mouth shut. It was always stated that when he went around to the River Authority you could hear a pin drop if he was speaking because he'd quickly tell people to leave the room otherwise. And, when Sir Kenneth interrupted, he said to him point blank, 'Who's making this speech?!' and, at the same time forgetting I'm sat next to Her Ladyship, *I* said, 'Well, *that*'s a damn good thing to say!' and Sir Kenneth, who'd only done it for fun, wriggled himself up and almost went in under the tablecloth. So Mr Tuckett went on, he said, 'We're all new. Adams have had experience of the river, knows quite a bit about the fishing, and I'm sure he'll help everyone. If there's any member of our Syndicate that's not up to scratch, Adams will put him right. He's a good bloke...' He praised me so much I felt embarrassed.

Then *I* got up. I was terrified. I didn't say very much, just, 'Mr Tuckett, Ladies and Gentlemen, thank you for your invitation to join you all for a drink. But asking for to have a drink is one thing and to give a speech is totally another. So many of you is prominent speechmakers here this evening, one wonders how to start. If any one of you watched BBC a few weeks ago you'd have seen a well-known Endsleigh fisherman.' I mentioned that Sir Kenneth had been filmed making a speech in a special programme called *Speech Making*. '...So you see what I'm up against!' And then I went on and I said, 'We've lost quite a few fish this year through inexperience and carelessness and broken casts and people not doing what they were told, and some of your faces are new to me and I'm still concerned about my job, so it's been a year of ups and downs. All I can do is thank Mr Tuckett for his kind remarks, and I'm delighted, I suppose, in a way, to be allowed to run around the river bank and assist you. I hope that I shall be with you for years and years to come.' I was very, very nervous and it was a rotten speech.

If I can come forward to a speech I made during Mrs Thatcher's first term of office. I said, 'Well, thank you very much, Mr Chairman, for your kind remarks. To me, the autumn, the end of the season, is always a little sad because for most salmon it's the end of life. But they spawn so it's also the beginning of life, and new fish will have the same taking mood as they've had for centuries. We all know that the salmon is as fickle as a woman, that salmon fishing is a gamble. But what other sport can give hours of undisturbed pleasure? Drainage is so good now that rain produces an extremely rapid rise and an equally rapid fall and the water level for fishing is only held for a very short period. Yet in spite of this everyone seems to enjoy themselves. After all, fish or no fish, one must not get downhearted. All of us must be thankful for the opportunity to be able to fish this beautiful river of ours. We're living in an age when all around us is turmoil. The papers are full of sad news. Strikes everywhere. Unions demanding more money where there isn't any. Margaret Thatcher being accused of union bashing. Maybe it's not really for me to say, but the unions need some bashing... In my speech last year I indicated that we had turned the corner as far as fish was coming into the river. I still believe that your river is far from dead. It is, though, being put at risk by those who regard it as a convenient drain or a dump for refuse and wastage connected with modern manufacture. It's true that Industry is essential to the life of the nation, but it must not be allowed to destroy our rivers. We only have to look at a case not long ago: eight hundred fish killed by poison from a factory — the fine, £500. A poacher killing one wee trout? The fine, £470. Although we must clobber the poacher, we should get our priorities right. Industrial poison is not affecting our river at the moment but it could be in time. Now, in conclusion, a story, which is a true story, of a lady fishing with me. She asked me, "Adams, what's the best piece of advice you can give me about salmon fishing?"

171

I thought for a moment, then I said, "Well, madam, find a river with water in it, water with fish in it, water with many fish in it, water with many hungry fish in it and water with many stupid hungry fish in it! Then, madam, you *and* I might have a little bit of luck!" '

You can see how I'm more confident than when I first started. My twenty-odd bosses, they're butting in all the time and I get a little confused. But I'm pretty rude to them and they have a laugh. Someone will say, 'I didn't hear that!' and I'll say, 'Well you should have been listening!' When it's time to sit down, *that*'s when you should be standing up because fear's gone out the window and you don't give a damn for anybody. Major Russell Dore is our oldest member — he's coming ninety-four, a little tiny wizened man, half blind, and I'm sorry to say he now fishes from one of those folding chairs. In 1979 I crossed him in the boat and helped him catch a ten-pounder at Parson's. I brought the story up in my speech that year, and everyone kept clapping him all through. He always calls me 'Professor'. At the finish he got up to the table and said, 'Well, my friends,' he said, 'the Professor was with me so I couldn't go wrong. Thank you very much, Professor.'

Nine

My speech, typed by Jill, two year ago was about poaching. I said, 'There's been a lot of talk why salmon are getting fewer every year. We all blame illegal fishing off the west coast of Ireland and Greenland, but what about the illegal netting off our own shores and estuaries? Oh yes, it's right on our very doorstep! A lady staying in this house decided to take a trip down to the public nets at Cotehele and she bought a seventeen pound salmon for £17. In 1982, I ask you! £1 per pound when in the shops it was almost £4 per pound! That fish was poached, make no mistake about it! But how was she to know? How true when the restaurant menus read: "Poached Tamar Salmon"! And, fish or no fish in the estuary, a suspicious character was spotted about 4.00 a.m. a couple of months ago on the *river*, just above Gunnislake Weir, and, when the police were called and dogs brought in, they found twelve salmon and three sea trout though no angler was having sport! There are so many gangs of poachers these days that the bailiffs are hard pressed. The papers say poaching is big business. The South West Water Authority shouts, "War on poachers!" but, when the bailiffs have a bit of luck bringing a poacher to court, what does the law do? A fine of £5, £100, £500! Well, he's just laughing! On a good night's poaching a gang can make £1,000. 283 nets were found in the West Country in the last twelve months. I do really believe one's got to do something about this. In Canada, as I understand it, a fisherman, if he wants to sell a fish, must tag on where that fish was caught and the date, or the fish can't be disposed of. Well, why don't they tag fish here?! It's still being debated apparently in Parliament and Roy Mason is saying it's about time the salmon poacher is hooked by confiscating his car and £1,000 fines or imprisonment. Here's as ex-minister for the Labour Party shouting the odds! But, like they all do, he's doing it when he's in opposition...'

In years gone by, before the days of the River Authority, there wasn't any poaching as such: the poacher was out after 'one for the pot', he might even spear it on the spawning grounds right up in the shallows. I remember before the war a bailiff called Tommy Landry was tipped off that a gentleman had been fishing a certain stretch down near the estuary on a Thursday afternoon which was half-day from his business. So this bailiff kept an eye on the river and, sure enough, there he was in the middle of the river, trying to gaff a fish. He failed and, when he came to the bank, the bailiff sprung on him, he said, 'Excuse me, sir, but', he said, 'I've had you under observation for the last half hour and you were trying to gaff a fish.' He said, 'I wasn't trying to gaff a fish!' He said, 'Well. what have you got the gaff for?! I *seen* you trying to gaff a fish!' He said, 'Do you know who I am? I'm the Mayor of So and So!' He said, 'Well, I'm sorry, sir. It doesn't matter to me whether you're the Mayor or the Queen of England because I were watching you and you were trying to poach a fish, so therefore I'm bound to ask you for your name and address and report it.' The Mayor said, 'Here you are. Have a drink,' and he took some money out and offered it him. The bailiff said to him, he said, 'It's bad enough you trying to gaff a fish but this is what we call corruption, you're trying to bribe me now and that's worse than ever, so I'll just take your name and address! ...' He was the *Mayor* of a certain town! So it wasn't just the down and out; this was one the down and out or the working person would look up to and trust and take advice and guidance from!

The situation really began to deteriorate in the mid-Fifties — you couldn't just sit on the bank and exchange stories and laugh. Two gentlemen, Mr Bennet and Mr Salkelk, were driving down to Weir Pool from Endsleigh when they met a bloke with a small sea trout net. They said, 'What's on, then?' He said he was trying to catch butterflies. They thought, 'Well, that's far-fetched,' and then further down they spotted two queer blokes and a net across the river. In broad daylight! From then on so many as fourteen of us bailiffs and ghillies from the riparian owners upstream would go down there by night and watch.

Sir Philip du Cros was fishing here one day at Lowley Run and a gent came walking down and said to him, 'Oh, I'm sorry,' he said, 'I seem to be on the wrong beat.' So Sir Philip said, 'Yes, this is *my* beat.' The gent said, 'I see you're fly fishing.' 'Yes,' said Sir Philip. 'I'm trying to catch a

174

salmon.' The gent said, 'I understood it was spinning for salmon and fly fishing for trout,' so Sir Philip said, 'Well, you've got it all wrong. You fly fish for salmon and you fly fish for trout.' The gent said, 'Well, I'm sorry but', he said, 'I must be poaching. I've fished at Hardstone and I've caught a sizeable fish on a spinner. Would you like to come up and see it?' So Sir Philip reeled in and drove up with him to look at it.

The gent said he was a butcher from Somerset and he was staying in a caravan down at Wadebridge and he'd come up purpose for the day. What had happened was he'd collected a ticket at Launceston which said that he was allowed to fish from Polson Bridge upstream, but when you come out of Launceston you come to a fork road and he should have took the left fork and, instead of that, he took the right, came down to Greystone Bridge, parked his car at the gate, cocked his leg over the gate and walked down and fished when he got to Hardstone Pool. So he produced the fish for Sir Philip, weighed it, and it was sixteen pound. Sir Philip said, 'My God!' he said. 'That's a good fish!' and he allowed him to keep it as he said he'd made a mistake.

Well, I never knew anything about this, and the day rods, if they fish here on a Monday, next week they're fishing on a Tuesday. So, the Monday evening previous to the Tuesday, Sir Philip gave me a ring and he said, 'What's the river like?' and then he told me the story. I said, 'Well what the hell's the good of telling me the story now?! That could have been a proper poacher!' 'Oh,' he said, 'he's no poacher,' he said. 'He's a real gentleman.' I said, 'Yes, but how do you know he's a gentleman?! You can't say he's a gentleman at face value! I'll have to intercede.' So I rung up the River Authority and they said I should check at the shop in Launceston where they sell the licences, so I checked with that and the story was true. But he'd got the salmon under false pretences. What Sir Philip should have done if he didn't want the fish himself, he should have said, 'I'll take it,' and give it to me and then I could have given it to the farmer that owned the Hardstone fields. You've got to follow the rules, otherwise everything breaks down.

Herbie Symons, he's a hell of a good bloke really but he was of a nervous disposition when it came to poachers, especially at night. Of course, you're all brave before the event. But, as daylight's coming in or if it's a moonlight, it's quite creepy and you'm always visualizing shadows and you think 'tis a poacher and probably it's a bullock or a cow. I know Herbie on one particular time — this was getting late in the season because the squirrels were at the nuts and there was a lot of shells in the hedgerows — Herbie whispered, 'Go quietly, quietly!' and then I'd step on some nutshells and they'd crack and make a tremendous noise in the night and echo in the valley and he'd say, 'Watch where you're stepping!' Well, how the hell could you watch where you're stepping?! It's pitch black! Herbie and me had one or two scares together but we were never in on the kill.

Fifteen, sixteen year ago, myself and my namesake Jack Adams, a River Board bailiff, we'd been out on the river all night and I was lying in the bulrushes between Hardstone and Lowley Run and Jack was behind a hedge back in the wood. It was half past five, quarter to six of a mid-June morning and we were both using binoculars. It's beautiful in the summer mornings out like that. It's better than lying on your bed. The birds start to whistle and sing, the sun's coming up and it's lovely to be alive. You know, you feel fresh though you'm starving and you'm longing for that fried breakfast. Trouble is, after you've been home late and ate it, you don't want to get up on your hinder legs and go out again.

Any rate, there I'm lying on my mac in the bulrushes and Jack's behind the hedge and there's all these sheep in the field and if these old sheep see you they'm liable to go maaaah and give the game away. And now the farmer came down on the old tractor. Thank God my position was a bit marshy, though, at one period, he came so close he damn nigh drove over me and I didn't want to show, we were so well covered — he'd have stopped and had a yarn and probably said, 'Seeing you've been out all night, come up and wet your face, bring yourself back to life and have a breakfast.' What he *did* do was go home and ring the wife. She said it was about half past seven the telephone went and he said, 'Is Horace home? I've seen his Land Rover tucked under the bushes up one of my fields but I haven't seen *him* anywhere.' She said, 'Well, he and his pal's somewhere on the river because there's something happening.' But we never seen anybody and we'd been around on the river bank since eleven o'clock and sacrificed a night's sleep.

Occasionally I stay out still, though I've never done it alone. You see, poachers stay till after daylight, knowing that Endsleigh guests aren't

176

likely to arrive to fish till nine o'clock. When you go out now, you hope it's something you can contain and not the dangerous big organized poaching that's going to kill the rivers if something isn't done about it soon. Someone's usually been spotted by a fisherman. It might be just a man poaching with a rod and line or a spinning rod. If you can catch him, you whip his stuff away and say, 'We're going to report you.' If he panics, then you think to yourself, 'Well, this man's not going to do this again,' so you automatically say, 'Look, we'll forget it. But we've been out all night watching for you. Let this be a lesson to you.'

Early one Sunday morning in the Sixties I was walking down river between Hardstone and Lowley Run and I saw people had been pushing down through the bushes on the Cornwall side where none of our rods had been. I rung up Jack and he said he'd come and have a look around. In that day and age the more poachers the River Board bailiffs could catch the better — it gave them a good name. We marked in the area with cotton on sticks. This was on the Monday, and we watched with binoculars and the naked eye till the Saturday and nobody moved. I thought they'd broken in the previous Sunday, so we anticipated they'd do the same again and we decided we'd make a pounce on the Sunday morning. He arrived at my home at quarter past three. Fishermen were snoring away, dreaming, and we were out of bed, starry-eyed. We proceeded in his car the six or eight miles to get to this pinpointed place. To our astonishment there was a car parked where we were going to park in a little lay-by a long way from the river. Jack said, 'We'll have to push our car into a field.' When you put a car into a field you've got to make sure there's no cattle there and that you're going to get away quite easy. Also, the farmer can come along and report a stolen car. Any rate, we parked the car and walked down through Greystone Wood. We were still a long way from the river when we saw through our binoculars two youngsters spinning. This is now about quarter past four, quarter to five, and it's daylight because it's mid-summer, mid-June.

We kept these youngsters under observation for a little while and then my mate said, 'I think we'll pounce.' I said, 'Why not let them go for a little while and if they *do* get a fish we'll pounce as they land it and, then, if they don't throw the fish away, that'll be a fish for one of my farmer tenants easily caught.' At that period I had to catch fourteen, sixteen fish a year for the farmers — each one was given a fish. Now

177

they'm lucky if they get any. Right. We decided to wait, but they didn't catch a fish and then we lost sight of them. There's so many ways for them to get back to their car we've got to retrace our steps and lie in the bushes with the car in full view. We presumed it was the poachers' car. A good way to injure the poacher is to let his tyres down but, after saying that, this wasn't very far away from a farmhouse and the farmer could have had guests staying and it could be their car, so you don't *do* they sort of things though you're tempted, because then *you*'re breaking the law. The law is so funny.

So any rate, here we are: we're lying amongst the bushes with the car in sight so we can pounce on it pretty smart. And we hear voices and then we spot the boys and they can't see us because we're well covered. It's now coming about eight o'clock so we'd been lying around a long, long time. This is where patience comes in. And now they were in full view so we were able to size them up. They were total strangers and they'd taken their rods down, put them in their rod cases and they were carrying of them. Now we've got to make sure that they come right up to us so we can see if they're carrying a salmon. Well, they were carrying nothing but their rods: they'd caught nothing. We let them almost pass us, then we jumped; we said, 'Good-*morning*! Bailiffs!' And they were gone and my pal was gone after them. Jack was about three times my size, a hell of a chap with a hell of a gut on him, but he was well off the mark. I was left trailing; I was shocked with the speed that he got away and the speed that *they* went. Between us and the car was a stile. Well, *I* had to climb gently over the stile.

They'd beat Jack, but they didn't go to the car, you see, they were gone out of sight. Now is the car in the lay-by theirs or who does the car belong to? Jack climbed the hedge on the other side of the road where steep fields run down to the Lowley: he thought they must have jumped it and gone there. But God knows where they went: they'd disappeared. We wandered up the road, still keeping the car in view. Then Jack said to me, he said, 'You sit on the car and I'll go and get *my* car.' Well, probably he was only away five minutes but it felt like an hour. I was a little bit panic-stricken because I'm on my own and it's two blokes and they were quite tall fellows. Jack came back and parked his car and we'd got to sit in it waiting or throw the sponge in. Jack said, 'They may come back to tow their car away, pretending it's broken down.' And, within half an hour, three parts of an hour, the two young men appeared, walking quite naturally and carrying their rods in their cases. They said, 'Good-morning,' you know, as though nothing had happened. We said, 'Good-morning,' and then Jack took over because he's got his warrant with his photograph whereas at this stage I'm only classed as an honorary bailiff so far as arrests is concerned: I *can* arrest a person, but he's paid by the River Authority, he's the boy in charge. He said, 'We're water bailiffs, both of us, and first of all we want to see your licence.' So one produced his licence and the other couldn't, and my mate took out his writing pad and scribbled their names. The one without the licence said, 'I've got a licence at home.' They both lived at Bude in North Cornwall, approximately twenty, twenty-one miles from where we were.

Jack said, 'Well, to start off with, we've had you under observation and you were fishing the Tamar.' They said, 'We weren't!' He said, 'You *were*! Don't come that with me! Now, come on! Be truthful because this is for your benefit! If you want to be fussy and rough, well, you'll find that *we* can be fussy and rough!' — we'd got them sized up by now; we knew they were chicken and we could handle them. So they told us a fairy tale that they'd been to some casting competition in the locality. We weren't concerned about that; we didn't recollect that there'd *been* a casting competition — they always come up with some tuppeny-half-penny tale. We said, 'We presume you've been here before.' 'Never!' they said. We said, 'Well, do you know the reason why we're here? It's because we'd already pinpointed marks last Monday of someone who fished here last Sunday. Now did you come here last Sunday or didn't you?' They said, 'No, we didn't come here.' Then my pal got a little bit hot under the collar so they said, 'Yes, us just want to come clean. We came here, but that honestly was the first time.' Well, God help us, we don't know if they'm telling the truth, because you cannot be watching the full stretch of the river every minute. You've got seven miles of water to watch; you've got to be here, there and everywhere. This was only spinning so it was a minor sort of thing, but it was causing me a lot of trouble, it was causing me a hell of a lot of restless nights: getting up at three in the morning I was missing a little bit of shut-eye.

Any rate, we got down to details. My mate said, 'I want all your tackle. I want everything you've got.' Well, they hadn't got very much in the way of flies, they'd got their spinning reels, their spinning rods

179

and a net. So, all out of the blue, they opened their car door and produced two Thermoses of tea and some sandwiches and turned right around to us and said, 'Would you like a cup of tea?' Well, much as we wanted a cup of tea, we couldn't accept because this could have been a bit of a bribe. We said, 'No. We'll push off now,' and we left them drinking and proceeded to my home where the wife wasn't very long in knocking up a breakfast. We'd got all their tackle so we didn't bother about *them*. One side of the law at that period said you shouldn't take the tackle and another said you could. We kept the tackle.

That morning I had to meet Lord Boyd at Endsleigh at half past ten. He said, 'Horace, my friend, how are you?' I said, 'I don't feel all that good. I've had a night out.' He said, 'What's been on?' so I told him, I said, 'We caught a couple of poachers.' 'Good,' he said. 'Did you pinch their tackle?' I said, 'Yes.' He said, 'Good.' But, that same week, I was in conversation with Sir Leslie Peppiatt, who'd been President of the Law Society, and he said, 'I don't think you've got any right to take their tackle.' I said, 'You, a member of the Syndicate, saying I haven't got the right to take their tackle! I'm out trying to protect your fishing so where do you go from there?!' I said, 'I was talking to a solicitor, Mr Mundy, only yesterday and he said, "You hang on to it!"'

So I hung on to the tackle and, in September, the Chairman, Sir George Hayter-Hames, decided to send these boys a letter saying that if they would promise in writing not to come on to the river again they could come to my house and collect their tackle, which they did before I joined them at the Edgcumbe Arms. In conversation one of them said he'd spent his honeymoon three doors from where we used to stay in Southfields, London. It's unbelievable, isn't it?! I said, 'You ought to have known better than to poach.' He said, 'We were tipped off that there was fish in the river. You just don't think about your wife and the infant baby. If my boss got to know about this I'd probably get the sack.'

You could control that sort of poaching, but it's gangs now. At the start of the Sixties we heard of netting on other rivers, but we didn't think they were raiding the Tamar, though they probably were. There was a breakthrough in the early Sixties. Two of the Bridport Boys, the biggest gang, were in a dinghy under Beam Weir on the Torridge and the dinghy got sucked into the weir and capsized and one of the boys was drowned; he was washed up well downstream at Weal Gifford. Because he'd lost his mate, the other boy reported the matter to the police. They was just two or three in the gang in they days. Now there's thirty of them, real tough boys, well organized, and they don't just do the Torridge and the Tamar and the Tavy and the Dart, they do *all* the rivers even in Scotland and Wales — any river that holds a salmon or a sea trout. They've got it up top: they know exactly where to go. On the Tamar it's the tidal stretch below and above Gunnislake Weir. They were spotted there first in about '63 — through a stroke of luck someone was fishing late at night. A cave was found later full of empty baked bean and milk tins. Usually you get the fish and don't catch any of the gang but, Rodney, my son-in-law — he's a private bailiff like myself — he's only been on the river five years and he's been in at the kill six or seven times because he's right on the vital section. It's dangerous work. We're not allowed to carry anything to protect us, not even a priest, because in court it's classed as an offensive weapon, yet these boys can carry flick-knives they've bought in a fishing shop! How can you control poaching when these things is on the market for sale and we can get stabbed in the back when our wives is home in bed?!

Luckily, Rodney's never been injured, barring a few weeks back when he was punched on the nose at Hawkmoor Weir. It was pitch black on the morning of the 26th [July]. He and Ron Rowledge, the River Board bailiff, were sat waiting to pick up the shock waves. They'd only got Rodney's black labrador with them, though Ron owns a savage Alsatian which'll have your leg off if you move. As they never heard a sound, they risked shining a torch and, almost immediately below them, they saw a net across the river! They gradually creeped upstream, knowing where the poachers would have their next net — when the river's low and there's no flow of water, fish can't run upstream so poachers normally have two or three nets, stone the pool and the fish swim around and get caught in them. Right, they saw another net and they decided to sit it out but, though time passed and the light was creeping in, nobody came. Ron said, 'We've had it,' and, right on the same, they spotted two blokes walking up the far, the Cornwall, bank so, without kicking a stone or disturbing a heron, they got back to their cars and, while Ron contacted the police on his walkie-talkie and directed them where to come in force with their dogs, Rodney went upstream on the Cornwall side and kept the poachers under observation.

One started pulling the net; the other was folding of it. Very professional. Two other fellows were there as well. And Rodney and Ron are together again behind a wall this time with Ron's Alsatian. The police are in the locality and they've encircled the poachers' car. Everything is blocked off. Everyone is out of sight… So Rodney and Ron decided to pounce. They jumped from the wall and grabbed two immediately, and Ron stayed put with these while Rodney chased the other two who'd bolted. One jumped into the river, flinging his arm around and striking Rodney on the nose, making it bleed. But Rodney grabbed him by the scruff of the neck and dragged him out, marched him up to Ron and then went in search of the other. He couldn't find him and went back to his car, and there he was, pale and shaking, leaning up against the car with a hurt back. Soon the police were in and they were all arrested and taken to Launceston Police Station.

There's trouble with poachers practically every day at present on the lower stretch. The week before you came here, the police had a tip-off and came in before the bailiffs at Impham Meadows and found two dinghies, five nets, two pairs of Wellington boots, two Barbour jackets, a pair of trousers, a shirt and two pullovers and twenty salmon from the weight of five to fifteen pound plus seventeen sea trout from the weight of one to eight. Here at the hatchery the River Board's now got an electric warning system because the Bridport Boys will even go into a pond. A gentleman in North Devon had a pond with a lot of big rainbow trout in and, about six year ago, and the Bridport Boys — or they *think* it was the Bridport Boys — went in there one night and had the lot. Then, a year later, someone pulled the sluices of the trout farm over in Tavistock at the back of the Market. They thought they'd catch all the fish as they came out, but something went wrong, the poachers fled. The town owns a stretch of the Tavy and, for a very small fee, the local lads are allowed to fish there. One night a boy caught a three, four pound rainbow trout and, in a matter of a few days, he'd caught eighty, ninety fish. His parents couldn't understand it — the freezer was full up. Come to, the parents got frightened and informed the police because they thought their son must be taking them from a little reservoir. But he was allowed to keep the fish. They'd run down from this trout farm into the Tavy and he'd caught them in good faith.

The hardened poacher's wits is pitched against the bailiff's or the policeman's but often the poacher is the cleverer, and he's got the wide world to disappear in. The thing is to pinpoint the car and sit on it, keep it under observation, cut off the means of escape. You must ask to see their licence which they won't have because they're criminals, but there are so many laws today you've first got to catch them in the act; and you can't even get them for trespass unless you prove criminal damage. Some people say photograph them at work, but again it's a theory that can't be put into practice. How could it be? There you are in the pitch black, creeping in the bushes and there's a poacher a hundred yards down the river and it's raining streams or the bushes are moving and you'm trying to take a photograph and all you've got is a bramble in front of you with two or three blackberries hanging! It's as simple as that.

There *are* machines that the River Authority place in the grass or in the bracken on the river bank and, once you walk past this machine, a bleeper goes in a bailiff's home. But all these things cost money and the Conservative Government's way of saving money is to cut public spending, so you've got to have private money, and the private individual, he wants everything but he isn't so quick to spend.

A way to curtail poaching would be for *all* private bailiffs and *all* riparian owners to co-operate with the police and the River Authority who's only human and who's thin on the ground. There's several bailiffs or ghillies upstream, and they should have to do their turn. Why should we further down have to go to all this expense and go rushing around for the benefit of people that's ten, fifteen, twenty miles up river?! The riparian owners should club together and put some money in the kitty so they can employ people, spend more on protection — it's for their own enjoyment and, in the case of hotels and guest-houses, it's their livinghood as well. Otherwise, I'm afraid, the poacher is going to overrule. And not just the gangs. With so much unemployment, poaching is perks and adventure for someone on the dole. In the moorland rivers, the cleaner rivers such as the Dart and the Tavy, they're wearing a snorkel and swimming right up to the fish and snaring them with a wire loop like a slipknot. And some are swimming around in wetsuits to get the same results as stoning. You should be out watching all the time — weekday, weekend, day and night. Particularly after rain. *That's* when they're likely to jump. They think, 'Well, as the river's risen, fish is moving from A to B and we'll get them.' We had a low river last year, too, and the bulk of fish didn't run till November. Right. The poaching boys don't care if they're full of ova or not; they get up the river and net a deep pool where the fish have settled. Of course, given the number of eggs one salmon can lay, I'll be dead and you'll be dead and the River Tamar will still be going on with salmon — unless the sea trout take over. Yes, that's the rumour: a lot of people want to see the Tamar as a sea trout river. Well, once that day dawn, that *will* be the end of it.

The trouble today is there's so much printed. If hundreds of fish run into Gunnislake and the newspapers get hold of it, it's spread nationwide so the poachers say, 'Right. Plenty of fish down there. We'll go there tonight.' Or people talk loud in the pub that they've read about cyanide being used like you used lime in the old days to bring fish to the surface. A couple of locals then may say, 'Us'll get some cyanide.' It haven't been used yet to my knowledge on our stretch of river. But if it was used through someone talking loud it would kill everything — the baby fish, every living creature. It takes six, eight weeks or even longer to wash through. Over the last twenty years, because of the poaching, you're almost afraid to discuss anything — even with your wife. When I leave Endsleigh I try never to talk about fishing unless I'm in the company of a fisher. I *never* go in a pub now. Someone might say, 'Well, what's the fishing like?' and you might answer, and there's always somebody sat in the corner and they'll say to a poacher, 'We heard from a bloke called Adams that there's one or two big fish up at Hardstone,' and the poachers will go to Hardstone to pull them out. If you don't blow it, nobody knows.

The wife will very often say to me, 'You soon won't have a friend.' I say, 'What do I want friends for? Half of them are friendly when you've something to give them. When you haven't got anything to give them is the time to have friends — when you need help, when you're down and out.' Though I'm a friendly sort of person, it's bred into me not to talk in the village where everybody knows everybody and there's a type of woman knows more about you than you know about yourself. It's like here at Endsleigh I find out more about the people than they know about *their*selves! I was sat with a Mrs Dower this year in the boot of her car

— one of those hatchbacks — and we were having a drink. She said, 'It's pretty grim this drought, isn't it? It's going to ruin the fishing for the rest of the year. It's got to rain and rain and rain and rain and once it rains and rains and rains and rains it'll put the river out for three or four days. Every day counts now. There's no tomorrow.' She poured me another little drop of hard stuff and then she said, 'You know, Horace,' she said, 'I started fishing when I was five year old and that was seventy-two years ago.' So I said, 'Well, it's quite a time,' and we went on discussing things and discussing other people and what sort of sports they were and how on average we get all the nice people at Endsleigh and, if they're not nice, they don't come back the second time because you don't encourage them. And then she said, 'People fish down here right up until they die. Lord Hollenden is ninety-one and Major Dore is coming ninety-four. Of course *you* must be knocking on now because I've known you for a long time.' I said, 'Yes, I'm seventy-one.' She said, 'You don't look bad for seventy-one.' I said, 'No, and I wouldn't have thought you were seventy-seven.' She said, 'Who told *you* I was seventy-seven?!' I said, '*You* told me, about five minutes ago in conversation! You said you were five year old when you started fishing and that was seventy-two years ago. When *I* went to school, five and seventy-two was seventy-seven, but', I said, 'with the computers and ready-reckoners today, it could be *eighty*-seven because a slip of the finger either reduces or increases it.'

What worries me is that, when these different cottages is let out to the Landmark Trust and whatnot, the right of ways is gone and the tenants have the right to use the drives and you don't know who's who. You'll often see Mr Tuckett's farm manager in a white van. All right. But you don't know who some of the farm *tenants* are. Not only Dairy Dell Cottage and Swiss Cottage, the *farms* could be let to poachers. You meet cars going hell for leather — nobody from Endsleigh. People are allowed to come and go too freely. I'm not around all the time and there's no one to stop them. In the Grandfather Duke's days the gate was kept shut and locked and you either had to have a permit or a written permission to come in. Even under the Trustees you had to ring up the Manager or the Manageress of the house. Things have become more and more relaxed

185

as the Syndicate have gone on. People just motor down and ask if they can walk around the grounds. Under the Trustees they'd have been told No. And, what you've got to remember, in my younger days, though there wasn't so many fishing, nobody could break through because there was always scores of workmen around — the woodmen, the gardeners, the people trimming the river banks. It was a community, all interlocked. It's the motorcar and now the motorways, the dual carriageways, that's opened up the West Country and made it easily get-atable for all this thieving.

One drizzly afternoon about six year ago there were two ladies — Mrs Bodman, a member, and Mrs Hazel — having a cup of tea at Inny Croy when three young men walking by said, 'Good-afternoon.' I motored down shortly after and the ladies said to me, 'There's three young men gone down here,' so I said, 'Well, there's a dilapidated Land Rover, a long wheel-based one with a hard top and fitted out with everything including the kitchen sink, in the stables yard, so it's probably forestry students, Lord Bradford's people, taking a look at Dunterue Wood.' So the ladies asked me would I like a cup of tea and a piece of cake and I said No and I came on down and, when I got to Gravel Pool, there was three young men walking along and I slowed up so as not to splash them with the puddles, and they stood in and thanked me and I went on.

Well, some time later — it was gone five o'clock — I was helping a pal start his car stuck at Fishery Bend when the three young men walked passed us, saying, 'Good-evening,' and went up Fishery Cottage way. About ten minutes after that a car came down with these men in, driving over the grass verge and blowing their horn and giving me the V-sign. I looked at the number and I said, 'My God! A Bridport number! The Bridport Boys!' And there I'd been earlier driving steady so I wouldn't splash them! I'd have bloody drowned them if I'd known who they were! It shows you how brazen poachers are. They came here mid-afternoon when everybody's fishing and they'm bound to be spotted! And I, of all people, spoke to them on two occasions. If they can trick *me*, they can trick any fisherman easy. They can come up to someone and say, 'Any luck?' or 'Have you seen any fish?' 'Yes, there's twenty or thirty fish here but we can't get 'em,' and, in the night, there you are! You can see why I don't speak to strangers about fishing and why I've stopped visiting the pub!

Dr May Reed and Mrs Best are very good members for keeping their eyes open. They'll say when they see an odd person, and they'll take notice of an odd car and give you the number. They're better than the gentlemen: the gentlemen don't pay no attention to this sort of thing and then they grumble if anything goes wrong. Mrs Best is inclined to overdo it. Two year ago she was sat writing late one evening in the library and she glanced towards the window and she saw a light flash. She kept watching and she saw the light flash again so she rang me to say she thought there was poachers down the river over in the Cornish woods. I said, 'I don't think you can *see* the woods from there!' 'Yes, you can!' she said. I said, 'All right,' and left it at that: I said to the wife, 'I'm not going down because she *can't* see a light in the Cornish woods from where she's sat.' And, when I came down in the morning, I went straight into the room and I realized I was right. And, come to, I investigated, and it was a farmer out looking at his sheep in the fields on the Devon side.

Last summer there was a scare. I'd gone to bed early. The telephone rings and this was a farmer. He said, 'There's a car up at Carthamartha. I saw the lights from my bedroom window.' Quarter past eleven this is! I said, 'Well, it's not a poacher because they wouldn't have car lights on to start with, *and*', I said, 'there's some youngsters gone out sea trout fishing from Endsleigh, so I won't come down.' I thanked him very much because it was very good of him to ring up — you must liaison. So I went back to bed. The phone goes again. This is Derek Bradbury, the Manager, at Endsleigh. 'A car coasted down through the yard.' I said, 'That ties us. There's a farmer just rung me to say there's a car down at Carthamartha. There could be something on. I'll ring one of the River Board bailiffs and get him to come down, and I'll come down too.' 'Oh,' he said, 'you don't want to do that! *I'll* come with you!' I said, 'Right. See you in ten minutes.' — I'm usually on the ball: I don't take very long to put a pair of trousers on. So I rushed down in the Suzuki and Derek jumps in, and he brought his dog with him — the worst thing he could have done.

We reached the fisherman — he was fishing at Inny Croy. I had my headlights on, which I shouldn't really. 'My God!' he said. 'You frightened me!' He'd been there since half past ten and it was now quarter to twelve. He said, 'I've been hearing peculiar noises all evening. Could it be otters?' And, right on the same, there was a damn great Alsatian dog

187

stood right in my car lights! I said to Derek, 'Right. We can't hang around. I want to find out whose dog this is.' The dog ran along in front of us and turned into the river at Inny Ford Junction where it was dark as a sack. I shone my torch and whistled, which I shouldn't be doing, but he carried on across. So we proceeded hell for leather right up to Greystone Bridge. I was out for to catch the number of the poachers' car: I wasn't going to stop because you mustn't pick a fight. At Greystone Bridge there's a wide, wide field and, if there's anybody poaching, they can park back under the trees. I swung the van around and I've got a spotlight I connect up to the cigarette lighter and I hold him out the window — he's such a powerful beam you can see for miles. I said, 'Well, there's nobody about. Let's go home the road way.' Derek said, 'No. They might be gone *down* river.' So I agreed to drive back and go down river.

We gets down to Black Rock where there's a stream goes across the field. I inspected there. No good. Oh, Derek couldn't understand it: 'I heard this car come down!' We get down to Leigh Wood where I searched the water with my light. Nothing. Then we got down to Southcombe Field where there's a lot of cattle. It's now coming half past twelve, quarter to one. It's bumpy and your headlights is jumping up and down and they make it fantastic because you see rabbits hopping and insects flying and hundreds of different coloured moths. The lights catch the eyes and the horns of the cattle and they're all glistening like a lot of ghosts, and of course, Derek's dog, which is only a house dog, spots this and goes berserk — bark, bark, bark. Any rate, we go right down to Horsebridge. No good, and it's now quarter, twenty past one so we decide to come back.

Next morning I was talking about all this and a gent said, 'Well, I went to The Royal at Horsebridge for a drink last night and, afterwards, I coasted down the drive here to the Cottage end of the yard and went in the bottom door.'

So it was a false alarm!

Ten

Yes, I *am* listening to you! You'm exactly like my daughter. She's talking to me and she'll say, 'Father, you're not taking a bit of notice of me!' I say, 'I've heard every word you said.' And she says, 'Repeat it!' and I repeat it. It's like when me and the wife visited the Old Bailey on one of our London holidays, the judge began to rock as though he was in a rocking-chair, and I said to the wife, 'It's no good stopping here. The judge has fallen asleep,' and as we walked out the door, the usher said, 'Are you coming out for good, sir? There's a young couple would like to go in.' I said, 'I would advise the young couple not to bother, because the judge have fallen asleep.' 'Ah,' he said, 'that's where you're wrong! He's concentrating.' ...

In June, 1966, Lord Chief Justice Goddard stayed at Endsleigh. He came with a fisherman called Mr Schuster but only for a break, not to fish himself. They weren't members: they were paying guests of the Syndicate. There was only fourteen members with six rods fishing at that period so there was rods going a-begging — now it's eight rods and thirty-one members. Everyone was on good behaviour and I was very, very nervous about meeting him because, though he'd retired by then, he was named 'The Hanging Judge': you used to go up in front of him and the black cap was placed. Very often when one's talking about crime even today, they say, 'It's a pity we haven't got the old Lord Chief Justice back, the old Lord Goddard. *He'd* swing 'em up!' But it turned out he'd a wonderful sense of humour. On the table in the hall I've a yearly Height of the River Diary I fill in between eight and nine from the gauge-board and, after breakfast, I'd find him and Colonel Macintyre, who he met here, laughing and joking on the settle. The settle's in the Staff Room now. You know, one of those settles with a high back they used in the old days so they wouldn't catch a draught; an old boy and an old girl would be quite happy there, sat beside the fire. We called the settle 'the throne'.

189

Any rate, June the 24th, the river was out of order and Colonel Macintyre said he was going to Launceston to have his hair cut and I'd better go with him and have mine cut too. The old Lord Chief Justice was stood in the entrance hall doorway and he said, 'Alistair, where are you and Adams going?' and the colonel said, 'I'm taking Adams to get his hair cut because he's such a bloody disgrace with you in residence!' Just like that. The old judge laughed and waved us goodbye and, at the barber's, I gave the colonel first go and he went off to do some shopping and eventually we met up in the Square and went into the White Hart for a drink. There, standing beside the bar, was one of his best pals, Colonel Lethbridge, who he hadn't seen for fourteen, fifteen years. There wasn't very many in the bar so Colonel Macintyre said, 'This is one of my long lost friends. I think we'd better have drinks around the house!' and one word brought another and I had too many drinks and so had the colonel and on the way home he asked to meet the wife. She came to the door wiping flour off her arms and very furious because she thought it was a hawker and, when she found it was me with the colonel, she was all confused, she didn't know what to say. He said, 'I've heard a lot about you, Mrs Adams. We've been on a drinking session. If it's not asking too much, we'll have a cup of coffee.' He was an enormous man, about six foot two and damn nigh so broad as he was long and, the first thing he done as he walked in, he hit the top of his head on the hall lamp and nearly knocked it for a six… The wife could have killed me.

We arrived back at Endsleigh, and there's the judge sat on the throne. He said, 'Well, Alistair, you and Adams had betterway come up to my room and we'll have a drink.' We were having a drink and he said, 'I don't go much on *either* of your haircuts. Why's that bit of hair, Adams, hanging down over your forehead?' Said Colonel Macintyre, 'We'll have it off!' and he cut it off with the fishing scissors on the string around his neck, whipped it around a plastic tube, tied it with a bit of silk and varnished it and caught a fish with it after lunch almost immediately. So he was the first person I'd ever seen tie a tube fly and he tied it with a bunch of my hair and called it Hairy Horace!

Though now I mostly use plain brass tubes which I interweave with black and yellow bucktail — a tube seems to have better movement, expand the fibres — it's in the mind a lot of it, the fish doesn't know any different. I've always read that they're colour-blind and don't know what the colour of the fly is or whether it's an Esmund Drury or a Clive Murphy or an anything-else-type tied fly! I'm outspoken on this through experience. I hate to see people buying stuff which isn't going to be any special use to them. I often tell the story of a gentleman with a certain ghillie on a certain river in Scotland, and the gentleman produced a certain fly and one of the feathers had dropped out and the ghillie wouldn't use it because, he said, 'It's not tied properly. You won't get a fish.' Well, that's utter nonsense.

Six or seven year ago, Mr Egbert Barnes couldn't buy a General Practitioner in the house. It's orangy red. Some people call it a Prawn fly but the proper name is General Practitioner. Right. On the Saturday evening he got a little brass tube of about an inch and tied on a bunch of red hackle, some kind of bucktail that had been dyed red, to get as near to this here fly as possible. He goes up river on the Sunday morning and he's into a fish immediately and, on nine consecutive days, there was twenty-two salmon caught on flies identically patterned. He tied up three or four and gave them to people. He *gave* them to people like I do. I can't afford it but that's what I've done: never sold a fly in my life. Ever. Well, people wanted to know what to call this fly. Someone wanted to call it Little Egbert — because he was a big chap, you see. I suggested Red Barrel because he was in the brewery trade, but that was the wrong brew. So it was called Red Devil. If the same thing happened now, everybody that came into the house would want that identical red fly and then I would come up behind them with something bright yellow and do just as well. It's all a gimmick. Jubilee time I caught a fish with a tube I tied up with bucktail dyed red, white and blue and called Patriotic. It was no more like a fly than a butterfly...

In October, 1967, the year after The Hanging Judge came here, Mr William Tuckett died, the *local* celebrity, the man on the spot, the man who was doing so much for the Syndicate and enabled it to fish the Tuckett Trust's two miles. I was working in the allotment at home and the wife come running down to me. She said, 'I've bad news for you. Mr Tuckett's dead!' Oh my God! And, the same year, there was *another* tragedy — Sir George Hayter-Hames, the Chairman, was taken very, very ill. One Sunday, coming up to the end of August, Her Ladyship

191

rang me up and asked me would I help him to fish Hardstone Pool, one of his favourites. So they both arrived in the afternoon with a private nurse and the nurse's husband and I went upstream with them and Sir George sat in a chair. I put the rod up and I said to Sir George, 'When you go to make a cast this chair's going to overbalance.' The nurse's husband said, 'I'll hang hold of the chair.' I said, 'Yes, but you don't really understand. As soon as he puts the pressure on, the chair's going to tumble over!' Any rate, he had two or three casts and then he slipped out of the chair. I said, 'Enough is enough,' and Her Ladyship and the nurse took him back to the house to get a cup of tea while I fiddled around with the other young gent trying to teach him as he'd never fished before. Well, you can't teach a person in two or three minutes and he soon got fed up, so it was an afternoon thrown away.

We came back to the house and dear old Sir George was sat in the car and I went in and sat by the side of him. Her Ladyship brought him out a cup of tea and a piece of cake and a piece of bread and butter, and he couldn't feed hisself, I'd to hold the piece of cake to his mouth. He murmured to me — I could just understand him — 'You seem to be used to this,' and I reminded him that my dear old father had been in a Home. Any rate, Sir George was driven back and he was expected to die. Then all of a sudden, in the middle of December, Mr Keith Bodman, who'd taken over as Chairman, rang me and said, 'Georgie is much better. He'd like to come to see you today. He's got a Christmas present for you.'

Bert Moore and myself were in the tool shed in the stables yard. I heard the car arrive. I whipped out to meet Sir George and Her Ladyship, and Sir George was walking towards me! He said, 'Well, Adams boy, how are you? A happy Christmas to you!' I said, 'It's one of the best Christmases I'll ever have to see you walking again!' He said, 'I've brought you and Moore a brace of pheasants each, and next year', he said, 'I'll be all right, I'll be fishing.' Well, he was one of those people if he could walk he wasn't going to stand still and if he could fish he wasn't going to sit on the bank so, in '68, I would go in the river with him though he worried me stiff because he worked like a Trojan. Of course, illness overtook him again and he died on the 21st of October.

I hate losing nice people. I've to go to a funeral tomorrow [August 9] — the wife of Claude Masters, the best man at my wedding, the gardener who looked after the Duke's budgies. She only lived three door away and I hadn't been in to have a yarn lately. You know, you see them in the garden and just put your hand up and say, 'How are you?' and now I regret it. I'm to be a bearer. I've been a bearer for so many pals and old people in the village in my time. Mr Bodman once said to me, 'You want to be careful. Otherwise there won't be nobody to carry *you*!' It's not a nice job but you've got to have somebody. Some of the graveyard is a bit steep and if you're not carrying with a person your height it's a little bit awkward, especially on the narrow strips between the graves. The first body I carried was on a gate when I was thirteen. Three or four of us kids were stood about in the village one Sunday afternoon after lunch and the policeman come along with a farmer and he said, 'You, you and you, come with us!' Just like that. We had to walk three parts of a mile up over the hill to the old gravel pit where a man who'd released himself from hospital jumped in the rainwater and drowned hisself. Somebody'd seen him floating there and pulled him out, and we'd to carry him down to his house.

I always think about the wife's mother when I'm wanted on the phone. She's ninety-three, and you never know, do you? You hope to hear they're dead rather than seriously ill: you like to remember a person as you saw them the last time they were reasonably well. Bert died in Derriford Hospital last year. I went to see him before Christmas. He'd just had his supper and the nurse, a darkie, said, 'Bert,' her said, 'you haven't drinked your tea.' 'All right,' he said. 'I'll drink it,' and he took the cup and he drunk it down like drinking down a glass of beer. About five minutes later he brought it all up and he was in such a hell of a state they had to get the pan. And from then … bang. Within a matter of a week, ten days, gone. I was sad that I'd been there.

On *my* deathbed I'm going to blame *you*. I'll be gasping for breath and I'll say, 'If I hadn't used up so much breath talking to Clive Murphy I'd have lived another fortnight!'

Mr Bodman, who was tied up with Barclay's Bank and hadn't been retired all that long, died in '74. For *him* to go! I was worried: I was losing all the nice people and I was getting older. Mrs Bodman, who's now become a member, she caught her first fish with me off Inny Croy. She was really dressed up and I remember saying to Mr Bodman, 'Will you give me permission to take your lady out and show her the tricks of the trade?' and she got hold of the rod and I stood behind her and caught hold of the rod as well and I said, 'What we've got to do is just cast the fly across the stream and let it swing around.' It was a very, very short cast, only a matter of three or four yards, and she was getting the rhythm so I stood by the side of her and said, 'Now go on! Do it on your own!' and, as the fly swung around, bang, fish on! A newcomer's dressed in her Sunday best and she hooks a fish almost immediately! Then you've got another person can fish twelve months and hook nothing. So there's a lot of luck in fishing though there's got to be several fish *in* a pool and they've got to be 'hungry', as I call it, though they don't feed in fresh water.

Before Mr Bodman's death, Lord Trenchard asked me to join him for lunch. He told me Mr Bodman wanted to pull out as Chairman as he wasn't feeling up to it and there'd been some talk of him taking his place. He said, 'What do *you* think of the idea? You know me better than anyone probably on the river bank.' I said, 'I would have thought you'd make a good Chairman if you remember one thing: not shout so much. Because,' I said, 'if you start shouting like you do to Porgy and to me, you'll frighten the hell out of everyone.' Then in October, when everybody was dispersing from the tables after my annual speech in which I referred to Lord Trenchard as 'your new Chairman', Mr Bodman called me into the Quiet Room. He said, 'If you get any trouble at all and things don't go like you think they should go so far as the river's concerned, don't be afraid to get in touch with me.' The following Saturday, October the 21st, I went away on holiday to Paignton. The wife went to bingo that evening and won sixty-four quid. On the Sunday our next door neighbours, the Lukes, joined us and they'd got a note with them for Jill. It said Mr Bodman had died the day before, sudden — he was sat watching the racing on television when it happened. I couldn't eat my lunch. I was all to pieces...

But you've got to forget Mr Bodman, you can't do nothing about it. Life must go on and Lord Trenchard took over till 1980 and, though he's a bit stiff and dry, he was well respected, and everybody stopped and listened, jumped to attention — you know, he's so loud. I suppose he's one of the most conscientious fishermen that's ever fished the Tamar. He catches more than his share. He'll catch a fish when it's high water,

194

low water, no water. And this is because he keeps on keeping on, he never gives in. When another person rushes home to lunch, he's still fishing. When people's home to dinner, he's out having a cold supper on the river bank. He's so keen that when he goes to bed he probably thinks he's got the fishing rod in his hand. First thing in the morning he's up roaming the terraces in his pyjamas and dressing-gown, looking down the river to see its condition or if a fish jump. He'll walk up and down studying the pools and the best ways they should be fished. He'll pinpoint a fish from the high bank through his polaroid glasses and think to himself, 'Now the battle's on!' and he'll move that fish — he'll get him to rise to him or he'll frighten him away. He's got the patience of Job. He isn't casting his fly all the time; he's pitching his wits against the fish's and he's sizing of it up and he thinks *he*'s going to win. And unlike so many youngsters who are in and out of their cars, doing ten minutes in this pool, quarter of an hour in the next, five minutes in the next, Lord Trenchard is at the same pool sometimes for so long as three hours.

Now *Lady* Trenchard, she's quite opposite to him. He's large and dominating, and she's tiny and unassuming. And so pretty and young looking! You'd never think she's got three grown-up sons and two grandchildren. And, though she's patient like her husband, her patience is liable to forsake her. If she puts a fly up a tree or gets it stuck in a rock, by God, then she starts fussing because she doesn't want Tom to know. And, if she should have been lucky and caught two or three fish before him, she's inclined to close shop and go to a place where she knows in the back of her mind she's not going to catch anything. I always say, 'Well, now at last you've got him in his place so, come on, let's have another go! Keep pulling of them in, never mind about His Lordship!' Lady Bailey, her mother, she's only ever caught one fish in her life and that was on the 14th of September, 1963. She'd never fished before and I got her into a pool and she was into a fish. *I* was telling her how to play it and Lord Trenchard, who was taking photographs of her from the bank, *he* was telling her how to play it, and she kept on saying, '*I* know! *I* know!' so we nicknamed her '*I* know'.

The trouble with Lord Trenchard is he's full of theory. He wants to get the mud out of Edgcumbe Pond so it can fish better. He was talking to me about it early this season and we've been talking about it ever since he took over as Chairman in '74 which is a long, long time. In '74 I said to him, 'How can you get the mud out of Edgcumbe Pond?! Edgcumbe Pond hasn't been cleaned out since 1940, just after the outbreak of the war! That was one of my father's last jobs. In they days it used to be done every five years with shovels and a wheelbarrow so it was easy!' Well, in '76, one of those damn great excavator things with a long arm to it was brought here and a hole was made to fish in about eight feet deep — in places it was only two or three — whereas in the old days the pond was *twenty* feet deep. A complete waste of time. The silt went on gathering and it's now almost level with the edge of the bank! Down at the outlet I have an eight or nine inch plank, a thick board, part of an old staging, which I've let down into the grooves where the iron grating used to drop in years ago. That raises the water depth to only eight inches, nine inches at the most. Yet we're still putting fish in! — for the last ten years Major Hill of Dorset has provided so many brown and so many rainbow trout for Edgcumbe and Dairy Dell Ponds and the Bathing Pool. It's embarrassing. A gentleman comes to me and says, 'The brochure says there's trout in Edgcumbe Pond. What's it like for fishing?' I have to say, 'Waste of time. There's trout there and only about six, eight inches of water. It's full of weed and full of mud.'

Lord Trenchard has suggested that I attach a chain to a tree on one side of the pond, try to get the Land Rover on to the opposite side with the chain attached, and then just drive fore and back, hoping to clear the mud. But how could it clear the mud?! All you'd do is stir it up and it would be only the effluent that would run out over the outlet and it would go into the river and pollute it! Even if you had the Rotovator there stirring of the mud, it would still only be the effluent flowing out over! All right in theory only — the same old story over and over again. This is the trouble with these people. So many bosses with so many bright ideas which you can't put into practice. Major Hill took fifty or sixty fish up there again this spring — they've been taken off food for some time before they're brought here and then they live on the food they find in the pond. He said, 'Well, some of these fish will be dead in six weeks!' There *is*, though, an odd fish to catch there still — a Mr Booth caught a couple only the other day. I say, if it's got to be a pond, have it for youngsters to put a worm on and see if they can catch eels. Better still, pull the board out leaving a stream through the centre and the mud to harden off for vegetation to grow on naturally. Of course, you *could* temporarily divert the stream — there's a bypass already which runs into a large tank to feed the hydrants in case of fire at the house. You could cut a channel, have a bulldozer in. But it would take two or three years for the mud to dry out and God knows where you'd put it, and the expense would be colossal. No, Edgcumbe Pond is now a hopeless proposition, a false economy.

What His Lordship's name will go down on most as Chairman of the Syndicate is his work for the Roadford Reservoir Inquiry in 1978. The inquiry lasted six, eight weeks. Fishermen and the general public could put their views, and Lord Trenchard and Mr Philip Tuckett represented The Tamar and Tributaries Fisheries Association. Roadford is near the River Wolf which is a tributary of the Tamar, and the reservoir will be able to supply Plymouth with water — they're going to start building it next year. It could have been built on Dartmoor but certain sections reckoned it would spoil the beauty. I think the Ministry should have overruled them because now they'm taking away agricultural land, although it's secondary, not first class.

Lord Trenchard fought tooth and nail for the Tamar as a salmon river of the future: he made sure there'd be a flow that fish could move through — say a million gallons of water a day instead of the proposed five hundred thousand — for the benefit of fishermen *all* the way up and down the river, not just at Endsleigh. The river will be unbalanced and I think a lot of fish will be pulled away from the lower reaches — in 'lower reaches' I include my lower pools. But the riparian owners should be grateful for someone as knowledgeable as Lord Trenchard who spoke on their behalf. As I keep saying, there's not enough liaison. A lot of them couldn't care less about anybody else.

I call Sir Ernest Woodroofe, who became a member/director four or five year ago, 'the lieutenant'. He's Chairman of Unilever, retired, and a scientist and, like Lord Trenchard, he keeps his eye on the Tamar as a whole, he's got the Tamar at heart. His motto is 'It's better to have a friend than an enemy' and he does a lot of liaising between all these here fishery officers of the South West Water Authority who are a little bit scientific theirselves. It's so complicated with scientists you don't know where you are with them. They're terrible for figures. If I said to Sir Ernest, 'There was fifty fish poached last night,' he'd say, 'What's fifty out of two thousand?!' Figures, figures, figures — it gets beyond you. He'll watch a river when he's fishing and, you might depend, if he says, 'I saw ten fish run through Hardstone Croys,' well, there was ten fish, there wasn't twenty.

In June, '76, the lower seven mile stretch of the river kept by Herbie Symons was sold because Mr Walton died. The auction was by Knight, Frank and Rutley and our Syndicate (the Endsleigh Fishing Club) put up a third of the money so far as the fishing was concerned, which enabled Endsleigh to have two rods per day down there like before — they fish in rotation one of the three beats from Lamerhooe Boathouse No.1 to Impham Meadows inclusive. The purchasers were another syndicate: the Lower Tamar Fishing Club. Its Chairman is Mr Michael Beecham. He's one of those gents that collects first editions. He's got a *tremendous* library and he's written his autobiography. Though Beat 2 down there looks quite attractive because it's full of damn great big rocks, I still prefer the top water for myself. As I told Mr Walton, in *my* opinion it's more picturesque — it hasn't any mine dumps and chimneys: apart from the croys built by McNicol under the Grandfather Duke, man hasn't tampered with it, and the river is banked with more trees. Also, without any tidal water, we're less open to poaching. Beats 1 and 3 down there may be easy for the elderly but on Beat 2 the river drive is probably fifty feet in places above water level so an old boy of eighty, when he've gone down the steps, he don't know if he's ever going to get back. In Walton's time, the last freshwater pool of Blanchdown on Beat 3 was named Symons Pool after Herbie. By the way, each beat's given a stretch of the tidal below Gunnislake Weir, but that's all I want to say in definition of the Lower Tamar Fishing Club and the Lower Water. Too much detail, like when you're talking about the Bible, is a waste of bloody breath.

Herbie retired in March, '79, though he still runs around helping fishermen on special request. He's an exceptionally good fisherman, in his day probably the best fisherman in the valley. The interesting thing is that it's Rodney Hill, my son-in-law, who took over as Warden of the Lower Tamar Fishing Club in his place. He doesn't like passing on information to Rodney. It's sad really. But Rodney's quick and he's picking things up from me and he's working for a good crowd that helps him. I'm on the way out and I can't teach a person all I know in a few months but, when I get rid of *you*, I'll be giving Wesley Lee even more than I give Rodney. I know I'm definitely here till the end of next year [See editor's note, p.6].

Jill wasn't interested in boys in 'that way' till she met Rodney at the Jubilee celebrations in Milton Abbot in '77. They met around the roasted ram in the Playground, went to the dance in the Village Hall, danced together, got friendly, and it went on from there with one or two ups and downs. He was a gardener for Mr Taylor in the Harragrove Gardens which had become a nursery — he lived in one of the old chauffeurs' cottages, next door to Bert. He's very artistic and he loves flowers and he's a good landscaper. In fact, he's been good at whatever he touches. He was loaned out to people say they wanted a big rockery. And he went round the different markets, selling the products of the nursery. Like up at Holsworthy in North Devon there's a rough market where the old farmers come in off the moors. They might want a couple of apple trees and they'd say to Rodney, 'Could you bring them home in the van and pop 'em in for me?' so he'd say, 'Yes, I'll be pleased to. Give us your address,' and on the way back he'd spade out the turf and bang them in. That's the type of person he is, you see — a good mixer and dedicated and always willing to help people.

Years ago, I taught Mr Beecham how to fish when he was a paying guest at Endsleigh. One day in '78 he came to see me in my home. He'd got a briefcase and a notebook and he sat down in the chair and he said, 'Now I want to know all about Rodney Hill because', he said, 'he's done some gardening for me and I want him down on the Lower Tamar to look after the fishing.' I said, 'Well, I'm not getting involved. He's friendly with Jill and I wouldn't think of it. Anyway you wouldn't pay him enough money. He's getting a pound a week more than the average gardener where he is.' Mr Beecham repeated that he wanted him. I said, 'You won't get him, so you can put your pad away and have a cup of coffee,' so he went off from me just the same as he came. But, in the end, he *did* persuade Rodney and he took over from Herbie Symons though he didn't yet know the first thing about fishing.

Jill and Rodney didn't get married till 1981, at the end of September. But, before that, they weren't pushing of it, and one morning, eight o'clock in November, '80, Mr Beecham rang me and said, 'I'm coming to your house. I'll be there in about twenty minutes.' I said, 'Hang on! I've only just got out of bed and I haven't even washed, shaved or had my breakfast!' He said, 'I'll be there in twenty minutes.' About ten minutes after, the phone rings again. He said, 'It'd be better to talk in private. It's very important. Meet me at Pridham's Garage as soon as you can.' So I went up to Pridham's. He said, 'Right. Get in the car.' He said, 'Isn't it about time Rodney and Jill got married?' I said, 'Yes, but the wife and myself can't dictate to them to get married! Jill mightn't *want* to marry him. He mightn't want to marry Jill.' We agreed he was henpecked. He lost his father when he was quite young and he was now living with his mother and two sisters in a small cottage in Gunnislake. Mr Beecham said, 'The Lower Tamar Fishing Club will provide them with a mobile home until we can get them a house.' I said, 'He's a very nice fellow but it's not for me. If Jill want Rodney she'll have Rodney. I'm not telling of her to marry him!' He said, 'All right. We'll say nothing more about it. Our conversation is a secret.' That Christmas, Jill was sat on the sofa in the kitchen. We always have twelve, fourteen of the wife's people on Christmas day for lunch and she said, 'Probably this will be my last Christmas at home.' I said, 'Why? Where are you going?' 'You know because I know what Mr Beecham told you about the mobile home!' I said, 'I don't think much of Mr Beecham. He said our conversation was a secret!'

In the end, the Lower Tamar Fishing Club didn't supply them with a mobile home, they supplied them with a tied house. Coming on into April, the wife and myself, we'd been out for the evening and Jill was gone to bed and she rushed down in her nightie and she said, 'Oh, Mam!' she said. 'Mr Beecham's got us a house in Gunnislake! I've to go down and look at it tomorrow night. Rodney says it's pretty dilapidated. Father won't like it, but it's nothing to do with Father!' — Father was me. She went down and had a look at it. There was a lot of work to be done — it was condemned and the Club had picked it up quite cheap, for about twelve thousand.

So eventually Jill and Rodney got engaged. They went to Plymouth and Rodney bought the ring. Then they came home, had a drink and went up the pub with their pals, not us, to celebrate. Next they started working on this house, working on it, working on it. They worked damn hard. I've never known Jill work so hard. She wouldn't do the painting at *our* place — you know the girls today, with all long nails. Sewers had to be laid; a door had to be blocked up and a window put where the door was; a new kitchen had to be built on and a door knocked through the main house to go to the kitchen. They'd to pay for nothing themselves.

The house was almost ready in time for the wedding. Jill was brought up in the Methodist Chapel and she went to the Methodist Sunday School, same as I did, but Rodney's confirmed C. of E. and he's a bell-ringer at St Constantine's, Milton Abbot, so they wanted to get married at St Constantine's and they wanted the reception at Endsleigh.

Nowadays they take a hundred and ten, a hundred and twenty at Endsleigh for a reception. Then we were told they could only take ninety. The wife wanted her relations but they couldn't *all* come. I wanted my second cousins and some of my friends and couldn't have any. We sent an invitation to people going to be in residence — also to some members and whatnot around, knowing they wouldn't be able to accept, or that's what I was hoping so as to keep the numbers down to ninety. And then the presents started coming in. One day the wife had just come down from the butcher's and a damn great Roadliner pulls up and the driver said, 'Could you tell me where Jill Adams lives?' She said, 'Well, I happen to be her mother.' He said, 'I've got a package for her,' and this was an eighty piece Royal Doulton china dinner service from the Syndicate — Mr Peter Medd, our Chairman, was then the Chairman of Doulton's China. The Medds also gave her an individual present. Well, everybody gave presents. The Lower Tamar, they gave them a clock inscribed 'To Jill and Rodney Hill from the Lower Tamar Fishing Club'. We couldn't come up to all this so what we gave them was a colour television.

It was a white wedding. Rodney was in a blue suit. It was a Saturday and the river was out of order so the people that was staying here came to the church. There was Lord and Lady Trenchard, Sir Kenneth and Lady Peppiatt and all this and that. There was Mr and Mrs Beecham. He's an offspring of Beecham's Powders. To get they sort of people in the church to Jill Adams' wedding, you know, to just an ordinary peasant's daughter, was overwhelming. Back at Endsleigh, Mr and Mrs Bradbury really laid it on. I got everything for half price but the drinks cost money because there was so damn much bubbly. Then, on top of that, we had a hundred and twenty in the Village Hall in the evening.

There was stacks of telegrams and cards and presents and more presents and more presents. Mrs Bunyan, the wife of one of the more knowledgeable Syndicate members, sent a telegram which read: 'Though Horace accused him of treason, Rodney went poaching with reason, And by hooking the daughter from off the Top Water, Landed the catch of the season.' Quite good that, isn't it? She can knock off a poem in five or six minutes. It's a gift.

In one sense we were out of our depth but in another we weren't because most of the people who come here are so friendly and unassuming. Lord Blakeham, you wouldn't think he was a Lord: you'd think he was just an ordinary fellow from a comprehensive school.

Jill and Rodney hung on late, before they set off on their honeymoon to tour the Cotswolds and the Lake District in the Lower Tamar's estate van — they were still dancing when it was eleven o'clock. They collected their suitcases from our place and went to the Arundell Arms in Lifton for the first night. Mrs Voss Bark who runs the Arundell Arms is a member of the Lower Tamar, and she gave them that first night, and breakfast, on the house. The Lower Tamar started Jill and Rodney off better than I'm *finishing* off! And now they're really, really looked after. I'm over the moon for them, but sometimes I worry if there'll be a crash. If a Labour Government took over they'd try to jump right at the throats of the people they think have the money and the Lower Tamar Fishing Club itself might be in danger. And I hope Jill and Rodney never get spoiled. But then, when early on I was taken from the old ramshackle house in the village and put in Fishery Cottage, it seemed like a palace, and I expect people said, 'Adams don't bloody deserve that! How's he got in *there*? He must be creeping!'

After the wedding I was having a lie-in after all this entertainment and the telephone rung. It was Lady Trenchard. She said, 'I'm coming to help you bring the presents home from the Village Hall.' Most of the presents were on show there. For the big ones we put cards. I said, 'It's all laid on. Jill's pals is going to do that.' She said, 'It doesn't matter,' and she collected some of the presents in her car and brought them home and stopped and had a cup of coffee with the wife. The wife mentioned she was on her way to the Village Hall to wash the dishes with the girls so Lady Trenchard said, 'I'll take you,' and, when she got there, she took off her coat, turned her blouse sleeves up and washed or wiped *all* the dishes. She stayed there till about twelve o'clock that Sunday morning, mucking in with the girls and my wife. That's Her Ladyship.

The presents stayed with us for weeks while Jill and Rodney was finishing their renovations. I was afraid that somebody was going to whip in the window when we was out and pinch them. It's got terrible now. Roughs from the big cities come down and live in the West Country where they think everybody's weak at the top. Older people that have been saving stamps to pay the bills, they stick them on a card, put them in a cupboard or in the wardrobe and, when they go there next time, they see the card is gone. A lot of them won't put their money in the bank where it's safe from robbery and fire. Only recently there was a person down at Plymouth and a robber found six or seven hundred pound under his bloody mattress. He was sleeping on it every night but he wasn't sleeping on it by day, you see.

I always remember — an imaginary case was shown on television — how *easy* it is. This thief parked his car some distance from a semi-detached cottage. Then he went around to the back where there's a dustbin and he picks up the dustbin lid and lets it fall just as he bashes the window so the next door neighbour says, 'Oh, the wind!' or 'Mrs Adams (or Mr Murphy) have let the lid drop!' and they take no notice. Then the bloke's through the window and in the house, and he goes straight upstairs where there's a chest of drawers. Now *I* would start at the top drawer. But not the criminal. He starts at the bottom so he can leave them out, not have to push them back in, for speed. Whatever he wants, so it goes into his haversack. It's all done in a matter of seconds. Down he goes and out the front door. Over the hedge there's a lady gardening. He comes outside of the door with his hat in his hand, turns around as though he's speaking to Mrs Adams and says, 'Well, goodbye then!', shuts the door, puts on his hat and walks away. The lady in the garden looks up and he touches his hat and says, 'Good-morning' or 'Good-afternoon' and he's out the gate and up the road. The lady thinks it's Mrs Adams' friend yet he's robbed the bloody house! ...

Going back to Lady Trenchard helping with the presents and the dishes, working-class people still say to me, 'Oh, you're with the snobs!' Well they've got it in the wrong perspective. *They*'re supposed to be your

203

friends and pals whereas it's often the people they call snobs is the ones that will turn around and say, 'Can I be of assistance?'

That's where I disagree with Dr William Medd. He's one of our directors and he first came here as a student doctor in 1954, the year after the 12th Duke was killed. In '78, when he took over the bookings for the fishing side (his wife does all the donkey-work), he put a series of ads in the game magazines which asked 'Are you the Endsleigh type?' along with general information about fishing, the food, the courtesy and the attention you get here. Well, that question seems to me a bit stuck-up. Is Clive Murphy 'the Endsleigh type', running around here in plimsolls and jeans? What's *meant*, of course, is 'Are you friendly and well-mannered?' It's nothing to do with the real snobs, what I call the fly-by-nights, the jump-ups, the ones that know all the answers, the ones who think they've got everything but haven't got anything. They're *not* welcome. We're unique here because the members are very polite. People like Mr — would never get into the Syndicate — they've the wrong outlook and we don't want people that's going to offend. Almost all the *staff* here is polite, too. I'm inclined to put my hand to my brow and say 'Good-morning, madam' or 'Good-morning, my lady' or 'Good-morning, sir' or 'Good-morning, my lord', whereas Clifford, who replaced Bert Moore as general handyman, when he comes into the hall with a basket of logs, he just waits for them to say 'Good-morning, Clifford,' and answers, 'Mornin'.' ... As part of the good manners, there's no preferential treatment on the river. Just because you're Lord Trenchard or Mr Peter Medd, that doesn't mean a thing. Clive Murphy's got just the same chance of fishing on the rota basis and he'll be just as well looked after.

So Dr Medd's phrase 'the Endsleigh type' can boil both ways. People who don't know better can pump into it the idea of 'the idle rich'. I got a letter once saying, 'What a superb holiday we had at Endsleigh. Hope to come back if they'll have us. Are we the Endsleigh type?'! My fear is Dr Medd will also try to make more pools, like we had for a short while before coming in on the Lower Tamar Fishing Club. All right in theory, but no good in practice. There *is* room for more fishing up here — there's room for twenty rods, not six — but, after two years of commercialization, the numbers of visitors would go off. People who like the bags of elbow-room would complain there wasn't room to hold a cup of tea.

There's a photo of Dr Medd in the new Endsleigh brochure. He's holding a net and chewing a finger. If the fish don't come in, he's bound to chew that finger off. When he gets into a fish, it's got to be all hush. *Nobody* within the vicinity, if he's what we call 'fishing to the gallery', can speak, nobody at all. I remember we were up at Carthamartha once and he was *on one knee*! I said, 'My God! Whatever are you doing, doctor?!!' and he just told me to keep quiet. His wife, Julia, was with us and she was afraid to open her pretty lips. She's very, very pretty and she's one of my favourites actually. I've known her a long time, since just after she married him, and it makes me feel old because I've watched their four children — Natalie, James, Lucinda and Jessica — born and grown up. Lucinda caught her first salmon with me when she was eight year old. I don't think she's fished since — she's mad on horses. James is a hell of a good fisherman, a lovely lad. He's shown fishing on an Endsleigh postcard. I'm just an old ghillie up and down the river and everybody now knows him nationwide... Any rate, Dr Medd's on the shingle on one knee and there's Mrs Medd on one side of him with a net and me on the other side of him with a net in hand, and he's telling both of us to net the fish! In the end I said, 'Enough of this! Off your knee! You want to stand up and your lady stand back and I want you to bring the fish to *me*! Come on, us got to do things properly!' So, on my instruction, he brought the fish to me and I netted and killed it. He said, 'Thank you, Horace, very much indeed. That fish was played beautifully, wasn't it?' And he said this in all sincerity! Yet he's a marvellous fisher: he catches a hell of a lot of fish.

Endsleigh owes a tremendous lot to Dr Medd because, as well as his work on the fishing and publicity side, he's now turned his hand to gardening. Though I don't think he should have cut out the miniature azaleas or the miniature *Acers* or the miniature variegated shrubs from the big rockery by the greenhouses, he's doing a good job restoring the herbaceous border and the rose walk on the terrace. There's no mistake about it — he's a real Endsleigh gent: Endsleigh means everything to him; he's got Endsleigh at heart.

Eleven

Mr Peter Medd, Dr Medd's cousin, became Chairman in 1980. The members voted him on because Lord Trenchard was in Mrs Thatcher's government as a junior minister so he hadn't enough spare time. They couldn't have done better because Mr Medd's first class at the job — he isn't excitable, he's an exceptionally good mixer and he's right on the ball. He's very serious in everything he does — very, very serious. And if he's talking to you and you try to stop him in mid-stream, he's likely to say, 'I'm talking. It's your turn after I've finished,' or 'Now, *wait* a *min*ute, wait a minute! I haven't finished what *I* was going to say!' Just like that! He'll cut you off! But this is what you've got to take. *He's* in charge and you know he's in charge, make no mistake about it. If I played cards with him, I wouldn't like to play the wrong ace because I'd find out what he was really made of. He's a man of very strong character and very, very strict, probably the strictest Chairman I've ever worked for. So I'm always very, very careful.

Though it's mostly House, House, House, and the river's working on a knife-edge, he believes the river should have a little extra money for improvements. This year I've made a dozen new pairs of steps, and that's cost me over four hundred quid for timber. Last year I stuck my neck out and asked for boats as the old ones had gradually decayed and been smashed up for firewood, so we went down to Padstow where we decided to have a fibreglass one built for about £500 and picked out another for about £200, second-hand. He's also offered more stone for the banks. He realizes the river is the main artery of Endsleigh and the fishing's what the buggers *come* here for.

He came here first in 1970 and eventually brought his family. He's got three sons and a daughter. George, the second son, caught his first salmon ever in Underhill, and Nicholas, the youngest son, caught *his* first salmon in Underhill. In '76, Hilary, the daughter, caught *her* first salmon in Underhill, just before she left to live in Australia. I was on the staging, still holding the fish in the net, and she flung her arms around my neck and kissed me. Mrs Medd — she's called Sybella but to me she's Mrs Medd — she's marvellous. *That*'s the person who should be recording this book because the book would be full of smiles. She's *always* smiling. When she's in a mood — and, after all, everybody gets in a mood — she's still got a smile. She was smiling one time after she'd fallen in the river. I'd love to pop into her house and see if she smiles there, because here, you see, I must admit, everybody lets their hair down. When the other Mrs Medd's arranging the tables for the annual party and by mistake puts two people together that don't get on, the smiler of smiles will say, 'Leave them!' out of mischief.

So *you*'d get on with her. Like you, she can knock off a cigarette or two. A pal offered me a puff as a kid but I never fell for it. Yet *you* can't live without it! It's sad really. A clever man, a surgeon, told me the damage is done in the first twelve months. Smoking is company, they say. You'd be hopeless in my job — it would cost you a fortune because in the summer you'd have so many offered to you and you'd be accepting of them and it would grow on you so much that in the winter you'd want the same amount. The wife smokes occasionally; Jill very rarely. In years gone by, if a young lady in the working classes was smoking a cigarette, her would have been looked down on. It's the second war that brought the change.

Another person you'd get on with is Mr Brian Peppiatt who's taken over the late Sir Kenneth's rod. He's a stockbroker and I've seen him on TV dashing around the Stock Exchange because the pound's fallen or shares have gone up. Here he's in charge of the wines. He's a very, very keen fisherman and he's inspiring his two sons, Quinton and Giles, to keep up the tradition. His mother, Lady Pamela, she's a warm and generous lady, but she's probably one of the unluckiest fishermen that comes here, she never seems to get amongst the fish at all. It doesn't seem to bother her. She's always been surrounded by family or friends and she's happy so long as *they*'re enjoying theirselves.

Lady Caffyn, one of the directors, is another very kind and considerate lady. She's the wife of Brigadier Sir Edward Caffyn who's Caffyn Motors. She's the only person out of the Syndicate I've to keep on saying 'Pardon' to and it embarrasses me. She mumbles and she's got a habit of looking down at the ground. I've to say to her, 'I'm an old man now and getting deaf and my old boss, McNicol, always told me, "When you talk to a person, look at him." ' She's quite artistic — she painted the picture of Percy the gardener's hat and dinner bag that's in the Quiet Room — and when you meet her on the river she looks like a gypsy. She's got an old threadbare coat, you see. I often say to her, 'There's only two places for that old coat of yours — either in the dustbin or out in the field stuck on a scarecrow.' She says it's her gardening coat. Probably it'll be buried with her. But, on the more serious side, she's in charge of the welfare of the staff and the running of the house: she's really Derek and Jean Bradbury's boss. She runs around to sales and buys damn great velvet curtains and job lots of antiques. She's really arranged the rooms quite beautifully since the Duke was killed and stuff was thrown out or taken to Woburn.

She caught her first fish with me on the 11th of September, 1962, through Symons teaching her. But, when I say that, I think she'd be the first to acknowledge she also learned a lot from her friend, the late Mrs Owen. Mrs Owen was a tremendous fisher, a master. Although she was short, she was game. When she got into breast waders, all you could see was her chin and nose. She once fell in on the lower stretches and she nearly drowned. The waders got full of water and it took a long time to get her out, though she stayed on her back. That evening Mr Owen said to me, 'Enid have learned her lesson. She bloody nigh drowned today. That'll stop her from wading.' But it never did. So Lady Caffyn's now, no doubt, the longest lady caster here, she throws a tremendous line. But when you see her fishing you'm inclined to see the action, the extra forearm push, of Herbie Symons. Some is humped like a heron ready to pounce on a fish. Some is upright in a gentlemanly fashion and just oozing with the greatest of ease. But Lady Caffyn really puts a bit of zip into it and she can bang that fly across. When she brings her rod up, she stops at twelve, one o'clock and uses her forearm, she doesn't go forward with her body.

Sir Edward, her husband, caught his first fish with me at Leigh Wood Croys on the 2nd of May, 1961. There was a great ash tree lying in the river across the croys. Now, if you know there's an obstacle, you can depend the fish will seem to aim for it. It's not the fish, it's your reaction, it's your mind, it's you and the way you're playing the fish, you're *leading* the fish into that obstacle. Any rate, he'd got this fish on and I said to him, 'Now be careful, because this is a big fish, an exceptionally big fish.' He played it and he played it well, though he didn't know a hell of a lot about it because he'd only fished for a day or two. I thought, 'He's bound to lead this fish into the tree,' so, when he'd got it a little bit under control, I said to him — I didn't mention the tree — I said, 'What you've got to do, you *must* try to keep him tight to this bank. If he wants to go downstream, put a bit of pressure on him and he might drown himself.' And, sure enough, the old fish turned and I netted him before he was really played out. Now, if Sir Edward had been there on his own, probably he'd have lost the fish because of the tree — the fish would have gone in under the tree and turned back and the line or the cast would have got tangled in the branches. So Sir Edward was lucky-lucky. And, what surprised me, this first fish Sir Edward ever caught was nineteen and a half pound. Now, I personally have only had three fish over nineteen all the way down and here's a gentleman that haven't fished for five minutes, as the saying is, and he's got a nineteen and a half pounder!

But the sad part of it is, when you gets a fish like that, whether you're a young lad or an old boy, and it's your first time, you'm inclined to get a little bit swollen-headed. I'm not saying that Sir *Edward* got swollen-headed but you'm inclined to. And, you see, after catching that fish, he thought it was going to be dead easy. Well, then he finds he's up against it and he's a very *unlucky* fisherman now.

So Lady Caffyn learned from Herbie Symons and Mrs Owen. Mrs Best, though, learned from her husband and myself. She ghillied for Mr Best for a time and then I said to her, 'You ought to start fishing.' She said, 'Will you show me how to tie a fly?' I said, 'I can tie a fly so well as the next person but I don't spend a lot of money on varnishing the head — I'm not getting big enough wages. I just pinch the wife's nail varnish,' — later I pinched Jill's because she'd more bottles. I said to Mrs Best, 'Why, as a beginner, spend too much money on a fly when the next thing he's up the tree or on the bed of the river?' So I showed her how to put the hook — a 1/0 single — in the little vice attached to her box to hold it stable and how to wax a wee bit of silk and wrap it around the shank with a whip finish, then wrap a thread of floss, then tie in different pieces of silk and floss with an Indian crow feather for the tag at the back end and a black ostrich herl for the butt and embossed silk tinsel for the body with orange floss silk interweaved and then golden olive and guinea-fowl throat hackles and then, for the wings, a black and white tipped turkey tail with orange swan or goose feathers and golden pheasant tails and, for the flank, a pin tail, and then a jungle black and white cock feather on the side or eye before varnishing the head. This was a Dusty Miller — there are as many as seventeen pieces in a Jock Scott. Then I showed her how to thread the cast through the eye of the fly, double it back, whip it around four times, tuck it in, re-bring the end, tuck it in again and pull it taut. That's a half-blood. I also showed her a double turrel, then how to tie the line to the cast with a figure of eight... Her fingers are more nimble than mine and she's so neat and tidy with it. She could do it all from the word go and, there's no doubt about it, she's probably the best fly tier that's ever visited Endsleigh. Like Dr May Reed, she's a fly purist and sticks to the traditional fly with the winged, feather tie. She hooked something a few years back in Hardstone and when she got it to the bank — this is straight up! — it was the carcass of a Rhode Island Red cockerel. She took some feathers off, dried them out and now she catches a lot of her fish with what we call a Rhode Island Red. It's not very nice to look at but, there again, you see, it matters not what you throw at fish, if you've got them in the taking mood you can catch them with anything.

Mrs Best is a very critical lady about other people. She's what I call a true old-fashioned fly fisher: her turns her nose up to the more modern brass type of flies. It's always been wonderful to be with her on the bank and she's the person who in 1979 thought up the idea of calling Carthamartha Top Pool 'Adams Pool' so people will say, 'Adams Pool? Who's he?' 'Well, that was old man Adams, the riverkeeper here.' She was one of the prominent speechmakers that year at the dinner and she announced at the table that the members had accepted at the AGM they should bestow a pool onto me. I mistakenly thought it was for me only — you know, nobody else would be allowed to fish there — because it's one of the hardest pools on the river. In the old days of the stiff Greenheart and the heavy cane rods there was only three persons able to hit the rock on the other side, and that was Lord Trenchard, Dr Medd and myself. Now, with carbon fibre and fibreglass, a youngster can do it after about five minutes.

Adams Pool is a flat pool, exactly like Hardstone but much smaller.

They should have named Leigh Wood Croys after me because that's my favourite. It was also McNicol's favourite. Mind you, it was easy to get at from Fishery Cottage! Carthamartha has a steep bank and it's very deep. Maybe they were hoping I'd drop in there and never get out again: 'This is where poor old Adams drowned.' I didn't want a pool really, but it was nice of the Syndicate to think of me. There should have been a pool named in honour of McNicol. He made the river what it is and I followed him on.

I'm only an employee. Like everyone else, you're asking me all about the people who come here: 'Ask Adams. He'll know.' But I don't probe. A non-member will come here with a blonde, and the others in the house will ask if it's his wife. I'll say, 'I don't think it is his wife.' They'll say, 'Well, he's sleeping with her.' I say, 'That's nothing today. Some men have three or four women. One's enough for me. I can't manage that!' Some arrive and say, 'Meet my wife.' I think, 'I've already met your wife,' and I put on my glasses and he's got a new one! The Richmond twins, though, haven't even been married once — they're inseparable twins. They used to farm in Oxfordshire but they've retired to Poundsworthy down on Dartmoor now. They're what we call 'Endsleigh day boys' — Dr Medd rings them up if there's vacant rods going which can't be let to anyone staying in the house. One's called John and the other's called David. They've got different voices on the phone, and John's taller and slighter than David so they're easy identified on the river bank. But — it's a bit uncanny — whatever one says, the other says with him: they say 'Yes' or 'No' in answer to a question together. They keep me supplied with tomatoes and cucumbers from their greenhouse because they know I don't grow them, and between seasons they always invite Rodney and Jill and the wife and myself to a meal. John's the cook and David's the bottle-washer. When we went over last they laid on a really good meal, a credit. In fact, Jill and the wife were so intrigued with the treacle tart they asked for the recipe. Two old bachelors giving two ladies who think they're good cooks a recipe! They do all their own house-cleaning, everything. Isn't it marvellous?!

The Harris twins, Mick and George, come twice, three times, sometimes four times a year — a fortnight, a week, another week, that sort of thing, and not always with their wives who don't fish. The house isn't open to the general flow of guests till the last Thursday in March but, because the fishing actually starts the 1st of March, they come down early with Mrs Best. They just have a little table for their food by the fire in the Small Lounge, or the Bar Room as we call it — what used to be the library — and they'll invite Rodney and Jill and the wife and myself down for a drink. The wife's a bit backward in coming forward and when I've had a drink or two the talk flows so the wife keeps nudging me. You stay from nine o'clock till about twelve telling stories they've heard a hundred times but with always a little bit more added. Like the Richmond twins, they'm liable to say the same thing at the same time. If one opens his mouth it's as though there's a bit of string attached to it and the other mouth opens. They look like little jockeys and they're two of the nimblest men I've ever met though they're six or seven years older than I am. They walk very fast in their waders from pool to pool and nip up and down the banks like schoolboys. George is the fly-tier. Ninety per cent they fish with a tube and they've been very, very successful. They came here first when Mr Bodman had taken over as Chairman. They were managers for Barclay's Bank. Sir George Hayter-Hames was Barclay's Bank. Mr Bodman was Barclay's Bank. This is how people get introduced to places like Endsleigh.

The Harrises have no children for me to teach. So many children of all ages come here and mimic me. Mrs Floyd, who's brought up six sons, she's quite a mimic herself, especially of the women guests. *She's* a good fisherman, a tough hunting lady from Wiltshire. Last year she went riding and she fell and couldn't get up. She'd got the dog with her and it roamed back to the house and brought someone out to her. Tommy Floyd, her son, was here in '67 when he was sixteen, seventeen, and I started him off with Mrs Floyd's help. I came along one afternoon while Mrs Floyd was having tea and he was fishing at Beech Tree. He said, 'Horace, boy,' he said, 'I've risen a fish here!' So I told him to put on a different fly and he made two casts and, bang, he was into a fish. But this fish took him a long, long time, and his mother was quite worried because it was getting dark. The fish had gone on to the bottom and we *couldn't* get if off — Tommy'd only a light cast and a fairly light rod. Eventually I brought the boat down from Inny Croy and got him into the boat with Captain David Bailey, who'd stopped by to help, but we *still* couldn't

212

move this fish. And then Tommy got excited and started dictating to Captain Bailey and myself. The cast had only a seven pound breaking strain and Captain Bailey said, 'If it's like that, Tommy,' he said, 'the fish will be broken, so I want you to behave yourself!' On the same, Tommy said, 'Would you go back to Endsleigh, Mother, and get some sandwiches?! I'm staying here all night if necessary to get this fish! When you come back you can put the car lights on to the river so we can see to land it!' And after an hour and three quarters playing of it we did land the fish and it was just over sixteen pound and it was Tommy's first salmon ever.

Mr Philip Tuckett, the local director, what I call my personal boss, he was married about four year ago. He's already got a daughter and a son — the son was born this year. I hope I'll soon be pushing the pram and having Mrs Tuckett fish. She's lovely. We've started her off and she's very interested, but at the moment she's tied down. They couldn't ask everyone to the wedding so they invited tenant farmers and intimate people such as the wife and myself to Leigh Barton two or three days before. I gave her a kiss, of course, and he said, 'That's got to be cut out from the word go!' He's a very charitable man like his father was: he's good to the Church, good to everybody. For local charities the Tuckett Trust have taken over really from the Dukes. He's not very fishy — I wouldn't call him fish hungry — so he gives a lot of his fishing to other people for their enjoyment. He'll even let me fish his rod sometimes so I can give something to the tenant farmers. I once said to him, 'What about your wife? Doesn't *she* deserve a fish?' He said, 'Forget about the wife. See your farmers is all right first.' Now, there isn't many people like that. Most are out for grabs, especially early in the season when the fish are fresh as a rose.

He's a gentleman of the first class with a lot of property here and in Cornwall, yet, I can't understand it, he's of a shy disposition. If he doesn't know someone he doesn't push himself over and say, 'Hallo' and 'How are you?' and 'Who are you?': he stands back. I'd like for him to be more domineering. I like for a person to come along and say, 'Look here, Adams! That's all bloody wrong!' but he'll say, 'Now can we correct this?' — you know, he's very gentle with it. Mind you, I've never seen the worst side of him. I remember his father sending contract people home for cutting up wood and banging it in the gulleys in Leigh Wood. When he pointed out the mess and they argued, he just said, 'Out! All the bloody lot of you, out! I'll employ someone else!' Of course you can't sack people now like you could then. If you complained I was rude to you, I'd wriggle out by saying, 'I'm trying to help Mr Murphy but Mr Murphy won't listen,' and I'd threaten to go to my solicitor. Mr Tuckett Junior is a little too timid. He'd walk away rather than pick an argument. I'd rather pick an argument, especially if I know I'm right — like when more than two rods is fishing one beat or someone's gone away and left their rod stationary, a 'fixed engine' as the saying is, or they're worming or spinning. No worming is allowed from Greystone Bridge downstream, and Endsleigh is really a fly fishing stretch so no one can spin except in April when the water is normally high and it's a bit dirty and the fish are deep. If I caught somebody spinning up here now, I'd have to report it and his gear would be confiscated. They're allowed to spin certain pools on the Lower Water at any time.

I've never spun in my life, I've always classed it as unsporting. Mr Bunyan, who's an extremely good fly fisherman, though he never seems to get amongst the fish in this part of the country, he bangs the spinner across with a leaded weight and he'll never catch a fish like that... Us don't want to discuss anything about spinning because I will be shot at dawn. It's not the done thing at Endsleigh, barring April. They might introduce it in May if the river is out of order, but the expert will tell you, 'One fish on a fly is worth ten on a spinner.' You weren't allowed to spin at all under the Dukes. It's only allowed now to bring the people in.

The river is two inches on the gauge — exactly the same as it was yesterday [Wednesday, August 8. By the 11th, when I returned to London, it was one inch and 'hopeless, a waste of time']. No use the short, sharp rise we had on Saturday: what *I* want to see is a *flood*! Then the fish will run through and we won't be only having fish at Endsleigh, they'll be having them at the Arundell Arms and all the way up the river. In fact, most of them might run *right* through, one doesn't know. But I'm not worried about that so long as it leaves our water a *bit* fishy. The fish now are on the bottom for protection: the river's in a terrible state, though we're lucky here because we've got all these croys which break

214

the water up and we don't lose very many fish through lack of oxygen.

Last Saturday I was walking through Tavistock when a gentleman said to his children, 'Look up there, look! See what that aeroplane's got on behind him?!' and he had a damn great trailer 'PLEASE SAVE WATER' going along in the air. Well, talk about gimmicks — eighty people in a hundred wouldn't have seen that! And then they've got all these adverts going along some of the main roads: 'SAVE WATER NOW OR ELSE'. On one part of the Bodmin Road they have them every seven or eight yards. If I wanted to put an advert up on the road, the County Council would say, 'That's attracting the motorist and putting him off his guard'! People's bound to be looking at these damn yellow signs and saying, 'Why have they so many?' and the next minute you'm over the hedge and then they've got to use more water when you catch your car on fire! It's as simple as that. It'll be good when the Roadford Reservoir is finished, because that will be pushing extra water down: when they get short of water in Plymouth, they'll release the water down the Tamar. That's supposed to come in 1989, but what about now?! There've been so much talk, talk, talk, and nothing done. It's like tagging the fish to beat the poacher — talk, talk, talk. But, you see, there are certain sections of parliamentarians, probably they've got in the back of their mind that the rivers and the fishes running up the rivers should be for everybody, which is like saying every individual house should belong to the Government whereas now the present government is trying to shed all their council houses.

There's some brown trout in the River Tamar but they're very, very small indeed — they only run about three to the pound. So, because of the drought, the younger guests have been concentrating on sea trout and fishing every night after dinner till about two. Eighty-odd's been caught up to now, and the more caught the better — they're pushing out the trout and, if we're not careful, they'll outdo the salmon. The young love night-fishing for the excitement. Some ghillies encourage them to boost the year's fish score for publicity. God help us when Endsleigh is commercialized like that! But if a person's new to the river and he says, 'Where's the best place to go sea trout fishing, Adams?' I tell them where there's a rock or shingle to stand on. It's better to fish for sea trout in the river, but you don't want to wade at night if you can help it. The Dukes didn't fish for them and they don't interest me so I

215

let people go on their own. Sea trout fishers are messing up someone else's salmon beat for the next day.

Don't think I'm being rude but, in this weather, I'd have been able to get away from Endsleigh and do a bit of gardening if it wasn't for this book we're doing. I like to go out in the garden because it keeps me busy: I've got to be moving around doing something or I'm on edge.

In the garden, drought or no drought, I never water anything. My father taught me two things. He said, 'With a vegetable, it lives or dies. Once you start watering you've got to keep on watering,' and he said, 'Always run around with a Dutch hoe and keep hoeing, even in a very, very dry time and you're killing two birds with one stone: you're checking the weed and if there's any dew in the morning the moisture can get in.' The advice pays off. One of my next door neighbours this year, his runner beans was about six to eight inches and he planted them out and then he was watering of them and he put polythene paper around so it cut the wind away from them. And I hadn't planted mine and now his is only half way up the sticks and mine's up to the top and half ways down again and I've picked four lots already! I've also got all sorts of cabbages, Brussels sprouts, savoys, peas, broad beans, carrots, beetroot, turnips... There seems to be everything this year but salmon and cherries. The potatoes will be coming up in a month, probably less, for storing in the shed with the apples. The wife's quite interested in flowers and we've a flower garden in the front. But I do all the rough work, even the planting. Her favourite is carnations and, after that, roses. My father was a damn good gardener but he didn't want no flowers. He said, 'Flowers won't make you fat. You can't live on flowers.'

When you're born in the country and you work in the open and you're up and down the river bank, you can become blind to a lot of the beauty all around you. A newcomer will say, 'Aren't they beautiful?' and he's talking about some bluebells you weren't aware of. Lord Boyd once said to me, 'Lady Richardson's been and picked a lot of wild flowers. If you can guess within twenty how many different ones she found I'll give you a quid.' Just like that. So I said, 'Twenty-seven, thirty?' He said, 'Well, you haven't got the quid.' Including grass gone to seed, she'd picked seventy-four different kinds of flowers that morning! I said, 'I didn't realize so many wild flowers existed!' So Lady Richardson said, 'Just have a look where we're standing!' and we were *standing* by eleven different types of wild flower! Jill was then at primary school and I thought, 'Well, I'll take her out for an hour or two on Sunday morning,' and we found forty different flowers.

One thing I always notice still is the mushroom. And when you see *them* coming, next thing around the corner is the blackberries and then it's the end of the season. Endsleigh Ham and Hardstone Ham are the best places for mushrooms now. Joel's Corner Field was best before Mr Tuckett turned it into corn. The wife don't like them, but I love them fried. There was a Czechoslovakian lady here in the first year of the Trustees' days with her husband, Mr Butcher. I was fishing with him at Lowley Croy one afternoon and I said, 'Where's Mrs Butcher?' He said, 'Gone picking mushrooms just behind us.' Well, come to, she didn't pick any mushrooms, she picked some of the fungi off the trees and she brought it back to the chef, Mr Young, for him to cook it and he was scared stiff it would poison her. But she ate it and it didn't kill her. I suppose it's called 'exotic'. None of the other guests would look at the stuff.

For our Ruby Wedding two year ago last February Jill said to the wife, 'We've decided to take you out to Sprytown on Saturday. Just the four of us — you, Father, Rodney and myself.' Sprytown's a tiny place out at Lifton. It's a farmhouse turned into a little restaurant. Well, Jill and Rodney walked in the door at seven o'clock on the Saturday evening and the wife had changed but I hadn't — I'd been watching something on television. Jill said, 'Come on, Dad! We've got to be out there by half past!' So I whipped up and put on a shirt and a pair of slacks and my velvet jacket, got the camera and off we went. It was a dirty evening, foggy rain, and Jill said she'd drive though it was our car. When she got to the top of Ramsdown Road, Rodney said, 'I want to go to the Arundell Arms.' Jill said, 'What do you want to go to the Arundell Arms for?!' and I said the same, I said, 'A moment ago you was in a hurry and now you want to go to the Arundell Arms!' He said, 'We're out this way and I've got to see Roy Buckingham.' Roy's the head ghillie for Mrs Anne Voss Bark at the Arundell Arms which owns twenty miles of fishing on the Tamar and some of its little tributaries. Any rate, we got down to the Ambrosia factory at Lifton and to go to the Arundell Arms you turn left and to go to Sprytown you turn right. Jill and Rodney were arguing like anything between theirselves, really going hammer and tongs. She said, 'You're stupid!' He said, 'Please, for my benefit! Roy's promised me some fly-tying material. It won't take five minutes.' Jill said, 'All right then,' she said, 'but', she said, 'we're not stopping.'

Now, when we got to the Arundell Arms and drove in the car park, there was a lot of cars, but I didn't think anything of it. I said, 'I'll sit in the back of the car and so will Mother,' and Jill said, 'You'd betterway come in now we're here. It's just as well to be killed for a sheep as it is a lamb.' So me and the wife decided to go in and say hallo to Roy Buckingham and, as it was drizzly, I turned my collar up and ran ahead to the back door. When I got there, someone shut the bar door quickly. I thought nothing of that either and, when we were all inside, Jill suddenly said to her mother, 'Oh, look at this fish!' Well, I'd seen this fish many times, but the wife hadn't. It's a big two and a half, three pound trout in a glass case and it's named Horace — nothing to do with me; Horace is a common name in the locality. We were looking at Horace when Jill said, 'Come on, then! Otherwise we'll be late for Sprytown!' and she opened the door to the bar and her and Rodney walked through with me and the wife following of them.

I looked and the room was full of people we knew and up sprang 'Happy Anniversary'. We'd been caught napping! Jill had unintentionally parked the car right beside Derek Bradbury's and I hadn't spotted it, though I remember wondering why there was no light on in Luke's house as we left Milton Abbot. And that afternoon I'd met a pal of mine called Herb Balsdon. He was chopping firewood in the garden and when I spoke to him he went red in the gills as if he was trying to keep back something secret. He said to me later, 'Didn't you see how red I was?!' He said, 'I was sweating like a bullock because I thought you was going to say, "It's my Ruby Wedding today and Jill and Rodney's giving us a quiet evening at Sprytown," but you said nothing!'

First to welcome us was the proprietress, Mrs Anne Voss Bark, who knows me very well and, as she's a member of the Lower Tamar Fishing Club, is one of Rodney's bosses. Her husband, Conrad Voss Bark, wasn't present — he's a very shy man. I said, 'I thought we were going to Sprytown!' She said, 'Whatever made you think of that?!' and gave me a kiss on the strength of it. Then after Jill had given everybody a drink

— there was forty of us all told — we moved to the Long Room where we had a chicken meal at long great tables. Oh, it was well, well, well laid on! If the others wanted wine they had to pay for it, which was fair enough, but Mrs Voss Bark gave the four of us two or three bottles on the house and served us personally, good as gold. Back in the bar everybody was giving us drinks. We went right on till twelve and, come to, Jill cut out and said she'd do the driving again. When everybody except us had filed away Jill wrote a cheque, paid on the dot, so when we were leaving we didn't have to look over our shoulders to see if Mrs Voss Bark was watching for us to pay.

That evening was a hell of a surprise for me and the wife: it knocked us for six. Now that we've been married for forty-*two* years I often wonder how Nesta will cope with my retirement which will have to happen soon. I'll have plenty to do, gardening and taking photographs and whatnot, but she isn't used to having me around all the time. I'm hot-headed — Jill's taken after me that way — but she's placid like Rodney: she never throws cups and saucers. I knew one wife who picked up cups full of tea in moments of frustration and threw them at her husband and then they'd to rip off the wallpaper because it was covered with stains. Except for *Mastermind,* me and Nesta don't like the same television. For instance, I'm tremendous for sport. I've already treated myself to a season ticket this year up in the Grandstand at Home Park. For the fifty quid I'll have every afternoon that Plymouth Argyll's home, that's twenty-three matches. I'll take the wife down with me and drop her off for bingo.

Of course, when my days at Endsleigh draw to a close, I *will* miss the routine of coming down in the season and telling old friends and people that's new the conditions and giving them advice and chatting about everything in general before picking them up later on the river and helping them there. I'm rough and perhaps I shouldn't have been mixing with the sort I did, though they seem to have enjoyed me for what I am. I'm pleased I was born when I was born and to have seen Endsleigh as I have seen it. I've never wanted too many here — they can all come after I've gone.

When, last year, I saw the Marquess for the first time since he caught his fish with me as a boy, I showed him some of the photos I've taken and he said

219

to his wife, Henrietta, 'There you are, you see! You never believed a word I said, but here's me with a fish and Gavin with his fish and Lorna with her fish!' I said, 'Well, it's wonderful meeting you again and to know you've joined the Syndicate. I hope you'll both partake in the fishing and the enjoyment.' This was after the party in October. I knew they was there when I made my speech so I put on a show, trying to use my aitches properly and not to put P's where it should be Q's. It wasn't very easy because I was stood right next to a lady who's got a habit of whipping away my notes and making me confused. All the members take the mickey. But 'I'm a fool and know it and you'm a fool and show it' — it takes a wise man to be a fool.

Editor's note: Several further fishing personalities mentioned in these pages have now 'passed on' (Horace's phrase) in addition to Victor Canning whose death is specified on page 3. Rodney now works for the National River Authority. He and Jill have acquired a new address in Gunnislake. They have two children — Victoria, aged five, and James, aged two. The present Chairman of the Endsleigh Fishing Club is Mr Brian Peppiatt. The Roadford Reservoir was completed on schedule.

February, 1994